Resilient Thinking

Protecting organisations in the twenty-first century

Second edition

To Chris
Happy Reading

Resilient Thinking

Protecting organisations in the twenty-first century

Second edition

PHILLIP WOOD

IT Governance Publishing

IT Governance Publishing Ltd
Unit 3, Clive Court
Bartholomew's Walk
Cambridgeshire Business Park
Ely, Cambridgeshire
CB7 4EA
United Kingdom
www.itgovernancepublishing.co.uk

First edition published in the United Kingdom in 2012 by IT Governance Publishing.

ISBN 978-1-84928-382-3

Second edition published in the United Kingdom in 2023 by IT Governance Publishing.

ISBN 978-1-78778-419-2

Images have been created by the author using Canva.

Cover image originally sourced from Shutterstock®.

PREFACE

The world is a dangerous and difficult place to live in for most of us, most of the time. We all want a peaceful and happy existence, but the path from cradle to grave is rarely smooth, and for some it's a real struggle. As individuals, families and social groups, we make single or collective decisions and choices that we hope will influence outcomes and ensure that what we get is what we feel we deserve, or at least that to which we aspire. Choices that we make can be instinctive or informed, and often we make our decisions more in hope than in good judgement. Later, when we look back on our lives, most of us will think that we could have done better with hindsight. For organisations that want to meet their business aims (usually involving optimising profitability), the correct decisions are important, and normally critically so. Even more important is the fact that, for businesses, hindsight is rarely an effective or desirable management tool, and the more proactive and forward-thinking the organisation, the better chance it will have of remaining viable and competitive. Not all organisations are businesses of course; society is also an organisation. Therefore, whether we are looking for profit or the protection of the assets that are our responsibility, we need to do the very best that we can. We need to think, plan and act.

Resilient Thinking is not about the mechanics of writing plans. You can download templates from the Internet for that, or even continue to update existing plans, which perhaps you did not write, as the organisation develops and the environment changes. This book is about intelligent approaches and the ability to operate smartly, so that you and your organisation are prepared for the worst. You won't find any checklists – they are for people who like to work within mental frameworks and, although they have their place, it's not here. Hopefully, as we go along, it will become clear that there are functionalities and processes that need to be checked off. However, the more valuable processes in the heat of an incident or event, and in the periods both preceding and following them, will be those that are flexible and responsive, carried out by a confident, agile and knowledgeable resilience team. Those teams should be led by and comprise resilient thinkers.

Another thing that this book is not, is a set text for resilience teams. You may have designated resilience professionals, semi-professionals or amateurs carrying out resilience tasks, but the truly resilient organisations are those that involve every single employee in the resilience process at some stage or another. If everyone has a responsibility, then *Resilient Thinking* is designed for them. And, if ever we needed to take collective responsibility for resilience, now is the time.

In terms of referencing guidance, such as standards, I will make some references but not many and not often. I believe that they are written in echo chambers and used as a vehicle for opinion and 'best practice' as decided by those who believe that they know best. I'm not one of those people who believe that they know best. I have simply written a book that is a collection of analysis, thinking, reflections and opinions.

Reading this book will not allow you to change the world. It won't make you an expert in the multiple nuances of resilience. But, hopefully it will allow you to step back, look at things a little more critically and add a little more to your overall capability. It will ask you to question, challenge and disrupt. That is what I would like to see more of. There are many who cannot and will not engage in that degree of activity. I believe that to be a shame, and I would like to see more argument, debate and discussion about resilience apart from 'when I was' stories, and the recycling of the same old case studies in relation to crisis and resilience challenges.

Resilient thinking is the aim of this book. Sometimes it wanders a little, and some aspects of it may or may not make sense to you. All I ask is that you think about some of it and consider adding anything that you do feel is a positive to your toolkit. If you can be a thinker, and add to that some common sense and an understanding of processes and organisational requirements and objectives, you can become very effective indeed. Ineffective resilience planning and action are not resilience at all.

ABOUT THE AUTHOR

Professor Phil Wood, MBE, is a resilience consultant and Academic Director for Frontier Risks Group, which is well known as a leading security and risk management training company in the United Kingdom. Formerly, he was Head of the School of Aviation and Security at Buckinghamshire New University. Before his academic career, Phil was a commissioned officer in the Royal Air Force Regiment, and deputy director of training for an internationally recognised corporate security training company.

Phil has developed and delivered resilience consultancy, higher education and training globally. He has worked in Nigeria, Bahrain, Bangladesh, Dubai, Kenya, Greece and Oman delivering security, resilience and business continuity education and consultancy. He is a member of the Register of Chartered Security Professionals, a Fellow of the Security Institute, an Honorary Member of the Business Continuity Institute and a Technical Specialist Member of the Institute of Risk Management.

ACKNOWLEDGEMENTS

In the ten years that have elapsed since the first version of this book was published, the list of people that I need to acknowledge has naturally grown. If you want to know who was acknowledged the first time around, and why, it will probably be better to have a look at the 2012 version.

Since then, like everyone's, my life has changed. And here I would like to thank Pete Lawrence and Duncan Godfrey, and the wider family at Frontier Risks Group who have given me a new lease of life and the opportunity to contribute to the organisation's continuing success, growth and excellence. Our collective mission is about being helping to develop capabilities in individuals and organisations while being different and disruptive in approach and ethos. That, for me, is what everything is all about. Hopefully you will see that reflected in this book, link to us and find out more about what we do.

To all my colleagues and the many students and learners who I have worked with and for, over the years, thank you for everything that has helped me to develop and deliver what I do. My only aim has been to do the best that I can and it's such a reward to see you doing great things.

I would also like to thank Alan Cain MA; Emergency Preparedness, Resilience and Response Manager, NHS Greater Manchester and Jason Gotch; Global Security Professional, London, for their help in reviewing the second edition manuscript for me.

Acknowledgements

Finally, and of course most importantly, thanks again to the love of my life Yvonne for everything there is; here's to more decades of disruption together …

CONTENTS

Contents

Contents

Contents

INTRODUCTION TO THE SECOND EDITION

The first edition of *Resilient Thinking* was written in 2012; since then, a great deal has changed in the world that was entirely predictable. As I write this second edition, it is fair to say that we are in a pickle. Basically and fundamentally, because of a combination of 'chickens coming home to roost', misplaced optimism, and arrogance and experience overtaking thinking; we have ended up in a very difficult place. Our politics and governance seem to be failing; economies, pandemics and energy have weakened us at every level. Social division is the norm rather than the exception, and the long-term adversaries of the West, and those who have been hiding behind their coat tails, have us firmly locked in their sights.

The core message of the book that I wrote a decade ago has aged quite well, I think. Its fundamental concerns were as they are now. I said this in my previous introduction:

> *"As we make the journey through the world of resilience together, we are going to look at organisations as vulnerable entities. And we're going to try to direct our focus firmly away from 'stovepipe' or 'silo' thinking. Business continuity, security, health and safety, emergency planning, disaster recovery, and so on, are all different elements of resilience. That's my view and I'm sticking to it. When an organisation is targeted, or an accident happens which affects it, the impact is not just in one area, at one time, at one level and aimed at one function, and your mindset needs to be as flexible*

and dynamic as the threats you face. Think in stovepipes and your organisation may well go up in smoke; go beyond frameworks and mental constraints and you may have a chance of coming out the other side in one piece, and, with some luck, you could end up in better shape than when the stuff hit the fan in the first place.

So, if you want to get through to the other side of whatever it is that may befall you or your organisation, it's time to be a little bit radical. Only a little. Do not tear up your current plans; they may need a little tweaking, or even just some effort to make them practicable. Do not throw away your checklists; they might be useful if you test them out. Do throw away rigid mindsets, adherence to the 'I'm a risk/security/safety/continuity/disaster recovery expert and my method is best' waffle and the belief that all resilience functions are different and separate. I'll quite happily argue with any number of consultants, advisers and niche managers about this, but in the end (and hopefully by the time we get to the end of the book you'll agree), I'm right and only by thinking will you achieve your resilience aim and avoid any number of terrible scenario developments."[1]

What I was driving at there was that we are not very good at being resilient, and in that book I tried to explain why. It

---

[1] Wood, Phillip, (2012), *Resilient Thinking – Protecting Organisations in the 21st Century*, Ely: IT Governance Publishing.

was short, and more of a collection of thoughts and observations than a weighty volume of archaic wisdom. In parts it was about the 'why's' and in others about the 'how's'. It didn't do as well as other books in the field; and didn't secure me any keynote speaking gigs to get my points across. Here we are a decade later and I believe more strongly than ever that we have not been able to make significant headway into resilience. With the lessons of COVID-19 already fading, and the public and politicians getting comfortable with ongoing war in Europe, we seem to be as weak in our thinking and actions as we ever were. It's odd, but because we can get used to anything, what may at first be seen and felt as a crisis can quickly become a memory or someone else's problem. That's resilience in some way; it's how we cope – we move on to something else and think less about problems. They are a challenge to face and to resolve.

The first edition was not at the top of the bestseller lists, then. It was a bit too short for that, maybe not seen as an academic treatise (it was not intended to be one), and the cover was a bit strange. However, it did have its moments and its ideas, and in this second edition I am expanding my thinking and writing to encompass more, challenge the reader more and to hopefully have more impact. I don't claim to be Nostradamus or Nicholas Taleb. However, you don't need to be a crystal ball-gazer or buzzword peddler to perform better. If we look around us, it is hard to see the benefit of any new resilience thinking in the quarter century that brought us repeated pandemics, truly global terrorism, mass displacement and migration, tsunamis and exploding reactors, and the serious risk of nuclear conflict, to mention a few big headline grabbers. Add to that the life changing, psychology-bending effects of social media at every level of civilised society, and we are looking at massive change that we have done nothing effective to anticipate and even less to manage. Social media is a 'Pandora's Box' that damages as much as it offers; and we let it do so. We're human beings and we like to see images in colour and share our egos globally for everyone to see. That seems to overcome caution.

In this book, I contend that my musings are as valid as any alleged revolutionary 'thought leadership' that is out there in the world of resilience, because it feels like there is precious little of it being used, delivered and communicated. Which is kind of my point. You can count thought leaders in resilience on the back of a microchip. If you can find a microchip of course, and that is another challenge; there's a shortage you know.

Back in 2012 I also said:

> *"You'll find that I repeat throughout the book that it is important to be a thinker. Why? Because for me thinking is everything that makes professionals effective and the lack of it is what makes organisations, large and small, ineffective."*

I absolutely stand by that statement. Everything that concerned me in the first edition concerns me now but much more. Why? Because there hasn't really been any *change* in thinking as well as capability. What we have seen is the growth of buzzword-led snapshot terms, and the development of a sort of industry by consultants and businesses around risk and organisational resilience. We now have operational resilience, which seems to me generally to be the same thing as organisational resilience, although those who are bought into it will maintain otherwise. They would, naturally, do that because it is their livelihood. However, in general, those who do profess to know about resilience generally have less knowledge than they profess. There has been so little change in response to decades of change because, basically, as humans, we have continued to exhibit the same old behaviours. Those behaviours and our lack of ability to face the challenges of the second quarter of the twenty-first century will cost us very dearly. So, in summary, we *think* we know more, and we *think* we have the answers. These span from building scenarios that lull us into a false sense of capability, to planning for issues in benign contexts without really understanding or modelling worst cases in extended detail. Optimism bias is everywhere in its ostrich-like glory. Overall, we do not perform well. Our thinking that we have the answers when we don't is the wrong type of thinking. Patting ourselves on the back when we have missed the mark and we don't realise it is an organisational liability.

In this expanded edition we will look at how thinking and learning can be applied to resilient thinking. We will revisit the areas and behaviours that mean that organisational resilience is seen as a phrase rather than a capability. It will encompass much more as there is much more for us to consider. And I will make no apologies for it not being an academic treatise; that would make it a tedious read and that's not my intention. My overall aim is to try to reach more people and induce a little more thinking and reflection. If we and our leaders had thought a little more and stripped away our biases and personal incentives, frankly we wouldn't be in the mess in which we find ourselves. And please believe me, the mess we are in now is not going to improve unless we make some changes.

On the positive side, it's not too late to open your mind a little and to think about how to do things well. Closed minds mean that we do things badly; and that's also how we got here. In this book I've brought together a lot of things, issues and ideas that I have been thinking about for more than ten years, and although I can't make much sense of the world and why things happen in the way that they do, I can comment on how I think we can do better. Or even how I would like it to do better. This isn't a textbook, and it includes some differences in style and approach depending on what I'm trying to say. If I repeat some points it's because I think they matter. Most importantly, what I have put in here is my viewpoint and my opinions; and the reader may well disagree. That's how it should be, and if you do disagree, please do get in touch with me and let me know what you think. It will let me know that we *do* think.

In this revision we will begin with a deeper look at the *world of difficulty,* because the resilience 'landscape' and those who are involved in it has definitely changed rapidly. We will then move on to reviewing the makeup of resilience sectors, how we think and behave, and consider the need to influence thinking. That is what the core of the book is about, and it bears significant further investigation and expansion. We'll then move onto wider discussions about resilient thinking and action. Hopefully, all this will lead you towards being that disruptive resilient thinker. I hope you enjoy reading it and that it at least helps a little in your thinking about how we can be better at resilience. I think we all know that we could do better. So let's do it.

CHAPTER 1: A WORLD OF DIFFICULTY

"We will bury you."

Nikita Khruschev

We are fully immersed in a changing, challenging world, and equally immersed in a global context for our strategies and organisational approaches, which has a constant potential to outstrip our coping ability. With a global outlook in mind, and the need to be able to live and operate in a dynamic environment, a fundamental starting point for resilient thinking is to consider the impact of that context. To what extent does our external context influence our resilience? A consideration of the growth and metamorphosis of regional threats and impacts, alongside the genesis and development of new types of risks with which the wider international community may not yet be fully engaged, is necessary, I feel, for all types of organisations and sectors.

Our societies and the links, interdependencies and conflicts that exist within and outside them are in a new age of (to paraphrase a past UK Prime Minister, Harold Wilson) 'White Heat'. In this dynamic arena of change, both innovation and surprises can challenge and unbalance us while offering new opportunities for the prepared and ambitious. When we think about the world, we are surrounded by and participate in much speculation, theorising, and pontificating about what is coming and how it should be influenced or could be controlled. From globalised business activity to changes in national and international power balances, from political reorientations to an emergence of technology enabled 'people power' – all merit discussion and analysis before we progress to thinking about how we might effectively live with them, and our responses to them, in later chapters.

In 'A world of difficulty' we begin with analysis and reflection on the cause and impact of some of the complicated resilience challenges that we have faced and will face in the future. The effectiveness or otherwise of our capability to respond to and manage the impacts of these challenges will form the core of the discussions that we then cover in 'Resilient Thinking'.

Thinking about the context

From any number of viewpoints, the world seems to be in a state of constant crisis; it seems that we are unable as a general, global and interlinked society, to free ourselves from a continuous flow of damaging, challenging and sometimes catastrophic events. These may affect us directly, indirectly or not at all. However, they do seem to be increasingly prevalent. This fluctuating, moving and dynamic modern world brings immense and diverse challenges, and raises multiple issues, and more so than at any time in history. We are facing a unique and unprecedented set of colliding and consolidating crises that we must face and overcome. These crises build, connect, connect again, consolidate and grow; and their size, extent and impact may overwhelm us to the point of extinction.

Of course, all of this is not strictly true. There have been events throughout history that have resulted in immense loss of life and that have had repercussions lasting for hundreds, if not thousands, of years. Wars, diseases, genocide and natural disasters have taken death tolls into billions combined. Despite the global scale of some of the issues that we now face in our connected world, a significant proportion of even local or regional issues in history would dwarf what we would term 'crises' nowadays. Certainly in terms of loss of life and infrastructure damage, even the two world wars of the twentieth century have been unparalleled before or since.

That, of course, is not wholly true either; it is simply a case of timescales and concentration; although wars between 'great nations' have certainly been less prevalent since 1945, there has been constant conflict with millions of lives lost around the world. We do remain, however, unstable and threatened by the actions of state powers that are themselves underpinned by manufacturing and trading complexes, and these are inextricably linked to economic and thus strategic national power and status. The further layer of change is through technological developments that are taking us to new ways of behaving, interacting and even thinking. From Artificial Intelligence (AI) polarising views from consternation to excitement, to cryptocurrency, blockchain and the metaverse, change is with us and pushing us ever further to cope and respond effectively.

In the twenty-first century, although the pace and speed of change can feel overwhelming, this has all been coming for some time. The economic issues and social changes of the first decades of the twenty-first century did not arise overnight; they are the result of activity that has been going on for a considerable period, and they have sown the seeds of debt and hollowed out the economies of many Western countries. The realignment of East-West power or what is economically termed the 'North' and 'South', and by that we are talking about the growth of economies such as China and India, are the result of a growing confidence by these countries. They are now using the significant investment of Western powers in them in previous years in the hope of exploiting the subsequent resource and profitability benefits for themselves.

There is perhaps also a justified view that the potential power shifts that we see in the world are somehow the result of 'karma' for the former empires and colonisers from the West. What we have seen as this realignment has continued, is that China, in particular, has moved at an unmatchable pace to secure its position as the world's dominant superpower. In terms of economic stature, China is moving towards securing the largest share of global GDP, and will finally overtake the US in the second half of the 2020s. This is an example of the effectiveness not only of China's foreign policies, but also of its ability to buy into markets to exploit and grow from the profits, building influence and aligned nations alongside and as a result of those policies. From the West, of course, there will always be an intention to challenge that. However, an effective challenge depends on the West having the capability, the will and the superiority to succeed. None of those are given; and will be less so as time passes.

As global activity continues, and the power shifts along with it, risks will not only emerge, but also develop in multiple routes and with multiple, sometimes multiplying, properties. Even in their initial form they will present difficulties. However, unaddressed and unmitigated risks will have the potential to become significantly challenging for all levels of organisations, and thus societies that are impacted. For nations, businesses and the consumers and citizens that they serve; and who all reflect the societies that they form together, impacts have the potential to be felt throughout. When conflicts take place and resources flow less effectively, it tends to be the end consumers who suffer most from cost and resource issues. Moreover, in our now rapidly changing world, risks that are dynamic require engagement, proactivity in thought and action, and a degree of intellectual understanding. This means that when we look at the world, we should see it less as a huge 'ball of crises', but as a lattice or network of shifting, changing and developing risks with potential for multiple, multi-layered impacts.

This being the case, and with so many risks and potentially negative outcomes 'out there', we need to develop the capability for resilient thinking before we move towards acting. However, conversely, we seldom have the luxury of time. There is little proven value in allowing risks to develop, compound and grow before engaging in responsive action; when that happens, a problem can become a crisis very quickly. When a crisis does occur, organisations must be ready to meet the challenges that it will bring. Is the growth of Chinese dominance a risk? It seems that it may be; and although China may be able to achieve what it needs while avoiding conflict; the likelihood of that, as I have mentioned, depends on how the West continues to react and seeks to position itself for the future. Another aspect of the risk problem is the consideration that, like some child's game that we never tire of, armed conflict is seen as the way for states to achieve their aims. As I write – and as you read – there are people dying in conflicts that we are aware of and some that we are not. For some reason, human beings are not very adept at risk-based intervention to stop conflict, but are very good at seeking violent resolutions using resources that those who make the decisions feel are worth expending. For me, that is fundamentally not a defensible human trait that will guarantee our future. When we run out of options, we often resort to violence; and often this is not the route to follow. For the resilient thinker, assessing and implementing our best options should be the objective. In every case of major conflict that I can think of, poor decision making under pressure, alongside mistakes, misjudgements and egomania, have led to the first shots being fired. From there, we know how it goes.

In our global context, where flawed human motives have always brought harm and impact to others, what has changed in our so- called enlightened times? What makes a difference and brings another dimension to the gravity and impact of threats and risks, and almost all their properties? The difference now, after all these centuries, is that there is a global, interconnected, real-time audience of populations watching on and asserting their right to consultation, involvement and assent. Not only are we watching, our dependency on a technology-based interconnected societal structure makes undesirable events much more visible to us *immediately.* We see, hear, recognise and understand, and are able to make judgements and act much more rapidly than ever before. We are also able to hear and recognise what the public now thinks and believes. Not only that, but we are expected to respond and act. Therefore, if we could reasonably be expected to understand that issues that arise can bring devastating effects, why do organisations and societies, nations and individuals still repeatedly fail to prepare adequately and respond appropriately? Fundamentally, I think, it is because we are all human and fallible. This is neither a failing that we can overcome nor something that we can criticise because all of us fit that mould to some extent. The problem is that fallibility can bring failure.

1: A world of difficulty

Resilient thinking is about overcoming our fallibilities, or at least offsetting and alleviating *their* impact by engaging with challenges rather than letting them happen without filter or intervention. It is a constant battle. Even the most intelligent, 'switched on' and self-aware humans are liable to be caught out by our hard-wired instincts. How, and to what extent we engage with what threatens us, is the main influence on mitigation of the risks to ourselves and our assets. There is a definite need to respond appropriately and effectively, but does 'respond' mean that we do nothing? It may. Does holding a music event to protest against war have an impact? When it raises funds for humanitarian relief, it probably does. Will it bring entrenched opposing forces to negotiation? That is less likely. Whatever responses we choose, I propose that we should spend a great deal of time thinking not only about what we do to respond, but also about what the extended impacts of our responses may bring. The problem is that in general and in hindsight, even our recent history shows that time and again we are unable to get our thinking right when we consider (or fail to consider) impacts upon us as individuals and organisations. And, because we do that, there is a recurring tendency for our fallibilities to haunt us in our words and actions.

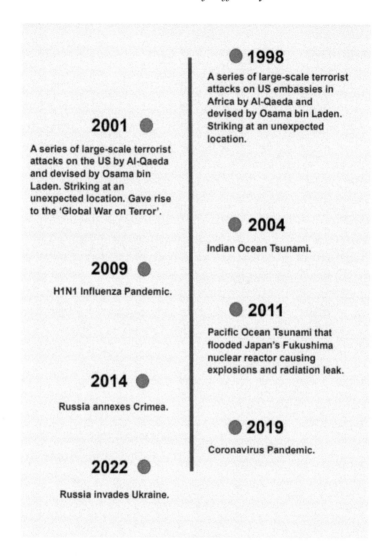

Figure 1: What we could have predicted

Given the fact that we had some quite clear warnings about the nature of developing risks, how did we let them impact us again?

It seems that even when there are clear indications that problems may arise, return or redevelop, the pattern of not learning enough continues to impact upon our resilient thinking. When we *should* have the ability to carefully assess, evaluate and implement effective mitigation, we often fail to hit the mark. An aspect of this cause-and-effect issue is a recurrent theme for us as we address and discuss ideas for resilient thinking. Human behaviours confound our ability to protect ourselves, even when we should know better. For example, how many times do we hear of compelling arguments and evidence being overlooked, ignored or dismissed because they did not fit the narrative, policy or in-thinking of the time?

In the cases shown in Figure 1, there was adequate reason to expect that following the earlier events, something similar or worse could happen again. These repeats of crisis types may have been in different locations and with significantly different impacts; but the warnings were there. The backdrop of history is always there. The similarities in the development of the second iterations were there. It is likely that some of the people in the decision chains for the first events were involved in some way in the development, or attempted prevention, of the second events. What we can see is that when things go wrong, the limitations on how much of them we review, revisit and learn from is a concern. In strategising organisational capability, quoting Marcus Aurelius, Churchill and von Clausewitz is not enough; the way to resilience lies in learning rather than parroted catchphrases and the framework thinking of the reticent and unimaginative. Our problem is that we are probably less orientated towards learning and its application than we are to optimism bias, making us think that we have learnt from the past, and that lulls us into a false belief in security and capability. In all these cases, lessons were there to be learned and acted upon. The problem is that, despite what I am sure were many positive attempts along the way to learn lessons, they would never be adequate; and be inadequately applied.

Onto this backdrop of our behavioural approaches are projected the multiple concerns, warnings and forecasts that are expressed to provide a 'picture' of the world. There are multiple ideas, ideals, scenarios and methodologies, theories and ideologies, and all contribute to the multi-layered lives that we live, and how we live them. If we cannot understand that it will lead in most circumstances and contexts to an inability or unwillingness to consider and act upon their impacts, this limitation will also compound the effects, sometimes to a point beyond which impacts may develop to levels that are beyond recovery. At every level, ineffective response to, and management of risks, crises and resilience challenges has a consolidating potential to contribute to the worsening of effects and the development of even more grave impacts.

Moreover, risks that can arise in isolation may become interconnected, and their impacts can reach beyond their geographical or economic points of origin, and this can therefore have a far-reaching effect both in effect and temporally. Recognising our many failings – and we should not be too negative – there *are* many successes – we need to develop the capability to be more active in taking ownership of thinking about our solutions. Nobody owns resilience; and thought leaders are not necessarily what they think they are. Therefore, nobody has the definitive list of definitive answers. Moreover, nobody is alone in being impacted by issues beyond our control. To take ownership we need to engage with what is going on around us and think about what we can do to alleviate, even avoid, the damaging effects. This is no easy task given the fallibilities and capabilities of all of us; but it is an imperative and something that we can take steps to address and rectify. Thus, the resilient thinker also needs to be the resilience actor, agitator, disruptor and influencer. The gap between eventually recognising that we need to act and then doing what needs to be done in a measured and reasoned way, can be quite wide and difficult to bridge.

In behavioural terms, we also need to think about ownership and the understanding that if we have responsibilities at any level, this is our problem, not someone else's. When considering resilience, our approach should be to think clearly and to understand that the whole concept is not just about 'blue light' emergencies, owned by others, that can and do arise and bring impacts. Impacts that will damage the organisation will be the responsibility of that organisation and the people within it. Resilience challenges can come in many guises and forms, and may not seem to be problematic for a particular individual or organisation when they first appear. A developing crisis may at first feel like something that does not necessarily affect us or our people. However, change can come with speed and pace, catching the unwary and unprepared, and resulting in any number of challenging impacts.

An additional dimension to this is our need to understand that an event that can have impacts that develop rapidly and do not necessarily need to have attributes and causes that appeared from nowhere and overnight. A crisis that develops from a problem to an incident to an emergency and then, just maybe, a catastrophe, may be as much a result of ineffective intervention and response than anything else. In a similar way to failing to learn our lessons, we may fail to plan for intervention and simply observe as risks develop over time. Or we may consistently avoid interventions because they do not align with our own world view, strategy or beliefs. If we accept and understand that this may be the case, we can perhaps see that there is ample evidence that we are potentially storing up the causes of a crisis, a disaster or worse. Any number of stories in the daily news since daily news began will illustrate that truth.

Rapid, considered interventions – and doing what is seen to be the right thing – are critical components of effective organisational resilience. Whether we are looking in the wrong directions, deliberately looking away or hiding behind our wall of cast-iron beliefs and prejudices; the result – failure – will be the same. Overcoming our hardwired human behaviours, some inherent, some learned and some that we soak up from our working environments, will help us to become more resilient. On the flip side and just as important, we tend to be slow to recognise good practice and the benefits of applying it. This can especially be the case when such practice is new, innovative, brings change, or is simply something that we didn't think of ourselves. In all respects, a positive change begins with reflecting on who we are and how we recognise our interactions with changing environments. If we are unable to manage the pace of change and respond accordingly to it, then again, we can expect impacts.

Slow and rapid onset – Changing pace

Familiarity and lack of apparent change go hand in hand. We tend not to notice the differences in the appearance of people who are constantly in the public eye, or who we see all the time, as they change and age. Conversely, if we haven't seen someone for a very long time and suddenly meet them or see a recent photograph, it can sometimes be quite shocking to realise how they have changed physically. It's happening to all of us of course, but the slow and indistinguishable changes that occur as we go through life can often only be apparent once they have accumulated and we see them afresh. We have a similar potential not to see and recognise slow onset effects when risks develop into impacts. These are, by definition, issues that arise over time and incrementally, and are not as evident and shocking as the immediate, rapid onset events that will tend to catch our attention and give cause for concern.

However, the severity of impact is not necessarily measured in the fastest time to the finish line; and the almost indistinguishable slow burners may be the ones that catch us out. They are no less impactful for that; it could be argued that they can be much more damaging as, by the time we have become aware of them, the impacts may be biting hard. Whatever the pace of development, the resilient thinker needs to understand and be prepared to meet the challenge – the *world of difficulty* has just as many slow-burning as explosive crises to meet. Furthermore, if we carried out an audit of the proportion of slow burning to rapid onset resilience challenges over the years, the slow burners would probably be responsible for most of the challenges.

Identifying the signs of slow onset events can undoubtedly be a challenge. Looking at interventions in our risk management processes to avoid the inevitably rapid endgame of slow onset processes is something that we should consider as a primary function and a priority – just as we should with the startling surprises. With this in mind, it is perhaps worthwhile considering the 'whys' rather than the 'what' of developing threats and risks from the viewpoint of the non-intervenor. Risk tolerance is something that organisations plan into their culture and processes. However, I am sure that you know that some risks are less able to be tolerated than others. Although many organisations will have the capacity and 'reserve' to be able to operate despite a developing and building risk, that does not mean that such tolerance is infinite. Organisations should therefore be able to make a considered choice, based upon the recognition of the potential impacts and the reasons why the risk is there. We should also understand that there will always be a degree of variation in our ability to absorb and manage them. Will the acceptance of risk make things worse? It is a possibility. However, it is important to recognise and emphasise the fact that to be effective rather than self-destructive, we need to understand the risk and its nuances, its causes and effects, and what we *may* need to do about it should the slow onset suddenly manifest itself as a rapid event that *may* develop into a crisis. Whatever we choose to do may not always be based on our choices – but we will need to decide what, if anything, our own final choices will be.

If we prefer lack of intervention, or an intervention that causes us the least possible inconvenience, over doing an informed, balanced and targeted *something*, we may find that not only is it too little too late, but also that it was never going to be enough or in time. Recognising and facing up to the slow onset of developing issues is something that needs to be a key skill of any risk or resilience professional. Importantly, this is not about prediction (we will look at prediction and its setbacks as we move on) but about clear perception, ownership of problems and the informed decision making that will blunt the effect and impact or partially reduce them.

What is clear is that whether rapid or slow onset; unknown or well-known proven impact, we humans are not uniformly very good at dealing with risks once they become impactful. And this brings us back to our mindset. The problem, perhaps ironically, lies in our human ability to absorb developments as they occur. In general, we humans have proven ourselves to be resilient, tolerant and accepting of what happens around us; and we sometimes fall into the trap of those changes catching us out and overtaking our ability to cope and respond. We live and thrive in a context whereby in our social and operating environments there are many uncertainties, with issues that we know of and issues that we cannot see. Not only that, but the issues that we know of still seem to confound effective response. And that being the case, there is significant merit in taking some control back. Once an incident requires a *significant* response, it may be too late to repair the damage; organisational effort goes into limitation and mitigation, and the chance for effective intervention to restore balance and recover is gone. However, while the cause is less important than what we can do about. it, we should be prepared to think about that also.

Whether dealing with the gestation and cause of indiscriminate and murderous attacks on innocent people, attempted government takeovers, wars and conflicts, or flooding and natural disasters, there is always a cause to go along with the effect. Dealing with the causes may be speculative, may require investment in resources for which there is no easily discernible short-term return, and may even go against our beliefs and ideals. It is probably a foolish person who looks on while the storm gathers or who makes a conscious decision not to engage with developing risks in plain sight. Unfortunately, there still seem to be enough of those in influential positions who, either alone or in self-affirming groups, do that. That in itself is something that resilient thinking needs to focus on countering; while recognising another important point of concern that bears reiteration. Impacts can be felt a long way from the point of origin. So, along with foresight and the ability to think about resilience, we also need an ability to think in long range. We can scan the horizon, but the horizon will always have something beyond it and out of sight. What may be a little itch somewhere way beyond our horizon, could become a major flare up and be right on top of us if it is not scratched early enough.

The flimsy connections that hold us together

If our thinking about context so far has identified for us that resilience challenges can come from many directions; understanding where they move to and from via connections and interdependencies is a key consideration. These challenges may be tangible or intangible; and they develop and move not only rapidly but in directions and ways that we may not be able to influence or anticipate. What goes on around us over which we have no control or influence can make our situation much worse; and therefore resilient thinking is not only about understanding our own business; but how the actions and impacts from others may impinge upon us. And our connections to risks in the new global context really do matter. It's my view that understanding that most aspects of our lives and what supports them are interconnected is a crucial element of effective resilient thinking. The lack of that understanding, or an unwillingness to 'lean into' the problem may, as with so many other issues, bring or accelerate failure.

1: A world of difficulty

A defining feature of the twenty-first century is that we have become victims of our own inventiveness, and the relentless drive towards technologically based societal progress. In that context, and in general, we are hyperextended beyond our ability to manage the impacts of our own success. The networks and structures that have developed over time to support our activities have traditionally (and it must be said effectively) managed to keep pace with demand. When we needed speed, we got trains, then automobiles, then aircraft. When we needed power, we had fossil fuels, then nuclear and now natural, renewable generation – with nuclear staying very much on the scene. When we needed food, we had fruit, grain and meat, and then we began to make our own synthetically. Supply has met demand, certainly in the West, and we have grown because we have been supported with what we need at our fingertips. How we got that support was mainly because of exploitation of resources, people and materials on a global basis. The empires of the West – in Old Europe we had the UK, France, Germany, Spain, Portugal and others, while of course the US in the twentieth century – was powered and fed by the resources that they could find, growing fat on the outputs of the lands that they conquered and colonised. The days of imposed exploitation of resources are now receding into history, with China, for example, buying its way into access to and control of resources. With much less than 50 percent of the global population having grown fat while the rest have been exploited by them, the impacts are now becoming evident. The invoice is being presented and we will be required to pay at some point.

In the new world order where independence and sovereign rights mean that countries can exploit their own resources, the supply lines are beginning to become less certain, less secure, less reliable and therefore less resilient. Added to this, with China conducting a global mission to invest in and own infrastructure and governments; the whole concept of resource access has changed. With Russia adding to the challenge by weaponizing and impacting on energy, food and other trading functions, we end up with consolidating problems. This, in turn, means that the infrastructures and networks that support us may be closer to breaking point than we would like; and when demand outstrips manageable and available supply, what next for our own societies and their structures? The supporting capabilities, national, economical and technological, may be less robust than we have led ourselves to believe.

We have an imbalance to address and redress; firstly, and primarily we should consider that we are reliant, absolutely, on the provision of resource in abundance, a long established and integrated supply routes from origin to consumption. This is one side of the equation; and on the other hand we have the fluctuations, dynamics and imposed changes that are happening in our interconnected world, where the supplies that we have taken for granted may be turned off or restricted. We are neither comfortable nor practised in dealing with that as consumers and societies, especially in the affluent 'everything we want now' West. Although we have become dependent on this availability, which has shaped our consumption and lifestyles, our societal capability, we have revealed ourselves to be vulnerable and much less resilient than we would like to think.

And of course the flow can be stopped by human hands or the 'Hand of God', where our supporting resources and the lines that bring them to us may be interdicted by malicious intent or simply by the fact that the resource is not available to us anymore. In history, we have gone to war in the search for resources. We often hear that Western involvement in the Middle East is because of oil; it probably is. However, we cannot go to war against climate change, natural disaster or environmentally engendered resource shortages. Fuel and food are basic societal security needs; and the lack of either or both puts us in a very difficult place indeed. Individuals will die and societies will fracture; and placing either of these out of the reach of those who need them can be a weapon for adversaries; and bring down governments. Moreover, we must consider the lines of support and the infrastructures themselves, and whether, even in times of abundance, they can work effectively to supply us with the resources that we need. Supply chain resilience is often discussed by supply chain specialists; but it is one of those specialisms that affect us all deeply, and perhaps we should be a little more aware of the consequences of breaks in the chain. The resilient thinker needs to understand that the administrative and supply chains maintain capability, and that without them, any resilience plan or approach is meaningless; or at least not meaningful.

Our Western, fat, society is precariously supported by a challenged structure, with the relentless pull of consumption and need linked by interconnected, vulnerable and expansive lines of delivery to the point of origin. When the linkages are broken, the effects upon us can be immediate, and we have numerous and illustrative examples of what happens to us when we lose that supply. In the UK, we have experienced fuel shortages brought on by strikes that have almost caused the country to come to a halt. When power fails in our towns and cities, our inability to operate without traffic control becomes immediately evident; when the UK suffers from more than occasional flooding and supply chains of food and fresh water are stopped, our return to the way we lived in the days before electronic technology can be rapid and damaging. Luckily, until now, because we have so far had the ability to respond to and recover within manageable timescales, the descent into mediaeval living has not yet fully materialised. But let's imagine; and it is not necessary to have extensive powers of imagination to think ahead.

Consider a changed world where power is not a constant and costs are prohibitive, both to supplier and consumer, such that priority is given to some sectors of government, industry or essential critical national infrastructure. This was a constant in the non-digital, strike-torn 1970s. But what would happen in a similar scenario now? What about our nuclear power plants, owned and run in part by China and France? How would businesses communicate – in fact do business – without the Internet and its supporting structure? What would happen if we were unable to maintain communication through our telephone networks, many of them owned or heavily invested in by overseas companies? Where does our food come from and how are the supply chains guaranteed and managed when interdicted and challenged – not in the short term when delivery trucks are stuck in roadworks or there is a shortage of drivers – but in the longer term when there is inadequate flow of consumables to the public? How much do we and should we trust a 'system' that we know so little about?

Risks are fluid and their impacts are uncertain; of course there are linked aspects and the loss risks can be extreme. Maths and formula do allow for the calculation of probability – but nothing is certain. For example, we can throw dice, but the die will roll a different way every time because of other unmeasured variables, such as who is throwing, where and with what degree of energy. There is therefore uncertainty that is additional even to the most scientific study and assessment of random variables. It is perhaps useful to pause and think about why, with all of our expertise, our awareness of Taleb's[2] 'Black Swans', our maths and our capabilities to gather information and intelligence – we keep getting it wrong. The hubris of humans can be staggering, and it is often brought into sharp focus when our looking at horizons fails us, or our limited human capacity for thinking is exposed. Examples of such limited thinking and about which we should know better abound. This is such a challenge that I make no apologies in advance for returning to it as a theme for this book.

If we look at any number of issues, geopolitical problems, conflicts and concerns, the fact that we just do not know is uncomfortable; because we like to be comforted by 'buffering' (my term for building in processes and ideas that allow us to follow our preferred paths and give us space to build our delusions of capability); or by dazzling ourselves with mathematics, or by putting in place theories, frameworks and 'best' practice that works only for specific people and organisations in specific circumstances. This is real uncertainty, compounded by the fact that we feel that our own certainties can influence outcomes. But only by controlling all uncertainties can we develop certainty in

---

[2] Taleb, NN., (2010), *The Black Swan: The Impact of the Highly Improbable*, London: Random House.

response; and we will never be able to do that. We therefore live not only in a difficult world but one of compromise, where we need to balance our thinking and response against our tolerances and, yes, preferences. What this compromise means is that we rarely find a clean solution to challenges that face us; and compromise always leaves gaps somewhere. In the face of deep and consolidating resilience challenges, compromise is not the best option for effective response. Although it may temporarily alleviate the pain of an impact, the bruise will spread over time.

COVID-19 and Russia

In the world of difficulty, we have developed our multiple interconnections and interdependencies whose weaknesses have only been fully exposed as such once we have come under extraordinary, new and challenging pressure. As we have mentioned, we can see examples quite clearly of slow burning events that have exposed weaknesses that have been with us for a long time. The prime examples as I write are the COVID-19 pandemic and the Russian war on Ukraine. In both cases, the first thing to note, probably fundamentally, is that neither of these challenging crises should have been a surprise, and therefore with collective and coherent thinking, it may have been useful to identify what may have been the impacts of such globally damaging undesirable events. What we actually saw was the result of optimism bias, 'groupthink' (more on that later), and an inability or lack of will to fully think about and put in place mitigation planning to reduce impacts that have gone much further than the 'trigger' events themselves may have implied.

At the same time we have seen governments and businesses take advantage of the impacts and opportunities to further pursue political and financial gain. In both cases, although death and casualties have been inevitable and tragic, the long-lasting impacts have been, and will be, economic, social and world changing. Blame is one thing; but an inability to act upon and intervene in a developing crisis leading to a catastrophe goes beyond fault and blame, and takes us into the realms of ineptitude, stupidity, arrogance and, of course, egotism.

Beginning with the pandemic, with hindsight we can see the scale of the impact. In reality, we should have seen that scale beforehand; but none of us did. COVID-19 has changed our societal thinking, and damaged trust and confidence in government, and to some extent, science. It has provoked a damaging shift in retail and commerce sectors for some, and has given opportunities to others. It has accelerated technological progress not only in relation to the development of vaccines and responses to the virus itself, but also to the way in which we communicate, and has projected us towards an even more digitally dependent future as our ways of working and living have changed. All of this could have been anticipated when national risk registers that were put together by 'experts' in response to pandemics in the first decade of the twenty-first century, actually began to acknowledge that pandemics do exist. In the UK our risk registers contained explicit mention of pandemics; and yet the national response to COVID-19 was less than effective in many ways.

Although the specific nature of the virus required an exact response, there were many other mitigation measures and potential impacts that could have been identified and were not. In effect, when the pandemic became what a pandemic really *is* – affecting all of us – our governments, planners, scientists and responders had very little to help us with.

They fell back on crisis management that rapidly outstripped what were clearly inadequate plans. The potential had been blocked out of thinking and the capability to respond was confused and weak. This is inadequate resilient thinking in action.

As the single largest ever global impact event short of the two world wars, to date at least, the COVID-19 pandemic was a once-in-a-lifetime (hopefully) opportunity for us to examine the true levels of resilience and preparedness at all levels of society. The concept of a global pandemic is neither something new, nor something that we should not expect. As we have mentioned, plans have been considered and scientists have often warned of the effects of a global, rapid spreading and impactful pandemic. The fact that became very clear very early on in the pandemic's life was that despite all of our talk and discussion concerning pandemic preparation, we were just not ready. The response to COVID-19 was so poor that not only were we not ready, but we had also not properly considered any of the implications of such a pandemic on such a scale, especially its wider impact once it could not be contained. Our resilience was not effective enough to meet the challenge.

It is probable that we considered the risk of a pandemic becoming truly global and having an impact on every level of every society to be such a remote possibility that our plans were simply a panacea to fulfil a planning need. This, in itself, is one of the major features of inadequate resilient thinking, and we will return to this as we regress through the book. Despite the word 'pandemic' being used in books and plans by scientists, academics and yes, resilience specialists, we were not ready. There were enough warnings; they went unheeded. COVID-19 was a resilience failure with clear, unequivocal lessons for everyone, not least resilient thinkers.

When the pandemic struck, there was no way of offering any form of inoculation or prophylaxis against the spread or development of the virus and its mutations. That came later. Also, there was a chronic lack of personal protective equipment (PPE) for both responders and the public. That meant that when the virus was in its most lethal stages and taking its heaviest toll, those who were required to treat its victims were put at considerable risk. Every business was affected in some way or another by the virus, and some have profited (many in China) but many have not. We have also seen significant damage to travel, tourism, events and hospitality industries that offer no little support to national economies; in some regions they *are* the national economy. This was foreseeable and perhaps could not have been avoided; but could it have been mitigated more effectively? I believe so.

Notwithstanding the significant numbers of deaths and the continuing impact of 'long covid', the long, long lasting, and chronic physical and psychological after-effects of the virus, which were bad enough, the economic effect will be felt for at least a generation after the pandemic has gone away. Of course, the pandemic may never go away, and may now be just another part of our new life processes going forward. And in among all the recriminations, blame-throwing and after-action reports, we simply need to learn that we failed and aim to do better.

In terms of what COVID-19 has done to us, and what it has allowed to happen to us, the list is long and crushing. Costs have risen, we have become used to unavailability and shortages. We have realised that we need to be able to manage our lives in different ways. There have been irrevocable gaps in education that were caused by the need to switch to online delivery when schools, colleges and universities were not only technologically ill-equipped to do so, but did not have fully capable and trained staff to deliver it effectively. These are slow burning impacts that will be felt in the long term. They are not intangible, but are something that will cause problems. The pandemic has damaged at least two generations: the old and the young, with both being vulnerable in different ways. There are real, enduring impacts – another type of 'long covid'.

More than anything else, the pandemic showed us that we are fragile, vain creatures who will allow our optimism bias to help us avoid facing details. If we have learned anything from COVID-19, it must be that for all of our conceits, supposed knowledge and 'best practice' that were in place for organisational resilience, crisis management and continuity, with very few exceptions, it caught us unawares in terms of size, scale and impact. It revealed to us that the hackneyed phrase 'people are our greatest asset' is absolutely true; and that people will prioritise their health and safety over placing themselves in risk situations, and the world of work and business has changed because of that. Conversely, it also showed that a significant element of society is more than ever, resistant to controls and restrictions for whatever reason, and will continue to defy legal and regulatory challenges in the name of freedom of choice and movement. COVID-19 was the salutary lesson from which we must learn to do better.

What the pandemic fundamentally showed us is that we need to be able to work effectively to anticipate, respond to and recover from the challenges we face, and we need to be *analytical and thorough.* This takes time and effort, and is probably the most challenging aspect of developing effective organisational resilience. However, the ultimate lesson was that this is essential if we are to be able to effectively face and overcome crises that may gestate in one way and then become catastrophes. At the same time, we must consider that only by detailed, analytical and open-minded thinking can we anticipate and thus act effectively. Without it we are dumb responders to stimulus, like insects.

DID YOU KNOW?

According to the World Health Organization the total number of deaths globally from COVID-19 as of 15 May 2023 was 6.9 million.

You can keep up with the increasing total here: *https://covid19.who.int/*.

Looking elsewhere, in the Russian/Ukraine conflict a very different exposition of what can happen when we look at a risk and decide not to mitigate effectively has taken place. Notwithstanding the fact that there has been wasteful, needless loss of life, and that the approach taken by Russia is redolent of German nationalist aggression before and during World War II, we should have seen it coming. In fact, if we conduct any form of research into Russian responses to the expansion of NATO following the dissolution of the USSR, we can see that Russia had been quite proactive in seizing and regaining control of territory that it believed belonged to it. Conflicts in Georgia, Crimea and, yes, Ukraine, demonstrated clearly that there was intent to reassert Russian ownership in the region. Western involvement in conflicts in Iraq and Afghanistan showed that politically, and to an extent militarily, there was a diminishing appetite to maintain a foothold in those regions for the long term. So, if ever there was a time for Russia to make its move, this was it. When the West began to doubt itself, the more patient Russia took its chance.

Perhaps also, the type of warfare in which the West had become involved, and convinced itself was the future, demonstrated that we had planned ourselves away from the ability to face what is termed a 'near peer' adversary. In the 'honeymoon period' after perestroika and the collapse of the Warsaw Pact, the US and the West may have felt that they were the winners. The reality is that we have been in constant conflict since then, and the vacuum of ideological adversary has been filled by Al-Qaeda, ISIS, the Taliban and Islamist problems. All the time the continued existence of a strong Russia focused on maintaining its previous international goals was there. The fact that the Cold War was an arms race between two superpowers that also conducted proxy wars in various parts of the world during that time is to me, almost irrelevant, when we get to the final outcome and subsequent changes to the world order.

Effectively, we had a world in stasis for a considerable period of time, when neither the US nor USSR really got the upper hand. From 1989, the world became fractured, disorientated and confused. Where there were certainties about the aims, objectives and ideologies of each side, there were many distractions; and that changed again in the

2020s. Most importantly, the West became complacent about itself and the world that it felt it owned. The new reality is that the West is having its identity and confidence crisis now, with a bewildering array of challenges posing a real risk to our current way of life, with a new world order beginning to emerge. Interestingly, this is not in Europe or Russia, but more widely in regions and countries that are now growing in confidence. The shift in global power is happening with the Russian war as just one of the many catalysts for change.

Because we are drawn to changes in headline news like moths to light, the lessons from the pandemic (the latest pandemic in any case) are probably being forgotten as we move further away from its temporal epicentre. Russia is destroying its neighbour and taking us back to a world of confrontation and distrust. Economies are battered, international relations are fractious and in the background China watches and waits. All of this has an impact on you, me, our families, our employers and our governments, and the tone is now being set for the remainder of the twenty-first century. For those who live throughout this century, this will be a time of change, the likes of which come along every few generations, where we move from dynamic change to some form of settled existence before major upheavals upset us again. These upheavals are happening now – the changes we face are and will be intense – and we will feel them. And as resilient thinkers we sit in the middle of all this. How we, as societies, working towards some form of future learn to talk to each other in this new world may save or sink us.

Communication in the interdependent world

As we progress through the book, we will consider impacts and events alongside the various multiplying factors that can cause further consequential problems for organisations. People are at the centre of that. Interdependencies are being played out against a background of huge societal change. If we think about the social media driven shift towards change that has accelerated in the second decade of this century, that change is now beginning to have significant impact. Although the initial consideration of the power and value of social media was perhaps focused on the idea that we are able to communicate more effectively; for governments and organisations in general, the ability of the public to communicate is very much a double-edged sword. With the communication-led change to the way that our world has operated in the past hundred years or more, the impact of the Internet has been such that even without conflict, we are accelerating those global power shifts. The 'traditional' power bias of the economic 'North' (the developed world) in relation to the economic 'South' (the less developed world) is changing rapidly; and social media is the driver, much more so than the traditional (geo) politics and the influence of mainly men in suits. *They* are losing control.

Fundamentally, and on the face of it, the need to control popular voices while governing can be seen to be at odds with the whole idea of democracy. However, in effect the controlling component, except in the most authoritarian regimes, has become something of a lost cause. The connected global population has a way and means of accessing information and sharing views in an unprecedented way. Our modern version of the Tower of Babel is less constrained by language barriers as we can communicate through emojis. However, as every opinion and idea can be expressed and aired, the voice is contradictory, multi-layered and confusing. Our social constructs and political decisions are now firmly influenced by the popular collective whose thoughts, ideas and values are centred on the personal and the self, and seen through the lens of mainstream and social media, with the immediacy and personal nature of social media being the prime tool of influence and expression. This confuses and dilutes decision making to the point of being almost ineffective, and certainly unable to reach its goals.

In the wider context of globalisation, technology (as has happened throughout history) has given us the tools to progress and develop, and the change of social makeup and interaction has gathered pace as humanity has progressed. With the interconnected technology that now underpins our globalised activity, populations have found a voice and we are beginning to see in younger generations a disregard for the concepts of national identity, and the lines drawn by nations in the nineteenth and twentieth centuries. Life is changing, humanity is changing, as is the physical world that we inhabit – and this leads to a challenging space in which we must live, work and interact.

The voice of younger generations that has been stifled by voting ages and political systems can now be heard, and has meaning and relevance, developing from something that central governments have steered throughout history. For the first time we now have an enabled and connected population that is able to make its own mind up and discuss what its own mind *is*. In the twentieth century those who ruled could avert their eyes and cover their ears.

Rheingold's (2007)[3] 'smart mobs' may perhaps offer a misnomer for the connected future; it may be preferable to think of 'smart government'. That government, in a resilient society will not only listen to, but embed the popular voice in governance. It is happening, with governments now developing policies in open scrutiny, and manifestos that must pass the test of public endorsement before they can be printed. It is not tenable to ignore or try to silence the outpouring of seized opportunities that the Pandora's Box of social media has released.

Let's look ahead. For at least a generation, we have been encouraged to link, communicate and interact; to express ourselves freely and openly using the social media voice that has emerged as a prime influence on our society This engendered behaviour has led to an innate need and requirement to remain constantly linked, and to have the opinions that we believe to be as valid as those of everyone else around us. Not only that but we demand that our opinions be both listened to and acted upon. The popular voice is now driving rather than responding to societal restructure. This has significant implications for government and societal cohesion, as social media is now facilitating a real change in political participation, with politics being less about what have been the traditional focus, and more about causes and ideas, such as climate change, human rights, inclusion and diversity. Governments and societies have been given a clear indication of what their future will be – and the resilient elements of both will without doubt be those who can manage the implications of

---

[3] Rheingold, H., (2007), *Smart Mobs: The Next Social Revolution*, Cambridge MA: Basic Books.

this change and adapt to them. Businesses that can demonstrate that they understand and can respond to this will be the resilient future survivors.

The accepted norms to date are not only challenged by popular voices, but also by what that voice will be saying about our traditional and rapidly changing norms and *mores* of national identity and culture. Boggs (2012)[4] asserted that there is: *"[...] a perpetual shrinkage of politics as citizen participation, public discourse, and social governance erode."* Communication and mutual influence are aspects of a wider manifestation in younger generations of disregard for the concepts of national identity and the lines of governance drawn by central governments. The generation born in the third quarter of the last century is probably the last to fully accept that politicians (and the parties that they represent) have automatic rights, mandates and authority. Later and current generations question and expect reasoned and rational answers where explanation overcomes direction. Gen Z, to be supplanted by Gen A after them, want something new. These generations are taught to question, to interact and to have something to say. This comes from the very earliest stages of their lives and education, and has and will develop a very different workforce, population and global society that is linked by the power and stimulus of social media.

---

[4] Boggs, C., (2012), *Ecology and Revolution: Global Crisis and the Political Challenge,* New York: Palgrave Macmillan.

Linking the cause and effect, there is no doubt that the power of the interconnected voice has had a significant impact upon the traditional view of where populations sit in the hierarchy of power and their influence on global thinking. The increasing confidence of those nations who have been relatively 'quiet' until recently is due in no small part to the interaction of their populations globally. Social media and mainstream online media provide unprecedented opportunities for the unheard to become heard and the unseen to be seen, and that opportunity is being taken with alacrity. What this means is that the authority of what is said, and by whom, is less important than what chimes with the collective voice. That voice may be ideologically extreme, it may be unearthing and looking for restitution for historical injustice, it may be linked to a particular fashion or trend. In all cases it will be interconnected and powerful. This is no longer controllable, and therefore it needs to be understood and accepted. More than this, the acceptance should not necessarily be of it as a threat, but simply as a manifestation of change, even progress.

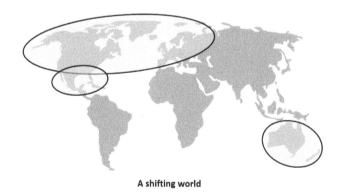

A shifting world

Figure 2: How it's going

1: A world of difficulty

The solid bordered areas are where the old money, the old thinking and the causes of our changing world order and recent history are increasingly felt to lie. In the remaining areas, in general, rising voices are challenging the old order; and there are many of them with a lot to say. The battle for the hearts, minds and deference of these areas of the world will lead to societal, organisational and individual impact, and continue to shift the power balance. This shift will change the way we all live and work.

The Gulf states, African nations, India, Pakistan and many others are now participating in debate and challenge, and finding their feet as Western technology capabilities become more prevalent in their own regions. They are taking control of theirs and our future. This is the state of a redeveloping world, and resilient thinkers should understand the impact of this accelerating change upon them. The idea that human association becomes more of a driver for international behaviour than any number of political parties, styles, beliefs and doctrines is an intriguing one. The movement to change fundamental large-scale organisational behaviours and interactions is ongoing, expedited by the way that we now behave and think in an information-led society, where borders are now irrelevant as far as communication and international relationship construction are concerned. The ability to persuade stakeholders has never been so important and so fundamental for organisational resilience and viability. The understanding that voices in societies cannot and should not be controlled is perhaps unpalatable for many; but, it is essential if we are to remain in some way viable and relevant to our future development .

Information and perceptions in society – Technology, messages and management

Resilient thinking is not just about business, but also societies. On the societal scale, and affecting all of us, the problem of protecting societies and their citizens has existed ever since society existed. However, the ancient method of building protective barriers to deter and protect against incursions across borders has (mostly) been subsumed into a less tangible and visible protective process. Our governments and their agencies that serve us operate on an 'arms-length' principle, whereby threats and risks are interdicted and contained at a distance. The way that we have become comfortable in doing our national business has been to outsource and offshore our activities. Our battles against terrorists, organised criminals and nation states are not necessarily (or desirably) conducted on our home ground, but in their states of origin or proxy, using all possible and available means of state to do so. As this approach and capability has developed and grown over time, there has been a sense of distance and detachment among the public. Despite the headlines and the sometimes horrific and unsettling scenes and situations that we witness through the media on an almost daily basis, we remain generally unmoved by what happens in other regions and countries, even if it is of our own making. That detachment dilutes the sense of impact that perhaps we would feel if we were closer and more involved. Not only that, but when we do experience impacts, we can tend to underestimate their nature and consequences.

This state of detachment or blissful ignorance can be helpful to those who wish to maintain societal stability, as it is probably counter-productive and certainly counter-intuitive in their view to induce a heightened sense of awareness that leads to panic. Panic leads to reactions that may worsen a situation; and certainly will render management of issues more challenging. But how should we be expected to behave when we realise the gravity of a threat? The threats that we do face, the configuration of our society, and again by inference those organisations that operate within it, mean that we should consider having in place, and educating and developing, capabilities to be able to build organisational resilience effectiveness and capacities at multiple levels. The very fact that risks and impacts are developed and generated before impacting society and our organisations at all levels, means that we should be able to develop a commensurate coping capability as the effects may be felt before they can be prevented. The question is, do those who manage our nations and the organisations within them need us to be more aware, or less aware, about what may happen to us when things go wrong?

The consideration of awareness, of the informing ideas that make the small changes that occur almost daily and that contribute to wider and more influential transformations, is perhaps more challenging and more stimulating than simply thinking that a problem can be 'ring-fenced' and managed without much consultation. I think that it is useful to realise that, although we would like to have a small, highly effective 'dream team' with all the answers and all the responsibility, that approach is less effective than it used to be. The ideas, thoughts and concepts behind the 'leave it to us/we know best/we have the answers' approach organisational and national resilience, are perhaps what bring so many problems along for the ride. There is recognition of this; and challenge of received information and instruction is increasingly a defining aspect of our societal behaviours and conduct.

Contributing to the issue, and key to this discussion overall, is the idea that we may believe that we are informed, when in fact (or in theory) we are receiving conflicting and ideologically motivated information that has been orientated towards influencing thoughts, ideas and consumerist and voting intentions on a constant basis. Of course, this is nothing new; advertisers have always advertised, and politicians have made their pitches. However, routes are now direct and persuasive. Complementary to this persuasive and what some may consider cynical approach; we are often informed through 'telling' rather than by explaining; this distinction is important, as psychologically deference to authority can tend to lend false gravitas to a particular statement, message or approach.

This deference to authority can be manifested in the idea that people are faced with and are directly influenced by what they consume via the published media. Newspapers and TV have the direct capability and capacity to make change and to swing public opinion; a role that, if not subsumed, has certainly been built upon by social media but in a very different way. Social media, viral and of course fake news, may be perceived by many to be the unfettered and impartial variants or descendants of the traditional and politically aligned print or broadcast routes. Whether this is true or not, it is perhaps partially true that human beings see a grain of truth and reflection of their own vision in many of the versions of the world that are put in front of them. It is for them to challenge or align themselves with that potential truth, regardless of the source.

But, there is a degree of further thinking to be conducted. To what extent are we informed rather than told, and to what extent is an explanation needed or required? And when we do hear an explanation, do we, or should we, accept it without question? Equally important, what do people hear and what do they choose to hear? Do they understand and interpret from the information that they are given, and is it beneficial to them or negative? We therefore are looking at and listening to a multiple format and multiple level media platform, involving many ways and means to influence not only the information that we would like the recipients to receive, but also how they may be asked to respond to that information. This multiplicity of communication issues brings complexity. When earlier generations were told to 'Keep Calm and Carry On' in the Second World War, they probably tried to do that to some extent. The questions now might be: 'What about, why, who says so and who is going to support me?' With inquisitive thinking and freedom of thought and action embedded in our societal aims and education, this is our norm.

Let us assume that information flow has a direct effect and that it is able to inform and influence behaviour. From that we perhaps should be able to recognise that the use of media and other outlets to provide the information and support that will improve our organisational resilience at a national level has the potential to be very effective. The ability to reach large sectors of the community through the delivery of authoritative information rather than in response to media stories (such as cyber or terror attacks) is now possible. Offering streams of important, updated information that will be able to deliver an enhanced societal response is something that has a capability beyond the simple transmission of words and images. It is of course important to consider that any such use of mainstream or even social media to develop this capability may be considered to be a 'double-edged sword'. The idea that perhaps there is a degree of manipulation or influencing involved in the delivery of important information is something that will immediately spring to mind. There is a reason that organisations of all sizes allocate significant budget and resources to public relations and communications; they want to get their message across, and they want us to believe that message.

The development of understanding of the necessary balance between what needs to be heard and the reality of a situation is an important element of resilient thinking. The ability to encompass and to understand what is real and what is not is a further influence on our capability and capacity. To manage the expectations and information needs of society and our organisations is becoming ever more challenging as well as important for organisational resilience. Where expectations are high, the complexities and challenges of communication remain at the core of organisational capability.

Another assumption, in this case something that is taken for granted and that currently supports Western society – continuity of infrastructure – is now also at risk. It is a sensible and realisable ambition to link our technology, systems and infrastructure; and the interface of humans and their relative contribution to the overall and future capability of the Internet is now woven into the information map. Time, effort and speed of information and data movement is increasing rapidly; an inevitable development of the use of machine learning and thinking to replace and support human thought processes. In terms of resilience and societal continuity, the interconnectivity of human beings brings risk where technology is involved, which is everywhere and at every level. It is an absolute indicator of the human condition and the constant need to think and consider more expansively that we now move from the mundane and accepted structures of the Internet into the next phases of our technological development and dependency. AI, the Internet of Things, blockchain and the metaverse are all within that next phase. They bring great opportunity, change and advancement; and bring particular and commensurate issues and problems. For those of us who are concerned with resilience, the exploitation of knowledge and capability gaps by determined adversaries will have a continued and continuing damaging effect long into the future.

DID YOU KNOW?

That about 99% of global data is transmitted via undersea cables. The longest, from Germany to Korea, is more than 24,000 miles in length.

You can see global submarine cable maps here: *https://www.submarinecablemap.com/*.

And it is not simply a question of how we communicate; but also of the change in human attitudes to work and living, at least in the privileged West. COVID-19 had a significant impact on the technology-enabled future, rendering remote working as the norm rather than the exception for many. This, in turn, increased awareness of the benefits of a work-life balance and the setbacks of the traditional focus on office working. The revolution in adoption of remote meeting capabilities has changed our working dynamic, and has proven to be a manifestation of reprioritised thinking by many sections of society. Why commute when you can work from home? Why not work at hours and times that fit your domestic and familial responsibilities? Why spend your salary on transport, coffee and lunches when that expenditure can be avoided? All reasonable and practical thoughts that were only made real by a pandemic. This, in turn, helped technology organisations to progress their thinking and development of support for new ways of working. The metaverse will further allow the development of detached, devolved and blended virtual, real and connected working and living communities, and thus societies.

This changed emphasis, and of course opportunity, is without doubt a form of progress rather than a negative, although it may clearly be seen to be so by some. Virtuality is now an aspect of life that we as societies need to embrace. We have lived in virtuality for some time. Blockchain based crypto currency has moved from a marginal concept to a mainstream viable and functioning basis for transactions and wealth development. As we continue to progress towards full digital immersion and the use of cash transactions becomes less commonplace, cryptocurrency is primed to play a much larger and influential part of our reality than it has to date. This is becoming another layer of complexity in our world of difficulty. In reality, we have been working with virtual currency for some time. When was the last time you paid for something using folding, real money?

We are continuing to move forwards in different ways. But, as with all aspects of digital reliance, there are risks to face that the resilient thinker would do well to consider. If our networks are in place, adopted, used and relied upon, they need to work effectively. Reliance on technology relies on power and logistics; and climate change and resource shortages (or denial) may have a part to play. The battle for the resources that power our digital age is under way, and is linked to who has them, who wants them and who will fight for them. Shortages of semiconductor materials and rare metals that form components of our technologies are being made more complex by the competition between important global state and business interests to control them. Resource shortage events, either temporary or long-term, causing problems at the point of loss, may also affect supply chains and operations through consequent shortages in much more extended ways. No semiconductors means that there are many other commodities and products that become unavailable. In the longer-term, social change may also be an issue, as market demand and values change to accommodate changes in supply. Taken to a more extensive and long-term conclusion, there is significant analysis and study to be conducted on the longevity of economies when pressured by the denial of access to the natural resources that sustain us. If we *need* these commodities to maintain our technological edge, how will we secure them? Is there a potential to revert to conflict?

These nuances and components will not only be limited to the processes that we write down in our lucid moments where calm and quiet allow us to think carefully and strategically about what we are aiming to achieve. We also need to think very carefully about the reactive, the emotive and the responses that will also have a critical effect upon our ability to be resilient. And, we also need to consider the effects of others. Stakeholders are not necessarily shareholders. They can range from suppliers to activists, and all will have some influence on what we do and how we do it. A stakeholder may be defined here as 'an entity that is interested in, or in which the organisation may have, an interest'. The spectrum of 'light' and 'dark' stakeholders can be very wide indeed. Stakeholders can come in the 'light' form: benign and supportive, or 'dark' non-benign and with less than supportive intent.

'Light' Stakeholders	'Dark' Stakeholders
Employees; partners; customers; clients; suppliers; aligned media; ideological and political matches; some competitors; collaborators; government; legal and regulatory bodies; general public; social media influences; activists; investors...	Competitors; criminals; ideological and political opponents; media; government; legal and regulatory bodies; general public; social media influences; activists; other nations...

Figure 3: Light and dark stakeholders

There are those who are interested in you because they benefit from some form of relationship. That relationship may not be benign or collaborative. There are also those who will benefit from malicious/adversarial activity. It's important to understand that they are interested, monitoring and seeking to interact. The more an organisation is active, the more its impact and the more stakeholders will be generated. The problem, then, is not simply one of communication, but also of management of them, and us.

Overall, we can see that the world of difficulty is effectively a world of complexity. And fundamentally, we need to set our thinking in the context of the new world; it will not change to suit our needs and expectations. The first quarter of the twenty-first century has shown that we can predict little and expect much in terms of change and impact. Alongside change and conflict, technology, education and new superpower dynamics has come the growing realisation and accusation that we in the West have been like kleptomaniac, violent babies for hundreds of years. We have stolen resources from other nations without conscience or thought for our own gain, and now it feels like it is time for reparation and for the North/South injustice, inequality and imbalance to be addressed and redressed. When it comes to paying the bill, we need to understand that the organisation that incorporates an understanding of the fact that we do need to pay, and that only resilient organisations will have the capability, and inevitably, the resource to contribute to that payment, our future perhaps becomes clearer. That future may neither feel attractive or comforting, but it is the future that we need to face, and I would contend that clear thinking and effective prognosis of the symptoms and impacts of the changed environment in which we live, will allow us to be best focused on what is coming in the future. It will certainly allow us to prepare more effectively than if we watch without responding.

I suppose the question for the resilience professional now is 'what impact does all of this change have on me?'. Firstly, it is crucially important to realise that the impacts that we are facing in the twenty-first century are, if not wholly unprecedented, of the highest level of challenge. The impact that will land upon individuals and organisations should not be anything of a surprise, nor should we be in a situation where we cannot see or anticipate the further seismic change that is coming. The development of our new world of difficulty is the demonstrable outcome of the changes that have happened throughout history and have simply brought us to this waypoint. Human beings are resilient, and we will adapt to change. It may not be the change that we want, but change that is inevitable and must be faced. We should also remember that anything that we can do only leaves us at a waypoint; and that further development, change and challenge are equally inevitable.

So that we can face change and make the best possible outcome for ourselves and our organisations, we need to understand how we might be able to look at problems and impacts. To understand, we need to think and analyse before we act. We need to move away from any form of reliance on checking through lists, standards and guidelines as the basis for our thinking. That's not what they are designed for; and in most cases they are designed by people who decide that they know what the outcomes are before they even begin. Of course, the reality test, as we have seen over history and yet again in the first quarter of the twenty-first century, shows that we are way behind the ability of life to surprise us. How we respond to surprises is what will make the difference as we go forward. However, it is complicated, and for me the over-complication of simple processes and thinking can be worse than the manifestation of a risk itself. We will look at this in the next chapter; but, before we move onto that, there is one final underscoring point. *A world of difficulty is also a world of opportunity.* Understand that and configure your thinking towards it and the changes become your differentiator rather than a millstone around your organisational neck.

Here are some points for the resilient thinker to consider from this chapter:

1. Change continues to come at a challenging pace. Based on your analysis and thinking, what is the most impactful change that has happened in the past ten years? Why have you made that choice?

2. Whatever your choice, to what extent do you think that there is an ability to mitigate the impacts from that change?

3. What do you think might happen if the change cannot be mitigated?

4. Given that you have identified a change and its impacts, what are your views on how we could and should have been prepared?

5. Of the changes and impacts that are on your 'radar', if you had the power to turn back time, which one would you have stopped at source (if any)? Reflect on your reasons and how, as a result, other impacts may be changed.

CHAPTER 2: LOOKING TO OUR FUTURE

"You cannot escape the responsibility of tomorrow by evading it today."

Abraham Lincoln

To allow further contextualisation of the ideas that will be discussed and developed as we move onto the attributes and challenges in resilient thinking, it is useful to continue by considering ideas about how we look ahead and why. With a multitude of varying, conflicting and competing ideas, ideologies, motivations and causes for thoughts, ideas and action, the complications of our environment seemingly continue to multiply. The global population, regardless of our international, national and individual situations, conducts transactions and interacts within that environment; and what happens in it in the future has the potential to affect us to varying degrees and with varying levels of severity.

In this chapter we will therefore discuss ideas about the influences that may engender or initiate change, and thus inform the shape of risk and impact landscapes. Also, although there is an immense amount of opinion and theory put forward daily from all quarters concerning human behaviour and its effect on others (such as, by implication, political, economic, social and technological impacts), it is also worth considering ideas, theories and opinions on the less easily quantifiable and controllable. We should ask questions. How effective are we at looking ahead? How effective are we at acting on what we see? These human behaviours will either constrain or enable us; and thinking more about this is a starting point when considering the potential for our future development as resilient thinkers.

The future and resilience

The world is warming up; the world is going to get too cold; we're going to run out of water; we're all going to drown in floods. Oil is on the way out; oil costs a fortune; the West is doomed, and it's all going to end this year or next year; cyber criminals, spooks and terrorists are looking to cause damage, death, and destruction; we are heading for economic ruin; there is a big asteroid out there in space heading for us. There will be a plague of locusts, there is (another) pandemic on the way ...

If we read the news, or listen to everyone who has a viewpoint, we will discover that there is a lot of conflicting and speculative talk about what could happen to us in the coming years, and the general view seems to be that we are accelerating towards destruction and extinction. This line of thought is probably not without justified reason; the problems and issues that dominate our thinking could all happen and are characterised by varying degrees of plausibility and urgency. In fact, everything in my short listing above has either happened before or is coming. However, the truth of the matter is that we just do not know enough about what will happen to us and how we might respond. There are some events that we can predict with a degree of certainty; there are others that we can deprioritise; and there are even more that make good copy in print and in broadcast mainstream and social media. It is confusing, challenging and worrying. However, resilient thinking can help us to try to make sense of it all. And from that, we can begin to devise the resilience attributes and responses that we need so that we, and our areas of responsibility, are able to maintain and continue.

Because all these challenges are complex; and because we don't know all the answers, we need to think about the mitigation or solutions. The challenge for the effective and committed resilient thinker is to try to develop and enable capabilities for anticipation, response, recovery and improvement based upon some foundation of thought and balanced analysis. Unsurprisingly, this is not an easy thing to do. I think that the key to unlocking the future capability of resilience is to consider what may come next, realistically, and then figure out what, if anything, you or your organisation need or wish to do about it. Although this may seem straightforward on paper, we need to engage with that thought process, then act on what needs to be done effectively and in a timely way. This can be a challenge and lead to failure if not achieved comprehensively, accurately and with diligence. The difficulty of transferring a problem into a solution through understanding, planning and then action should not be underestimated. I suggest that despite all our talk about how to be resilient, cashing those thoughts into useable capability is something that many organisations either cannot or will not do. This inability to put in place a real, resourced and tangible capability is much more prevalent, I feel, than we would like to think.

However, even with the most capable response and recovery organisational functions, and as we are learning daily, there are some things we cannot stop. No matter how powerful our senior management think they may be, they will never be able to stop an asteroid smashing into the Earth. Setting aside the issue of galactic disaster, there are many smaller-scale events that we cannot stop happening, and the main task, to begin at least, is to consider how prepared we might be and how we can come out on the other side of the problem in the best possible shape. From the organisation's point of view, we also need to do this cost-effectively. It also makes sense to keep in mind a sensible and logical but fundamental assumption and starting point: doing nothing is usually not an option. From then on, the degrees of anticipation and response that we are willing and able to put in place will be the most influential contributors to any final outcome.

Another influencing thought to bear in mind when we are discussing the future of resilience is that, although we have a huge array of threats facing us from multiple directions and with many differing levels of potential severity, not much is completely new. For as long as there have been human beings on the Earth, there have been threats. In fact, even longer, because it is fairly well accepted now that the dinosaurs' lack of resilience meant that they could not deal with the effects of their own galactic incident. The threats are there, as they have always been – there has always been conflict, there have always been criminality issues, there have always been succession planning issues. Nothing is new; it is the *impacts* of events on us that makes them a threat or a risk; much more so than the cause or probability – our understanding of risk management and resilience should be clear; how we are damaged or degraded is the quantifying aspect.

As resilient thinkers, it is our responsibility to have thought about this and to have anticipated and planned our solutions, because there *will* be impacts. Look at conflict; the Ukraine conflict is notable; and it is not just about battles and bombs. It is about political alignments, energy costs and shortages, food costs and shortages, and the inevitable long-term hits that we have not felt just yet. Although this conflict's gestation has been long and complex, it was a surprise to many. Even those to whom it was not a surprise did not act rapidly at first. Although observations like this begin to take us down a route where we see and understand the importance of anticipation leading to readiness, our impact awareness remains the critical element.

Therefore, if we assume that the threats that exist out there – regardless of their initial cause, motivation or origin – may have potential for significant impact, then the future of adaptable organisational resilience needs to consider its forthcoming threats. We also need to think about and be aware of the context and environment of the potential victim organisation and society it inhabits. We should then ensure that we are ready and configured to face these threats, while maintaining business viability and competitive edge. Naturally, whether we are a government, an army or a corporation, without a competitive edge we are out of business anyway as continuity failure is a certainty.

Let us underline what we began in Chapter 1. Here's an example. We all know that the Internet underpins what we do in modern, civilised society. Increasingly, it is at the core of everything, absolutely everything we do in terms of business, communication and knowledge development. It informs our thought processes, behaviours, interactions and social structures. We are dependent upon it, and related technology enablement in Industrial Revolution 4.0 is totally dominant in all human activity. The Internet is fantastic in that respect, and it gives us everything we need, and need to know about, in order to live effectively in the world that we have made for ourselves.

Let us take a pessimistic view and conjecture that one day, suddenly, we lose power globally (even partially) on a permanent basis. We will meet change. This could happen because somebody pulls the plug, maybe there is a solar flare that terminally disrupts power transmission and distribution, maybe we just run out of fuel. All of these are more obviously feasible to us now as we begin to realise that what underpins us is less robust than we would like to think. Among the many lessons that the twenty-first century has taught us so far about our propensity to make errors, there is one clear and standout lesson. Despite all our dazzling progress and our developed society, we sit in a precarious supporting infrastructure that is extremely vulnerable to interruption, disruption and loss. Because of that we need to be fully aware that failure is a constant, haunting option for us.

In the case of infrastructure failure, the cause, once an event has taken place, is unimportant and irrelevant at the point of impact – the further effect is everything. Those who enable and provide power to support the Internet would, of course, be interested in what caused the loss, and should be looking backwards to any causal and vulnerable points in order to protect them and to reduce vulnerabilities and subsequent impacts. But the majority of us, the end users, and that is essentially the global population, will end up without the essential life support that we have become accustomed to through the Internet and its associated business and social-support activities. And in the civilised world that means communication, infrastructure, food, transport: everything. As these vulnerable systems support us, their loss or degradation as a risk brings catastrophic potential consequences.

However, think about the average person, society and structure that exists now in less advantaged, supported and connected ways. In some countries and regions there is less reliance on support because it has never been there. There will be little power, limited infrastructure and no sophisticated communications system either supplied or required. Therefore, if there is a solar flare, if we run out of oil or if someone pulls the plug on the Internet, the average person may be slightly less concerned than we are in the fat West because it's not an issue that disrupts. If a society becomes dependent, as we have done, upon supply and services that are inherently weak or have inherent vulnerable points (and most do), then we need to ensure that we plan for problems and are prepared to work with alternatives, or not at all. And looking to our future means that we must consider realistic and achievable options. If there are no alternatives, we must consider what our future in the large scale will be.

To maintain our fantastic standard of living in our privileged Western world, we have developed and invested our time, effort and money in the most sophisticated, convoluted, interdependent and interconnected network of capability and supporting functions. As a result, our standard of living far exceeds that of our less-privileged fellow humans in less-privileged parts of the world. But, if it all goes wrong and we cannot rely any longer upon those developed and capable supporting functions and their interconnections, how long do you think we are going to last? In effect, we are investing in and building vulnerabilities into the system that gives us 'life'. And removing that removes our power, capability and confidence. Without those we lose our competitive edge. If we are compelled to 'level down' that may be just as beneficial for those who are beyond our borders and control and are seeking to 'level up'.

DID YOU KNOW?

As of May 2023, there were more than five billion Internet users globally, which is about 63% of the global population. 4.76 billion of those use social media.

You can see up-to-date statistics here: *https://www.statista.com/statistics/617136/digital-population-worldwide/*.

This is not even a doomsday scenario. All we are talking about here is the inability to plug in to a wall socket and to power technological tools. The future of resilience depends upon our ability to ensure that if we are going to continue to rely upon these technological tools as underpinning elements of our civilisation, then we must appropriately protect them, or put in place systems whereby we can continue to function if we lose them in the short- or the long-term. In that context, the future of resilience depends upon thinking about things in simple terms and then applying them to the complicated issues surrounding our everyday lives. It is our own advancement that is our weakness; if that is allied with an inability to focus on the consequential weaknesses and potential points of failure, then perhaps it is a doomsday scenario after all. Of course, there is an element of conjecture here. This will probably never happen because someone will have thought of all this already – won't they? I would suggest that the gap between thinking and planning and *action* is significant enough to confound many organisations. If we and our organisations cannot bridge that gap, we may face significant survival struggles.

Predictable and unpredictable

To begin, let us assume (at least for the moment) that we are going to maintain the view that we have thrown out the first option: do nothing. We also need to consider throwing out another consideration: 'it will never happen to us.' In reasonable probability, and we'll discuss probability more later, most bad things will not happen to most of us, most of the time. However, there have been enough incidents over the years with enough people affected in enough serious cases for us to realise that sometimes bad things happen and sometimes those of us far away from intended or unintended targets can be affected. Prediction of exact impacts and their severity can be difficult. Therefore, how can we predict what might be coming along and what can we do to ensure that we have considered the predicted effects upon our organisations and the individuals who work for them? The worst-case scenario is a good place to start, even if it is not a good place to stay. If we have considered throwing out 'it will never happen to us', that means that we understand that it *may* happen to us; and if it *may* then there is a chance that it will.

When things do go wrong there will always be a proportion of any organisation who can respond; and there will always be a proportion of the organisation that is properly resilient and that will come out the other side of the incident in good shape. But that proportion will be small. The complexity and dynamics caused by people who are the subject of resilience planning makes difficult tasks even more challenging. COVID-19 showed that people can make superhuman efforts in the face of adversity. It also became clear that there was an opportunity for many to take a more family-centred approach to life. Where remote working became the norm, it then became difficult to make a case for a return to the office environment and 'presenteeism'. Naturally, some businesses anticipated, adjusted and they and their people thrived. For those who could not or would not change, recovery became more of a challenge. Could this response have been anticipated and predicted? Yes, it could. The idea of remote working was not new when COVID-19 arrived, nor was the growing opinion that work-life balance in the 'always-on' world was becoming more important. What was needed to make the change was a catalyst; and the catalyst in this case was a pandemic that forced the issue.

Because we are human, we must deal with humans. And it is probably a good idea to consider the very worst thing that can go wrong and to put in place at least the thought process, so that we are prepared mentally and with a resourced capability to deal with what can happen. We can never predict with accuracy what is going to happen next, but what we can do is predict how we are going to respond and how we are going to configure and prepare ourselves to respond appropriately. And that will give us the edge in potential problem scenarios because we have taken steps to head them off at the pass. Heading problems off at the pass: anticipating and acting, is an absolute necessity. Waiting to see what develops is less effective, and while a problem develops it will generally worsen, which in turn can add to developing impact.

Here is a scenario. The next time you get onto an aeroplane (if the aviation sector ever recovers from the impacts of COVID-19) and the cabin crew go through the safety demonstration, have a look around. How many people are taking notice of what's going on? You will have a guaranteed 85 percent of the people on board every flight who will be doing everything in their power to ignore what is going on in the safety demonstration. There is a card in the seat pocket in front of every person that indicates where the exits are and what to do in the event of an emergency. People never read those. How many people do you see checking underneath their seat that their life jacket is actually there? Not many.

So, what we have is a thin-skinned aluminium tube that flies at more than 600 km/h at a height of 15 km. It is full of fuel and guided along by one or two people and a computer, controlled and supported by radar and radio. By 2035, there are plans for passenger aircraft to be pilotless. When you look at flying in those terms, it is quite a risky process to travel on an aeroplane in the first place. As for the 15 percent of the travelling population who do consider their safety, who *do* just quickly check where the exits are, who do put their hand on their life jacket and who do read the card – when it all goes wrong do you think they will have a better chance of survival than those who do nothing? It's worth thinking about – nothing is certain and nobody on the aircraft might survive an air accident despite all the measures that are in place to mitigate the risk – but it's definitely worth thinking about. Do you know the optimal 'brace' position? Probably not.

Height, speed, maintenance, routes and locations, pilot skills, weather, collisions, cleanliness, passengers, air traffic control, flag carrier, automation and technology, terrorism and crime, errors and oversights, airport facilities, fuel and range...

Figure 4: Aircraft

How risky is flying? There are many risk factors that are mitigated, managed and accepted when we take to the air. All of this doesn't stop us from flying. Naturally, the benefits must outweigh the risks, or we wouldn't do it at all. Would we?

When margins for error are small and fine, anticipation, looking ahead and preparation are going to give you and your organisation a distinct advantage when trying to figure out how to continue to operate and produce outputs. And if you put yourself in parallel to the aircraft scenario, if your organisation is one of the 15 percent and your competitors comprise the 85 percent, then, come the big day, you are going to have a competitive advantage over them. It does seem relatively straightforward when we put it in terms like that, but there are so many organisations who do not make any effort to take anticipatory steps and then find themselves wanting when the problems arise. There really is no excuse, especially for the resilient thinker working in any organisation. And if it comes to escaping from a burning aircraft, it probably makes sense to be one of the first people at the exit door! Thinking figuratively, how far away from that are you?

So, although we cannot exactly predict what can happen, what we can predict is that things will happen. We should also be clear that the impacts, rather than the granular detail of how they get to us, are things we should worry about. That is the stuff of business continuity and resilience, and some might argue that it is also the stuff of risk assessment. We'll discuss later whether we should consider risk assessment to be an exact or an inexact science and something that we can rely upon to ensure that we have decent resilience measures in place. Regardless of the degree to which we might consider probability assessment to be reliable, and the information that feeds into it to be of any value, we do need to make sure that we have something in place to protect against impact more than anything else.

What is certain in this world of uncertainty, and predictable in this world of unpredictability, is that those who are better prepared, those who have protected themselves, and those who have considered routes and methodologies for pulling themselves free of any problems that may arise, will be in a better place than those who have not. Forecasters get some things right, but they also get a lot of things wrong. However, the best forecasters, and the ones who are most successful, are the ones who have thought about issues, influences, components and dynamics of situations, rather than those who merely stare at the horizon and try to divine what is coming next based upon guesswork and cursory glances. Putting men on the Moon is rocket science – understanding that you need to be able to think about predictable and unpredictable events and considering what you're going to do about them is not. And even the history of rocket science has its fair share of disasters and very close shaves. That is because at every step there are opportunities for multiple variations of things going wrong. The resilient thinker understands this and needs to maintain the balance between readiness and worrying about every little aspect of every little problem.

Thinking about impacts

Once you've accepted that something is going to impact upon your organisation or its associated activities, then you need to consider what the further consequential impacts of any of those will be. That is – what the heck is coming next, and who else is going to get a taste of it? Nothing ever happens in isolation, and nothing ever happens without having that consequential effect upon something else. The impact upon your organisation may have begun a long time ago and a long way away, far beyond the areas of function and process upon which you've concentrated, and that you've encompassed within your business and organisational planning. Likewise, what you do as an organisation will have an effect, good or bad, deep or shallow, upon others way beyond the point of manufacture, design and sale. If you place yourself at the epicentre of any impact activity, looking outwards, hopefully you will see that everything that your business touches, everything that your business might affect, and any result that your business operations may cause, will impact upon someone or something else. In the most depressing circumstances in our litigation-crazy and blame-oriented world, someone will think that it is your fault.

It is staggering how many organisations do not look beyond their own four walls and fail to consider not only the effects of what they do, but also the fact that they sit within an environment that affects them. There are a million influences buzzing around you all the time, everything from the personal issues that affect your people to the huge geopolitical influences at work at an international level. There is an intermingled, dynamic and flexible sliding scale that operates on a global basis, which has multiple fallouts daily for all those who live on this planet. Some of them will have a direct impact upon your business and you; some of them you will never even see or feel. But, make no mistake, they are there and at work on someone and something somewhere. In that regard, you may not be involved; but you may be affected.

The next time you see a funeral procession, consider this: does it affect you in any way whatsoever? Did you know that person or their family, where they worked or what they did? If not, there is every chance that the death of that individual has no impact at all or influence on you in any way. To you, it is of no consequence whatsoever that the person is no longer alive. Granted, you may feel empathy or sadness, but for most people that passes in seconds. However, think about that person's family. Devastated emotionally, they may have lost the senior figure in the family, they may have lost the breadwinner, they may have been affected financially by having to support someone who had been ill for a significant time period – and so on. One person, two different sets of effect. And that's the basic, personal and human impact. Think about that person's employers and extended acquaintances, and perhaps business clients. Will they be affected also? Some things happen daily that will never affect you – some things happen that will have a profound effect on you forever. Sometimes, it is difficult to gauge what the effect will be until the bad thing has happened. And operating in this world, it is worth remembering that whatever does happen to you, you and your organisation may well be on your own. If you work on the principle that no-one is coming to help, you have a sound basis in the beginning at least, for your response planning.

So, you might have seen things coming, you might not have seen them coming at all. However, that has no bearing on the initial or eventual impact. To get clarity on how you may need to configure yourself, face the fact that some things are predictable, and some are not. Some will impact close to home; some of the impacts will be vaguer and more tenuous; and depending upon varied factors, some things may not even impact on you at all. There may be an opportunity for you there, especially if a competitor or adversary does feel a direct impact. Another point to consider is that even if things are predictable, is it worthwhile investing time and effort looking ahead, or do you just put up the shutters and wait for things to happen? In simple terms – are you an asset protector or a shock absorption set-up? Or can you be both? Is it possible to look ahead and defend ourselves, while moving ahead, or does the focus on protection impede progress?

How far ahead can you see?

In the good old days, when things happened more slowly, it was perhaps easier to predict what would be coming in the future, as events may have gestated slowly and over longer periods. The reason for this was that communication lines were slower, and the speed and suddenness of effect was generally less pronounced because things just took a long time to happen. But that was in the good old days, and they've gone forever; in our brave new world of interconnection and information, things are very different, and that problem or threat that has been lurking over the horizon can come without warning, with additional impacts and with devastating speed. If you think about strategic financial plans, back in the good old days organisations and companies would have been able to plan ahead for considerable periods of time in the almost certain knowledge that change in politics, social structure and other major influential factors would have been relatively sedate and predictable. That was a different age, and, although things may have seemed to happen quickly at the time, they really didn't when we compare them to now.

Thinking a little more about this, most things have happened before, elsewhere – but in different forms and in different circumstances. You could argue that both world wars have parallels in the Iraq and Afghanistan wars. They most definitely have parallels in Ukraine. You could argue that the latest economic depressions are based upon the well-known and understood cycle of boom and bust, and that the process by which realignment of power in the twentieth century went from the British Empire to the US-led West will be repeated. No different, really; it's happened before, and it is happening again. If we work on that assumption, then we can look quite a way into the future.

We know that there are going to be changes in the geopolitical face of the world, we know that there will be economic growth again, and we know that there will be economic failure to follow. It is pretty much inevitable, and it will affect all of us who live to see it to some degree or another. And if we do work on this assumption, then we must also assume that either we face the effects and impacts and take steps to avoid them or mitigate them, or we ignore them and take what's going to come to us. In the spirit of the rest of this book, you should start to think about which side of the thinking fence you will be on. And, as we are all 'veterans' of the war on COVID-19, most adults have at least some ideas of the need to do something when the unexpected happens.

If it is among the great certainties of life, a truism that you cannot foresee everything, you must be aware of the fact that you can foresee something. There are some things that you can avoid, and some things are inevitable – one of the tricks of effective resilient thinking is understanding this and ensuring that, avoided or not, whether you can escape it or not, there are levels of effect and response that need to be planned for and considered by the thinking and resilient organisation and its people. Having the will and taking the time to move beyond burying your head in the sand, and beginning to look forward and around obstacles and over the horizon, will allow you to consider at least what's coming next, or even beyond what's coming next, and then to figure out what to do with yourself and your responses. This, of course, assumes that you want to do something! There are some people who are leaders and followers in some organisations who prefer to avoid being blamed for their actions by doing nothing. The challenges of stasis in the face of risk, call it metastasis or homeostasis if you like, but simply put being ineffective through inaction or inappropriate action – will affect the best laid plans of mice, men and resilience forums. This staring at the problem and doing nothing is, well, nothing of value.

Do you want to see?

In among the aspects of resilience that we have looked at already, and remember we are considering conceptual thinking rather than the specifics of your organisation (you'll need to apply yourself to this a little), one of the things you will need to think about is your *willingness* to look ahead and consider what is coming to you. There are very many organisations, and very many people who are almost in a state of denial about the potential impacts of the activities of others and of the things that go on in the world around them. Frankly, if they want to effectively anticipate, respond to and recover from adverse effects and unwanted risk realisation, such organisations need to shake themselves out of this mindset and start being a little more aware and ready to confront the issues. This does not mean that to prevent damage you have to build high fences, put everything under lock and key, and, therefore, stop your business or organisation from doing what it needs to do.

The effectively resilient organisation will look forwards carefully and consider the commensurate application of mitigation measures and impact absorption procedures to ensure that it can continue to do what it does best with minimal disruption, and at appropriate cost. Again, the pandemic taught us something significant here. In a closed-down world there must be an alternative way to continue to operate and to live. The pandemic taught us that we hadn't thought deeply enough about that challenge; but to be fair, we learned quickly that the inability or unwillingness to do something would lead to failure, and everything that ensues. On the other side of the coin, and as many governments discovered, even doing something can attract negativity in the responses to it.

So, you should be ready to look forward and you must want to see what is coming and avoid the issue of denial. If you hide, and if you refuse to see the realities of threat, risk and unchecked impact upon your business, then, when those risks become reality, your business will have a real chance of failure. Although it is impossible to mitigate every risk, and equally impossible to fully recover from every issue that might have an impact upon the organisation, it is possible to ensure that you know as much as possible about what may be coming. So, this is the time to put down the checklist and start thinking outside the boxes (because your checklist has little boxes).

Free your mind; think of anything and everything that could happen. For the moment, do not assume that you can *deal* with everything and anything that could happen, just think about it all. If you are a small- or medium-sized organisation and you start to consider the things that could happen to you, and could have an impact, then you may find that there are more of them than you think. In academic and research work, we ask people to provide us with information concerning their assessment of what could happen to them, and it is amazing how many provide a cursory checklist or priority list of risks. Bullet points are offered in the place of reasoned thought because they are easy. Many organisations like to have a 'top ten' list of things that could go wrong. But number 11 could be the killer; and so could number 111. Clearly, very few organisations can muster the time, effort, resource and willpower to deal with so many problems in their tidy, readable plans.

Here's something: what if it's your unlucky day and number 11 happens? Because it's not your priority, have you put in place the appropriate resources to manage the incidents that may occur because of it? Have you properly and fully considered and managed the allocation of resources to allow you to recover, and to ensure that any consequential losses to the stakeholders and supporting activities have been encompassed and can be managed back beyond recovery? If you haven't, then, as a resilience professional, you haven't done your job. Neither have those who are in your resilience chain. Not so resilient now, is it? Resilient thinking is for those who have the capability and capacity to move beyond the human behavioural response of 'it will be OK'.

So, if you take the leap and put down your checklist, the challenge is for you to go back to your business and to look really carefully at the risk registers and the business impact analysis (BIA) work that your organisation is doing (you do have those, do you not?). Start to be critical; because, although you may find that you have encompassed everything that could go wrong, or at least have considered it, conversely, and probably more likely (yes, be honest), you haven't done enough yet. And if that's the case, then you are risk exposed. If you are risk-exposed, then you have gaps in your armour, or a weak spring in your shock absorbers. The result of that will be that you are vulnerable to injury or damage. And we know what happens next. I can guarantee that in this regard, many organisations have more holes than a Swiss cheese.

Whether it is unwillingness to look ahead, a lack of imagination or even the lack of time and effort that the organisation can expend upon preparation and planning, is immaterial. As far as I know, nobody can actually charge you for thinking; that is free. So, to get ahead and stay ahead – start to use your head. The constraints on that of course may not be yours. The people, departments and disinterested stakeholders, as well as the unknowledgeable managers who think they understand risks but really do not, become your adversaries. Their watered down, biased, easy-out solutions that appear in their risk plans because they either cannot be bothered or do not want to draw attention to vulnerabilities may bite back hard. This is a reality for many hierarchical organisations and an unavoidable result of working in organisations where people are vying and competing for power, recognition and kudos. Wouldn't it be refreshing if power, recognition and kudos came with doing things right?

Try facing realities – An example

In our world of resource demand, geopolitical turmoil and economic competition; the morality and justification for certain actions and activities will be an enduring topic. It is always quite interesting to me to read and hear of discussions concerning oil and the ambitions of various interested parties in obtaining it. How often do you hear reference to conflicts around the world in these terms: 'Really, it's all about the oil' or similar points about feeding the economies of the West at the expense of others? We have activist groups who want to 'Just stop oil'; which is perhaps a little naive. Well, politics are not my particular thing, but surely it is naive to consider that the search for oil is not a main driver behind many policies. Importantly, consider this: imagine a world without oil right now. No man-made fibres, no manufacturing, no Internet, and no plastics to produce the hardware it works on, no aviation – in fact, not much of anything that is usable. Despite the significant efforts to reduce dependencies on oil-based products (recycling plastics, natural and organically based packaging, and the ongoing move towards electric vehicles), the demand remains and will remain for a long time to come. We *are* changing, we *are* anticipating and taking our steps towards the new and alternative future; but we still need our oil thirst to be satisfied for now at least.

For as long as we require it, there will be a need to exploit any given resource and the territories that it comes from.

Prices will be set, wars will be fought and those who are either against the exploitation of the resource or in ideological conflict with those who produce the end product, may well engage in malicious activity. Follow it up: a simple, thought-provoking exercise is to get a piece of A3 paper and write 'oil' in the centre. Then link every aspect of modern life that you can think of to it. Think back to the point of origin and forward to its multiple uses – do a little research and see what oil can be used for – it is amazing, really. Then add in all the areas where our resilience on a large scale in society and on smaller scales, such as for individual business, could be affected. You are now building an interesting picture. Now, take the oil out of the picture and see what you have left.

Some alternatives: try it with eco-fuels, liquefied natural gas and fossil fuels, nuclear, wind and any other power source you can think of, and you may highlight some differences in overall value to society. Go further and do the same thing with 'the Internet', 'precious metals' or other commodities that we depend upon. This exposes some dependencies and frailties, and these matter fundamentally. In thinking about what we do to secure energy resources, my point is not that there is justification for conflict – but that there are reasons for things happening that are fairly clear, and there are consequences all round. Conflict for oil has often caused squeezes on production, which, in turn, causes shortage and price increase – and we end up paying for that! The cost in human life has been staggering and, unfortunately, there seems to be no forecast that there will be change. Our growing rates of consumption mean that we need more, not less, and the focus perhaps should be to consider mitigating effects rather than changing dependencies.

And in addition to the dependence challenge, there is increasing antipathy towards oil and our dependence on it, particularly but not exclusively from the younger generation. Think forwards and consider this: the younger generation will assume the mantle of power and control in the future, and will make the decisions about how and what we use for fuel and life sustenance. They will balance that need against global and climate impacts and whatever they decide will in itself impact on how societies are supported and maintained in the future. The impacts of those decisions will need to be offset against the opportunity they bring for a changed world. And those impacts need to be thought about now. Like death and taxes, change in the future is inevitable.

Nostalgic as some of us may be for the great age of steam and industry, those days have gone for the time being, and we live in this world of our own making. It makes sense to face our weaknesses and to live with them. Whether we look at our issues in terms of anticipating and identifying threats, risks or impacts, we do need to be honest and knowledgeable. And, very importantly, there are different views on the efficacy of risk and impact analysis, and there are definitely different approaches. However, both aspects of the whole are important, and excessive focus on one, or dismissal of another, will not give the balanced outcomes that you need.

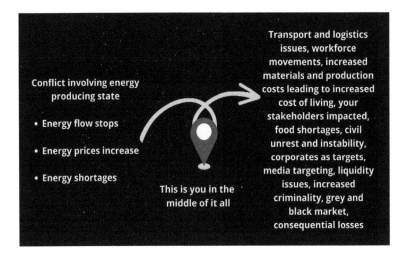

Figure 5: Integrated threats

This is an example of a consequence through oil shortage caused by conflict. Gas, evidenced by Russian control of supply management to Europe may not be as existential a product as oil for Western civilisation. However, look at the list on the right and think about the impacts of shortages there. Same cause, different commodities, similar effect. Dealing with those types of impact is at the core of effective resilience thinking.

To feel the short- and long-term impacts of change, it is not necessary to be part of the immediately affected industry, sector or even nation or continent. In the interconnected supply and logistics dependent world, we feel pain indirectly. Not only will we feel impacts directly, but we will also feel them at various levels of depth when thinking in terms of the qualities and attributes of those impacts. Not all impacts are the same and not all impacts are confined to one area of our organisation. It is a useful point to consider that each of those headline areas in Figure 5 has a subset of consequences and problem-causing issues that may have further impact. The crucial thing is that these things have the potential to happen, and that you will need to find a way of considering their sub-impacts and countering them. Given that we may have much less control over the probability and actual occurrence of a negative impact, our focus may more necessarily be on our own actions and how we can lessen or avoid the most damaging aspects and outcomes.

So, a little thought is required, and this is where the ideas related to thinking ahead need to become a little more concrete. We know by now that we are vulnerable to impacts from surprises. Sometimes they really do seem to come from nowhere; although everything does have a physical or circumstantial cause based on *something* in our world. It is not possible to know what is coming next in detail. However, we can look into the future with variable reliability, and when we can do that, we have options. Naturally, we need to ensure that the actions that we subsequently take are reliable and based on some degree of certainty; and that is where issues can become more complex still.

Bias, prediction and organisational failure

For the resilient organisation, the ability to think ahead is the key to success in effective planning and implementation of process. By making a clear assessment based upon judgement, history, experience, models, learning and foresight, the assumption is that the organisation will be able to orientate itself to mitigate effects and to anticipate where opportunities may lie. The opportunities may involve simply surviving, or they may result in improvements; whatever they are, we need to seek and exploit them. There may, for example, be an opportunity to assess where there is competitor weakness or the potential for the development of weakness, and thus exploitable gaps. Resilience can be seen as a comparative capability.

However, opportunity exploitation is not a simple process, nor is it guaranteed in any way to be anything upon which there can be a sensible and appropriate planning basis. In our next part of the discussion, we will think about how effective the whole concept of looking ahead may be as the basis of organisational strategies for operations and growth (and for that matter, resilience). Is looking ahead anything more than a guess, an estimate or an assumption? Although forecasting and prediction can be very specific and effective where data that informs them is rich and reliable; there may be dangers when a reliance on looking ahead is not supported effectively or where there are gaps. Seeing an opportunity to anticipate, respond and recover is a good thing; but only if the margins for error and mistake have been minimised. It is when we forecast and predict based on human instinct, assumption and bias that we begin to increase those margins. Interpretation can reduce in accuracy and utility the more we place our 'spin' on what we think the outcome should be.

There is also merit in applying some thought to the fact that not all organisations consider their future in the same amount of depth. In thinking about impacts and in broader terms, global interconnected risk issues, it is probably beneficial here to consider how things are done and how organisations configure themselves to make their own futures. There are, of course, many that will not expend any effort in the pursuit of future prediction and future proofing. There is a balance of expenditure, risk and mitigation that will exercise the minds and subsequent efforts to build resilience in some organisations more than others. This is logical; such organisations are taking a considered, or sometimes unconscious, decision to manage in the immediate term, rather than concern themselves with potential business impacts. That is also risk management, and part of the overall organisational picture.

Not all organisations have the ability or feel the need to consider their future in any detail, or in any depth. If they are successful organisations, they may consider that growth – and therefore thinking and planning for the future – is a necessity; after all that will have helped them to success in the first place. Conversely, the struggling organisation may be focused by necessity on what is happening to it now. Planning may be short term, which may be detrimental for overall resilience in the longer term. The struggling organisation may even know that; but stepping back, thinking clearly and looking ahead may evade it while the pressure is on.

Overall, whether looking ahead with clarity or struggling to do so, the main issue is whether our forward thinking is accurate and therefore reliable. Not all the information that we use is reliable; and increasingly in a world of fake news and disinformation this is becoming problematic. As the scale and speed of information flow continues to increase and dazzle, we should assume that not everything that we see, hear or are offered is fully reliable. It may be data, it may be analysis outcomes, it may be wrong; this additional complexity has the significant potential to impede our ability to see clearly and thus select the best options for action and response.

Figure 6: Where does your information come from?

There are many potential sources. What is true, what is reliable and what is filtered? How is information interpreted and repackaged? What effect does it have on you and your organisation? Are you an exploiter or a victim? The effective use of information has the capability and potential to build a real competitive edge.

Forecasting disadvantages

If we work on an assumption that there may be some issues with accessing reliable data and information, how can we provide a reliable basis for any of our ideas? How can our concepts of resilience and the building of it be a reliable basis for anything if we are unable to accurately consider what may be coming? The need to be able to understand and define what will form the basis of any threat and risk has been a subject for much debate, argument and pontification for many years and in many circles, and justifiably there are those who will not consider risk assessment to be anything other than a speculative approach to what may happen in the future. Conversely, there are other schools of thought that consider the ability to make a reliable assessment of future developments, which may affect our own responses to an intuitive human capability. And of course to an extent there is truth in both and any other viewpoint on this. That is because we decide on our preferences based on what we are taught by others who have their own standpoints, and on our own instinctive world view. It's another aspect of human behaviour that shapes our thinking, decisions and capabilities. Sometimes we learn well, and other times we do not.

It is not sensible and reliable to rely upon intuition alone to be able to provide considered and effective forward planning. To become effective there is a need to understand and ensure that there is some level of reliability based on true evidence and data in assessing the future. If we assume that assessing future capabilities is necessary; we then need to consider what the most effective method is, if such a method exists at all. There is merit in thinking more about a combination of approaches, methods and overall diversity in who does the thinking. In hierarchical and 'flat' management structures, does all the listening, discussion and thinking sit with managers and dedicated teams? Who filters the information and data? Who processes it all and how many changes are made because of personal inputs before the final version appears and is adopted as the basis or justification for action?

Do we exclude the innovators, challengers and disruptors, or those who tell us the truth that we do not want to hear or does not quite fit with the organisational vision? It is very much worth considering in that context how increased effectiveness may depend on moving beyond the mountains of human baggage behaviour that impair forward thinking and planning. Naturally, too, we humans learn from experience, and we should also consider the reliance on experience and learning from previous events as a bias indicator and as an informing influence on the development of resilient individuals and organisations. We will cover the 'experience trap' in a little more detail later.

Forecasting and prediction require us to rely somewhat on understanding the development of various elements and components of what we may consider to be our current and future world society. Influences and patterns occur and recur, and the reliance upon those influences and patterns to look forward and to assess how they may develop further (and thus influence our organisations) is at the core of thinking in terms of the shaping of organisational response. The application of forecasting based upon statistics, trend analysis and other influencing factors may be more reliable in some areas of activity than in others, however, total reliance upon a planning element that cannot be fully reliable by its very nature would be inadvisable. The effect on organisations of insufficient or inaccurate forecasting can be substantial, and perhaps has the potential to derail the organisation before anything else has happened. The reliance upon the prejudice and assumed prescience that forecasting can provide, has the potential to allow for the building of an unwarranted sense of security. Conversely it may cause us to expend excessive time and effort on caution and prevention when neither are necessary. It can be difficult to face the truth – that we do not know what may happen – and for various human reasons we may then find that we make the wrong decisions.

COVID-19, as we have mentioned, provides a case study to help our thinking. It was predictable, and we knew that a pandemic would come at some point. Being human, most of us probably thought at first that it was someone else's problem and that it could be contained and managed; after all we had not experienced anything else but a transient and short-lived pandemic. And of course if we didn't fall victim to it, or if we were generally healthy, we were (in general) OK. So we were surprised and caught out when an actual, real, make you sick and die pandemic appeared. As individuals and as organisations, we were, in general, not equipped to face the immediate problems; and we most definitely were not ready for the long-term impacts. As industries and sectors, the 'long covid' impact has been felt to such an extent that one of the core tenets of business continuity – recover and if possible, to a better level than before – has evaded many. Recovery became a 'reset' for some, a real reassessment of core strategies for others, and for many it meant closing businesses while salvaging something from what was left. Like conflict, major crisis initiates and accelerates change; and in that change there will always be winners and losers. The pandemic, predicted in books, movies and scientific studies, made fools of us all.

Bearing in mind that our focus is about taking a thinking approach, and that we are concerned with looking ahead, at this point it is useful to carry out a short (or long if you like) exercise. Using the table structure in Figure 7, expand it where you need to and complete it with your own thoughts on aspects of the pandemic's impact and what could have been forecast accurately. The amount of detail you put into this is your decision, but it is a useful exercise to think about the variables. Not only that; but think about what might happen if it comes back, or some other cause of similar impacts appears. Have you done the work? Why not start it now?

Issue	Cause	Predicted?	Response effectiveness
Travel restrictions put in place globally due to pandemic.	The urgent and overriding need to avoid unnecessary spread of the virus through international and national travel.	Restrictions predictable and probably planned but not on the scale required for this pandemic.	Effective and rapid measures implemented to reduce flights, travel and virus transmission.
		Transport sector impacted with aviation and its dependent sectors suffering most.	Ineffective in understanding and implementing business continuity measures. Sizeable number of businesses did not continue.
		Implications for all sectors modelled?	Loss and movement of skilled staff and employees, currency in essential skills, reductions in workforce and people assets.
			Long-term sector damage?

Figure 7: How well did forecasting perform?

Assess how well forecasting worked when dealing with unprecedented scale activity. What aspects of the forecast situations were missed – and why? It is a worthwhile exercise to try this retrospectively for any issue your organisation may have faced. It may reveal where you could do better next time. So try to apply it to potential future challenges.

Planning for long-term resilience is simply not straightforward. Although there is an ability to consider how events may work, and how models for development and predictability can be applied, the human element makes prediction a very difficult capability to enact and particularly to use as the basis for action. If we consider what has gone before, and the lessons from the past, we can look at how actions led to consequence; however, what no-one can do is make a true judgement on what would have happened in every instance on a different day, or if a different person or group of people were involved in the decision or action processes. In other words, if the causes and enablers, and of course the responses were different, events may have concluded differently. This is not only because of circumstances, capability and the uncertainty of the flow of events, but also because there are multiple influences on the ways that humans make things happen, react and interact with the situations that they face and the choices that they make. In his study of human behaviours some time ago but still relevant, Ajzen[5] considered the issue of control and intention:

---

[5] Ajzen, I., (2005), Laws of Human Behaviour: Symmetry, Compatibility, and Attitude-Behavior Correspondence. In: Beauducel, A., Biehl, B., Bosniak, M., Conrad, W., Schönberger, G. & Wagener, D. (Eds), *Multivariate Research Strategies*, Aachen: Shaker Publishers.

"[...] We should be able to improve prediction of behavior if we consider not only intention but also the degree to which an individual actually has control over performing the behavior."

Naturally, this calculation assumes that at least there is a degree of control in place or it is possible – even permissible – and indeed some organisations may well be in full control of themselves and of their assets. Full control will likely evade most; however, there is also a significant element of the organisational landscape that is not in any way in control of itself or its environment. The organisation is therefore vulnerable to the effects not only of what it is doing itself, but also of what may be done to it by others. If such an organisation is out of control, or unable to control in the first place, it is then no leap of the imagination to consider that it will become more vulnerable to anything that is neither known to it, or is outside its capability to look forward. This can be compounded even further by the illusion of control, where the organisation thinks it has a problem in hand when it really does not.

The organisation that is not focused on itself and what it is trying to achieve will not be configured to protect itself against the issues that may arise even now, let alone those that may arise in the future. The issues, of course, will be compounded by the dynamic of any threat that is not only outside the organisation, but also is internal to it. The ultimate and inevitable result of a dis-organisation; and one that refuses or is unable to at least consider how it will configure itself to manage impacts or problems related to it, is that it will put itself under considerable stress and unacceptable risk. Unacceptable risk will lead inevitably to excessive, unwanted and negative impacts which, if not mitigated, will have the potential to lead to failure.

For many organisations, especially those that expose themselves to risk without preparation, justification or the ability to mitigate such risk, this is a dangerous and irresponsible activity, and if it is in breach of any governance or regulatory requirement, it can result in sanctions that will be unavoidable and damaging. The consequence of failure can take many forms. Therefore, there is a core imperative – develop and implement approaches for effective anticipation of what may be ahead. There are ways to enable that capability. Also, there will need to be an informed response that continues, while responding, to anticipate the changing environment and contexts that are yet to come while the problem develops. COVID-19 variants demonstrated the importance of that need to understand that what we would like to happen often does not play out as we would wish. At no point was any illusion of control warranted until it became clear that it could not be ignored, would not go away and was not a simple, common cold.

Looking ahead

Organisations forecast to enable them to remain competitive and to consider where they should invest time and effort to ensure capability and competitive edge. In terms of financial cash flow and perhaps in market behaviours, there is reliability in forecasting that can be based upon the known behaviours of various components and actors who will interact in a certain way, and will move towards common goals and required conclusions as part of their overall modus operandi. We know that investors will always invest; we know that share prices fluctuate; and we know that markets will change in response to customer requirements and the amount of product that is available for customers to consume. These are examples that are relatively easy to bring in to forecasting, as we can predict to an extent the demand and the ability to supply throughout a year; or other period; particularly if we are considering seasonal products or traditional peaks in demand.

However, although these forecast components are relatively easy to predict, this is generally because the operating environment will be benign, and because the various stakeholders are able to move freely throughout the operating environment; and to react to incidents and changes as they see fit and in accordance with the various boosters and constraints that influence their overall outcomes. In terms of considering where resilience may be informed by forecasting, we are looking at a separate and different type of scenario. The malign or non-compliant risk that comes to fruition and develops in ways we have not anticipated or would not want to see is a problem. And if we have planned with optimism and perhaps with misplaced confidence about our ability to overcome impacts, then when the impacts overcome us, we need to be able to do more. I read somewhere that if a plan is good enough then you do not need a Plan B. Although that is a nice aspiration, the reality is that we need the ability to have a Plan B to Z; more than one at least. And if we do not have them all written down, we need to have people and capabilities in place to come up with something, and at pace. The better the value of the anticipation, the more beneficial will be the outcomes. No plan is good enough. Ever.

In planning, we need to make *informed* decisions; and key to our development as resilient thinkers is the discussion of judgement, and whether and to what extent it can affect the ability to forecast effectively. To what extent do perceptions and biases have an influence? There is bias in everyone; we make judgements about each other based upon appearance, race, colour and accent. Naturally, if individuals and organisations have a skewed perception of realities, their assessments will also be skewed. The chain of events can therefore continue to the inevitable conclusion; that their reactions and responses will also be skewed. In the world of resilience, the issues of judgement bias are serious inhibitors to capability. An incorrect, inappropriate response will not only be wasteful in time, effort and resource, but will importantly lead to points of omission or failure. Organisations make judgements and assumptions daily, sometimes based on a single person's observations or opinions, and that itself is not healthy.

There is then yet another potential consequential development, which is that the effects of the omission or failure themselves may be incorrectly or inaccurately judged, with a further chain of effects leading to even more failures and additional consequences. Consequential loss is the frequently underestimated element of many plans, in that the initial effect may be assessed and planned for, with 'chain impacts' ignored or missed in forecasting completely. At all stages and at all levels of an organisation that strives to remain viable, accurate assessment of threat, risk and impact is essential. When our assessments are incorrect, and we inevitably act incorrectly, it can be fatal. From customer confidence in product supply to public confidence in governments, judgements and responses may be very harsh and damaging.

One of the important issues facing organisations is the need to feel in control. The idea behind plans, policies and procedures is to put in place an element of control over the future; after all an organisation that cannot determine its own future is not a sensible proposition either as a business or as an investment. However, there is an issue, in that the ability to control should be based upon an understanding of not only what can be controlled, but also the level of control that can effectively be applied.

For many of us, the *illusion* of being in control may be more hazardous and damaging in the longer term than any contributing components or factors. The development of business and organisational practices that provide frameworks for activity are important; but they also rely upon acceptance and application by the organisation's people; and being human, those people will exhibit everything from inconsistency to underestimation of uncertainty. Similarly, the ideas of confirmation bias, support theory and familiarity will be prevalent in organisational activity and planning constructs. In other words, we talk ourselves into accepting our preference. We then build a justification to support our choices, and more often than not we will follow the route that is familiar to us.

It is not only individuals who are susceptible to human attributes, but also the organisations of which they are contributing components. The negative and disabling influences on the ability to accurately forecast can be (and I would suggest are being) transferred on a routine and constant basis into the organisational resilience and wider framework. The potential outcomes for reliance upon organisational approaches that are founded on unreliability will be damaging; more so should the organisation fail to recognise the serious long-term impacts on both itself and its stakeholders of the illusion of control. Management, planning, prediction and strategy will be fundamentally flawed and costly in terms of time and resource expended and, ultimately, wasted. This flaw, when it impacts on resilience, will have the potential to be even more serious and damaging, where inconsistency and an inability to recognise the illusion of control and its failings will leave the organisation open to process and human failings, which in the very worst cases will cost lives.

Scenario studies and strategic foresight

Many organisations like to train and test using scenarios. Scenario identification as the basis for strategic planning is well entrenched, and looking at the literature and ideas around its utility, effectiveness and contribution to strategy, identifies a general popularity among theorists and practitioners. Scenarios and planning have been linked for many years as some consolidated literature reviews have identified and analysed.[6] Ged Davis of Shell said in 2002[7]:

"Scenarios are coherent, credible stories about alternative futures. The process of creating scenarios

---

[6] Varum, C.A., & Melo, C. (2010), Directions in scenario planning literature – A review of the past decades, *Futures*, 42, 355–369.

[7] Davis, G., (2002), in *Scenarios as a Tool for the 21st Century*; Royal Dutch Shell. I'm sure he could have written 'problematique' in English but c'est la vie.

places a strong emphasis on the joint definition of a 'problematique' and on a synthesis of ideas, rather than just extended and deeper analysis of a single viewpoint. Because they involve using multiple perspectives to explore problems, scenarios can help us to create shared understandings of possible developments, options and actions."

The strength of scenarios as a planning aid becomes clear in this context. As in good research and analysis, the synthesis rather than the selective approach – which is choosing what we want to plan by selecting our outcomes and focusing on justifying them – is a strong basis for organisational resilience development. If we consider scenarios as a single basis; and a singular approach to take, with the steering of thinking – either consciously or unconsciously – being inherent from their conception, we may risk skewing and invalid outcomes.

When we think about looking ahead, we should also be clear about the differences between forecasting and scenarios; and again, going back further in time, Paul Schoemaker[8] pointed out that there is utility in both, with forecasting being more effective in stable situations and scenarios giving the advantage in instability, fluid and uncertain situations. I think that is because when we are unsure about something, we need to anchor our thinking to something that we recognise and with which we are familiar.

---

[8] Schoemaker, P.J., (1991), When and how to use scenario planning: A heuristic approach with illustration, *Journal of Forecasting*, 10, 549–564.

In thinking about looking ahead and its benefits, we should consider the influence of thinking, behavioural science, bias and collective illusions in approaches to both scenarios and forecasting. The liquid flow of thinking and planning along channels that have been pre-set, either by circumstance or intent, will have an impact on outcomes. If the results of skewed scenarios, set by those with the most to gain or lose from a particular outcome, are played into strategies – then those strategies may be as flawed as any autocratic *diktat* from top management.

As we evaluate, analyse and synthesise the enduring principles referred to here with many others, should we aim to situate what may have been analogue thinking into the world that has developed in the past two decades? In our planning for resilience, where have the societal and behavioural influences of digital development changed the way we develop scenarios and how we forecast for strategic effect? More importantly, perhaps, where have scenarios become less valid than alternative ways of assessing and strategising our future directions? Are the time-worn principles still valid or has change overtaken our capabilities for effective synthesis of multiple perspectives?

Although we may not necessarily know what is there to support us and we do not necessarily know how the land lies ahead –what we can most definitely assume is that nothing stays the same. There is also merit in applying some thought to the fact that not all organisations consider their future in the same amount of depth. In thinking about impacts and the global, interconnected risk issues, it is probably beneficial here to consider how things are done and how organisations configure themselves to make their own futures. There are, of course, many that will not expend any effort in the pursuit of future prediction and proofing. There is a balance of expenditure, risk and mitigation that will exercise the mind and subsequent efforts to build resilience in some organisations more than others. This is logical; such organisations are taking a considered, or sometimes unconscious, decision to manage themselves rather than concern themselves with potential business impacts.

Luckily for us, we are not alone in worrying about emerging risks and their potential effects. Each of the influences on our organisations will have their own properties and specifics. These will influence their development and longevity, while also identifying in what way and to what level they have the necessary power and strength to impact elsewhere and to pull the 'silken thread' that affects another area.

I found some old notes from 2014 when working on this second edition, and I've copied them here. Maybe I should have published them:

"In fairness some prediction and analysis of future threats may be difficult to conduct with accuracy. However, an example of a relatively recent risk (both to individuals and organisations), which has moved from the area of research and speculation into that of reality-based effect is the H1N1 Swine Flu pandemic of 2009. This type of virus pandemic had been widely forecast in previous years and there was no shortage of guidance or information available from government and academic sources, to assist in ensuring that the effects of a pandemic could be mitigated. The UK Government's Risk Register and the World Economic Forum (WEF) both identified such a pandemic as a most significant and compelling global risk, and the levels of readiness

that were advised and mandated during the last pandemic (even if not globally acted upon) managed the global effects to some extent. It is unclear from any of these works whether their assessments and guidance were of use to organisations in the face of the pandemic, and it may be that the main driver for increased protection against future pandemics may have been the pandemic itself and the realisation by many businesses that they were unprepared."

Even if it is noted and used within business, research and guidance is relatively rare, especially when moving beyond those risks with obvious potential for human impacts, such as disease and terrorism. The challenge for those who have identified the abundant risks to society has been to distil that thought process and research protocol towards an analysis of business readiness to protect against impacts.

If there are distinct views and approaches towards global interconnected risks, there is the further disadvantage in that there is much discussion but little published work that considers the effects that these risks may have upon the business other than stating that they *will* have an effect. There is a glaring absence, and thus lack of depth-researched guidance or academic influence available to resilience professionals, of identified impacts upon business beyond the identification of the range of threats and that their effects are either potentially cumulative, or potentially linked and to an extent 'mobile'. This lack of imagination and detail effectively leaves managers to do the research and forecasting of threat impacts alone. If there are linkages between the effects of, for example, resource shortages, population growth, a shift in public attitude to business and social exclusion, resilience thinkers should explore the implications.

What we have is the situation where many organisations are sailing ahead without any awareness of the 'icebergs' that may be ahead of them, and more dangerously, are not consulting or listening to those who could protect them against disaster. This can be rectified with careful thought and research, but vitally with the participation of resilience professionals themselves. Assessment and subsequent action must be based on this understanding, and where necessary and possible, elements of this understanding should be fostered within workforces. And it is not all about management responsibility; trying to gain traction and interest at all levels of an organisation for this resilience thing is just as difficult as getting the board's attention. I think that the impact of it is worse; because plans then simply become pieces of paper with no meaning, because nobody wants to play.

Organisations and their specific sub-disciplines often work in isolation rather than together. Although many organisations will be able to see that some disciplines of organisational resilience are complementary; my experience is that there are many that maintain separation between functions. Even within organisations that have disparate resilience challenges, we may find that disparate elements of the organisation deal with them discretely. Although there may be good reason for that, we can end up with duplication and a lack of understanding of interconnected risks. So perhaps, there is something to be said for the development of a more holistic approach that allows us to break out of frameworks and to understand our perception of bias towards a particular framework of activity, or to a particular preferred or higher priority threat, which may be hampering our ability to understand what is coming next and to be able to develop an appropriate approach to the issues that may arise. When considering emerging risks; it is probably sensible to ensure that we have a joined up rather than disparate approach. And of course, as I have said, the organisational attributes of the world in microcosm: apathy, disinterest and 'me first', will be the cause of more challenge to the resilient thinker than most other aspects of your role.

Summary

This chapter has briefly skimmed over the challenges and issues of forecasting and trying to figure out what is coming next. You do not need to be an expert to anticipate; however, you do need to understand your own organisation and what can go wrong. You do need to understand who depends on you and on whom you depend. You can be the most qualified, most experienced and, on paper, the most capable resilient practitioner there is; however, if you cannot think, if you are not flexible in approach and if you're not able to understand the dynamics of the world – how it is now and how it will change irrevocably in the future – then you will potentially find that you are unable to keep pace with change and capability needs. If you are not prepared, and if you are a little unlucky, you will be overwhelmed in a very short space of time, and the consequences will be more than likely at least damaging, and at worst business fatal. The concept of resilient thinking is neither new nor difficult – but it's amazing how many people either cannot be bothered to apply any real thought to this fundamental approach, or feel that it is neither their business nor in their interest.

Having looked in overview at our context, the world of difficulty and that which is to come, we will now seek to consider, and offer opinion and guidance on aspects of resilient thinking, and on effective organisational resilience. From how we are structured in organisations, to how we see the world and ourselves; all are aspects and differentiators when considering our resilience.

Here are the points for the resilient thinker to consider from this chapter:

1. To what extent do you think that we rely on predicting the future in risk and in business in general?

2. What do you feel are the levels of effectiveness of assessing future risks? How reliable is the process? How effective do you feel that those responsible for steering the organisation are at managing these assessments?

3. Reflect on and explain why we have a tendency not to respond fully effectively to prediction. If you agree, why do you think that might be?

4. There is a saying: 'hindsight is a wonderful thing'. To what extent is that true? How does hindsight help or hinder us?

5. Given all that we know and the technology at hand, what ideas and capabilities do you feel could best help us to look ahead?

CHAPTER 3: ORGANISATIONAL RESILIENCE – PRINCIPLES AND IDEAS

"Resilience can go an awful long way."
Eddie the Eagle

In this chapter, we will discuss the fundamental issues relating to organisational preparedness, planning and the organisation's attitude, and think further about the problems caused by our human traits, behaviours and interactions. Organisational resilience is not just about protection and 'bouncing back', but about a fluid, flexible and adaptive approach to changing circumstances. There may or may not be death and disaster. The issues that arise may come from nowhere; but they will come. As the umbrella for security, risk, crisis, emergency and continuity activity, organisational resilience needs to be able to work in multiple ways across differing types of organisations. This brings challenges that organisations and their specialists must face.

It is only really within the past two decades that organisations have begun to formally focus their ideas on the concept of 'joined up' resilience, at least in a structured way. Before then, organisations, regardless of shape and size, did not have coherent frameworks, guidance or structure on which they could base their resilience. The organisational resilience function would be reactive at best, and irregular in pattern and content at worst. The resultant inability to initiate coherent response to the extreme pressures of resilience requirements meant that organisations were exposed, vulnerable and liable to sustain long-lasting damage and associated or resultant debilitating effects on operations and business outcomes. The siloing of activities into the various disciplines that make up an organisational resilience function probably contributed more than any other single factor to this problem.

The resilience landscape is much better formed in the modern age. Our exposure to case studies and highly visible examples of the results of organisational resilience deficiencies has allowed us to evaluate and assess the cause and impact of expected and unexpected events and issues more effectively. Organisations can consider the reasons for, and flows of activity or inactivity, the elements of cause and effect and the risk implications of their own activity because they may have seen this somewhere else, happening to someone else and sensing the damage and consequences. With the constant and rapid flow of instant information, the observer can not only observe, but observe in real time. This immediacy should allow us to learn quickly. The global COVID-19 pandemic has brought immense challenges but also many learning opportunities. Why then, are we still so susceptible to the challenges to organisational resilience?

Our aim is to begin to understand what we mean by organisational resilience, and how it might work effectively in all organisations. In simple terms, organisational resilience defines some form of capability to protect ourselves against what may be termed as *negative events*: issues and challenges that present themselves – and we would rather they did not. However, before embarking on any kind of work towards identifying how organisational resilience may become something that is of much more value at societal, national, international and global levels, we must consider the influences upon organisational resilience capability itself.

We can use the term 'landscape', or any other descriptive metaphor, to visualise what organisational resilience in its breadth and scope and depth may mean to those who not only design and develop it, but those who benefit from it also. Whatever terminology we use, as with the development of any other multi-level picture for assessment of capability, we need to consider the contributory elements. What is it that makes up organisational resilience as a structure, a framework, as something that allows us to build the capability that we clearly need and desire? Where are the boundaries of a capability? What limits and enhances our ability to be able to provide and develop the structures, capabilities and organisational will – at whatever level that may be – to be able to develop organisational resilience and benefit from it?

There are multiple nuances of commonality and detail, there are differences and contradictions, and we should look to synthesise these ideas into some form of holistic picture. What exactly does a holistic picture look like, and is it more an embedded and conjoined structure than something that is the result of bolted together components? We will think about that. We then need to think about the relative importance and value, as well as any advantages or disadvantages of any of the functions and components to overall effectiveness, and the required picture for capability and long-term effectiveness. We will begin by looking at organisational resilience as a concept, before moving on to discuss criticality, impacts and the effects of human behaviour – both positive and negative.

Definitions

It is often useful to begin thinking about any subject or issue by selecting a suitable and useful definition to work with. Duchek's (2019)[9] excellent paper provides us with multiple examples and definitions of organisational resilience, and how they may be interpreted. However, to keep it simple, and to frame our discussion effectively; our definition of organisational resilience will be aligned with Kerr (2016)[10] in the BSI's position document on the subject, which states that organisational resilience is:

"The ability of an organisation to anticipate, prepare for, respond and adapt to incremental change and sudden disruptions in order to survive and prosper."

For the purposes of our discussion, it is then helpful to break this definition down, so that we can interpret, understand and explain organisational resilience and what actions may be needed to ensure that we can achieve the required and necessary capability to 'survive and prosper'.

Ability

If we begin by considering ability, it is useful to try to engage with thinking about what organisations think about themselves and their appetite to deal with negative events. Of course, there are many different types of negative event

---

[9] Duchek, S., (2019), Organizational resilience: a capability-based conceptualization. Bus Res 13, 215–246 (2020). *https://doi.org/10.1007/s40685-019-0085-7*.

[10] Kerr, H., (2016), Organizational Resilience: Harnessing Experience, Embracing Opportunity, London: BSI.

that may challenge an organisation, and therefore the challenge of putting in place an effective resilience programme needs to encompass many varying aspects of the business itself, and include analysis of threats and impacts it may face. This is a challenge in itself; and organisational resilience is an organisational and business capability that can be overlooked or 'skimmed' as a result – perhaps until it is too late. The main, and perhaps most common, challenge is that an organisation may not focus on its resilience until challenged by a particular problem. In general, it is fair to assume that most organisations will focus on the 'here and now' rather than the more distant issues that may affect it in the future or are affecting someone else now. Even a short distance in time or location can provide enough justification for detachment from the urgency that may be needed for effective management.

Clearly, for all organisations that wish to maintain a competitive or profitable edge, and are concerned about the impacts of negative events on their bottom line, or profitability, or even their workforce, there should be some level of importance allocated to the need to develop a resilient capability. However, organisational behaviour being what it is, such organisations may tend to be in the minority, and thus we as a wider society may tend to be less prepared than we might be for negative impacts. Given that there have been global, unusual, impacting events in the COVID-19 pandemic, to which all organisations can relate, and which has involved a clear manifested risk to all levels of the population, it would be reasonable to expect that we would be in a better position to prepare for resilience challenges in the future. However, we also need to consider the idea that human nature can sometimes allow us to override negative thoughts, displace reality and replace it with something more positive or palatable. In other words, organisational learning can be compromised by a desire for happier times and improved results.

Therefore, when considering organisational resilience, we should begin from a starting assumption that organisations and workforces will generally be less disposed towards taking steps toward resilience if they are required to move from their own comfort zone and cultural norms for working practices. And this may not necessarily be management-led, but at all levels. It is also worthwhile developing an understanding of the issues around organisational willingness to allocate resources and thinking to the development of ability, especially if there are multiple calls on those resources. The ability of the organisation will therefore depend not only on the risks, but its configuration and the parameters that it either sets for itself – or are set for it.

We shall consider organisational resilience as a system. This means that it is not only a framework and structure, but also something that interacts with human beings. This allows us to develop an understanding that any planned direction may be subject to controls, failures, interpretations and redirection. Those for whom the system is intended to be an enabler, can themselves disable the system; or cause significant deviation from its original route or intended processes. Some of these organisational resilience components and elements that comprise the system, will be more recognisable than others, and there are many who understand risk, for example, and see it as a crucial component. However, risk has variables, as do all the other components that we need to consider. In effect, the organisational resilience landscape is wide and deep – and has multiple elements and challenges involved in it.

Much of what we read and understand about our subject is focused on the system and its behaviours – organisational resilience is less a function of the organisation, and more an attribute. By reading into the subject, you will develop a more acute insight, which is *critical* knowledge for resilient thinking in the second quarter of the twenty-first century. Equipped with an understanding of what organisational resilience is, and why it has so many – sometimes conflicting facets – the resilient thinker will be better equipped to develop and support its successful implementation.

Ability

"The ability to simplify means to eliminate the unnecessary so that the necessary may speak."
(Hans Hofmann)

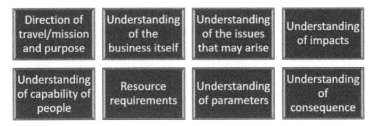

Figure 8: Ability

'Ability' depends on multiple factors, some examples are shown here, which are not necessarily related to any resilience plans but are more about the organisation's wider focus and business imperatives.

It is important to understand that ability will depend on the organisation applying the appropriate priority to resilience in among its other equally or overwhelmingly important prioritisations. To underline that requirement and need, it is equally important to understand that, in most cases, unless there is a negative and tangible effect upon the organisation, the ability to understand and engage with organisational resilience will be influenced, both positively and negatively, as shown in Figure 8, and in many other respects. Having all of these in organisational and management scope will help the organisation to understand that developing resilience ability is based upon them, and that actions will be needed to achieve success. Failure to address these aspects, will probably bring negative outcomes and the organisation has an equal need to recognise that limitation and risk.

An organisation

Although the use of the term 'organisation' is probably something that you will see more than any other throughout this book, the interpretation of what an organisation is and what it can do, especially in relation to organisational resilience, requires a little more thought than simply using a label. An organisation is essentially a collection of people, products and services, and can range from a group of people to a whole nation (or group of nations), with the whole range of activities that are required to support it and come from it. For our purposes it is useful to frame what we mean by an organisation and what it can achieve as a structure. We will return to the idea of organisations as *systems* later. But in terms of attributes, an organisation that is effectively focused, and has an ability to undertake activities related to the development and implementation of organisational resilience, there are some central requirements and dependencies that we should consider.

All organisations have, or should have, clear aims and objectives. For every activity that contributes to achieving those aims and objectives, the organisation should consider what is or has the potential to contribute to or detract from them. Regardless of the organisation's business, this consideration of what makes the organisation effective, is the foundation of success and growth; and where relevant, outstripping and overcoming competition or business adversaries. In a straightforward situation where there are few constraints on thought and behaviour; this can then lead to the invocation of straightforward action to ensure that the path to achieving objectives is smooth.

Naturally, there will always be constraints placed – and self-imposed – to avoid both controversial and dangerous activity, which could lead to wider ethical, political or ideological problems both internally and externally to the approaches taken by the organisation. Also, the necessity and requirement for organisations of all types to align themselves with others to achieve support, investment or funding, can bring opposition both internally and externally, which can lead to consequent problems; with organisational and management issues arising. These will also be the more prosaic issues caused by individual members of staff who do not particularly wish to be aligned with an organisation's approach; they simply see their employment as a paid transaction.

Organisations by their nature are based on some form of structure and framework. They need to be *organised*, something that may be overtly clear; or less clear because of the image of fluidity that more organisations are adopting in the twenty-first century. For any action to take place; there needs to be a structural framework within the organisation so that the various components within can interact and operate effectively. It is rare, in fact almost impossible, for any functional activity to take place without any form of interaction or co-dependency being required or acted upon. This, in turn, should generate either a reaction or a consequential activity that further progresses towards the necessary or required output or outcome.

Organisation

"An organisation's ability to learn, and translate that learning into action rapidly, is the ultimate competitive advantage." (Jack Welch)

Figure 9: Attributes of an organisation

Considering the focus towards the ability to deliver effective organisational resilience. Clearly, many of these attributes would be of value to any organisation, whether it is focused on organisational resilience or not.

In Figure 9, a range of organisational resilience focused attributes are included, which begins to give us an idea that not only does the organisation need to consider what should be in place to do its routine business, but also what it should focus on for capability to manage organisational resilience when unusual pressure is applied. This relates to the idea that organisational resilience is not a separate and distinct function of business; rather it is an attribute that enables capability not only in normal routine but also in extraordinary circumstances where a shift to a different way of operating may be required. We are therefore considering the organisation as something that is more organic, flexible and adaptable, rather than something that is strictly set up to manage and deliver its products and services in a benign, normal and non-threatened environment. This probably requires more of a step change in thinking and approach than we may first think. Organisations are built the way that we want them to look, not as they may look and feel when in crisis mode. Because of that, the gap between our desired and forced structures and responses may be significant.

Anticipate and prepare

The inability to focus on what we cannot see, to identify intangibles and to prepare for that which we will never be prepared for, will always be part of human behaviour. We are neither prescient nor do we have psychic power that allows us to see into the future. However, our ability to consider the future and to invest our organisations with the ability to become resilient, depends upon anticipation, forecasting and the expectation of the possible and the probable, while sensibly offering less priority to imponderables. However, this is neither exact, nor fully reliable, and as a result it can and will highlight shortcomings, and in some cases lead to failure, or a very high risk of it.

Before COVID-19, and in many cases still now, organisations had not been uniformly focused upon the need to be fully aware and to deal with and manage (mitigate) the effects of the multiple issues that could impact upon them. Both long- and short-term impacts are something that an organisation should consider and manage to allow it to remain competitive and effective. A resilient organisation will develop the understanding, capability, and moral and integral management authority to consider and deal with current and emerging threats. This may involve varied and multiple methods, at multiple levels of mitigation. Another aspect of the effective and resilient organisation will be that it will look beyond itself, and much more widely, to ensure that it is able to anticipate and, more importantly, understand where the issues may arise and impact.

The importance of *recognising* issues, and for specialist and non-specialist groupings within any sector to understand and manage the problems that may impact upon them, is a key consideration as we develop our resilient thinking approach. Mitigation planning needs to incorporate the confirmatory concept of anticipation, and the ability to understand and evaluate the *nature* of risks will also be of prime importance. It is timely at this point also to consider that the scope of our approach is not purely focused on loss prevention and organisational continuity (exemplified by disaster response and recovery, crisis management and security response to criminal acts). It is also considering the inherent risks that come from running an organisation, and the potential implications and risk caused by self-inflicted problems and issues. Even routine operations and activities can generate damaging risks and impacts without outside assistance.

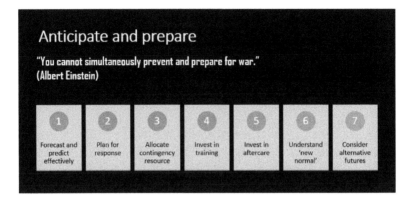

Figure 10: Anticipate and prepare

The organisation that can look ahead, plan, invest in trained resource, support its people and adapt will be well placed to maintain effective organisational resilience. This is not a one-dimensional or simple process, and the structures to enable such a capability will need to overlap across organisational activities and silos. Whatever the complexities, it cannot be ignored as a critical element of organisational resilience.

Respond and adapt

Despite its positive influence on organisational capability, anticipation is not sufficient for an organisation to be able to prepare and develop capabilities in relation to its resilience. There needs to be a resulting action based upon what has been anticipated, so that the organisation is able to respond effectively and adapt. Various methods may need to be employed to meet the challenges facing it in the most appropriate way. This will need the organisation to maintain its focus on not only what the threat poses, but also what its impact areas may be. This will ensure that the response and adaptation processes not only meet the immediate challenges, but also meet the requirements for organisational viability and continued competitive outcomes.

The key components that the organisation needs to think about may link to the following categories, but will not necessarily be limited to them.

Decide and do

The organisation needs to decide what it needs to do and then carry out actions to complete the task. This can be more difficult than many organisations and their leadership assume. The decision process will be influenced by many specific as well as wider issues that may limit or change influence and outcomes. A series of options, a planned set of processes to support those options can be considered; even if they change in response to the stimulus of the risk becoming a reality; or changing shape, there is merit in planning. The result should be that the idea of response and adaptation – deciding what to do and doing it, is not something that is 'set in stone', but something that is effectively subject to constant re-evaluation.

Use best possible thinkers and leaders

It is important that the organisation identifies those who can manage and deal with the types of problems that arise when things go wrong. This can cause problems for organisations that assume that those who are responsible at managerial levels during routine activity will be able to fill organisational resilience and related roles when the pressure is on. Individual and organisational stress factors can be significant, and even the most effective managers may find themselves struggling when the consequences of failure are facing them. Before a problem arises, organisations should invest in thinking. This is something that organisations and individuals tend not to do so well when under stress; and the time and capability to think and analyse is something that should be built into any response process.

Respond in the right way – neither over nor under-responding

The allocation of resource and response capability will be driven by many influences. However, the thinking process should ensure *appropriate* organisational responses. An overemphasis on throwing all resources at a particular problem early on may not be the best approach to take. Conversely, it may not be sensible to hold back on response in the early stages of an issue arising. This is where we should return to thinking about the ability to adapt. The design and delivery of plans should not preclude the organisation from responding appropriately to what it sees and feels. This should inform thinking, rather than using prepared matrices that do not effectively link to the issues that may arise. Sluggish following of previous plans will mean that in some instances the incorrect or poorly thought-out response maybe as much of an issue as an overblown response.

Avoid bias, 'groupthink' and risk stasis

Every human being is loaded with preconceptions, prejudices and ideas about the way things should be done. That is human nature. However, bias and preloaded thinking can have significant repercussions for an organisational resilience capability. Although we all have individual characteristics and traits that will affect our decision-making process, one of the most potentially damaging to an effective response is 'Groupthink' as posited by Irving Janis.[11] Janis considered that organisations and people within them will set themselves up into groups that think in a certain way, as a collective, and will consciously and unconsciously exclude what they consider to be thinking and action that goes against their own. If this idea of Groupthink has been embedded into planning and organisational approaches, and the preferences of a specific group or closed environment have been imposed upon planning without full consultation or assessment of the wider implications, then this can be problematic. We can see effects of Groupthink in most environments on most days. However, we can also see that if we look at various case studies in relation to risk response, the inability to think and act in an open and inclusive way, and focusing on preconceived ideas and conclusions, rarely provides the answers that the organisation will need.

Groupthink can also be a very pervasive issue when dealing with crisis and pressure. The response to a need to give rapid and correct answers to difficult questions, can evade the best of organisations and cause significant problems. When organisations argue themselves into a particular corner, it can often be difficult for them to convince themselves of the way out. More than that, in-groups and 'mind guards' as discussed by Janis in relation to Groupthink, are not simply a hindrance – they can be

---

[11] Janis, I L, (1972), *Victims of Groupthink*, New York: Houghton Mifflin.

destructive and completely negate the positive efforts to build resilience. If we can overcome the human nature and instinctive constraints that we place upon ourselves, we may have a chance at improvement.

Think about what needs to continue and what does not

There will need to be some difficult and challenging decisions taken in some instances when an organisation is required to adapt and respond to a particular series of events or a single incident. There will be a need to prioritise resources, to identify those who need to be in a particular place or location and – equally important – those who do not. Organisations should be aware of the needs of resource allocation, and what will be the priority to ensure that they are able to place effective resources in the right location to do the job that is asked of them. There are challenges: the organisation will need to specify which departments and activities are most important to it, and this may bring friction and issues further down the line. However, the time to think of core activities and to plan for those that may need to be relegated to a lower priority is not when the incident is running, but before it strikes.

Make changes to the organisation and operate in new ways

Complementary to the idea that we need to decide what needs to continue and what does not, we also need to be able to act effectively to make changes and change operational functions rapidly and effectively. Again, this is something that requires an organisation to think in advance and to plan effectively. If that is achieved, then the transition to a different way of working can be initiated and completed without additional disruption above that which is already being caused. Naturally, that, in turn, will compound problems. Therefore, it is important to ensure that there is some planning and scenario-based thinking that has been thought about, tested and validated. In this way the organisation knows that it will work and be acceptable to its teams and throughout its structure. It is important to note that such changes will have external stakeholder interest. Most importantly, any approach towards making changes and operating in new ways should not be introduced during chaos; that will only end badly.

Monitor and respond to how others respond and adapt

As issues develop, and as problems may arise that bring additional challenges to the organisation, it is important not only to monitor how we respond within the organisation, but also what is happening externally. There are lessons to be learned from looking at what is going on in the wider environment, and the solution to our problem may be much easier to see when someone or something else is taking a different approach to the problem and issues. We should also consider on a more micro scale how, within the organisation, we think about monitoring and responding to the adaptation, or lack of it, that our own people are able to make in response to the stimulus of a crisis, realised risk or issue.

Overall, response and adaptation are not something that happen when the issue has already arisen, nor should they be planned and thought about lightly, although the actual implementation of them may well be rapid and hasty. How, when and to what extent the response and adaptation take place depends on the nature of the problem facing the organisation. However, thinking applied and time taken on developing responses and management of problems before they arise, and including team members in the discussions and thinking, will provide significant effectiveness improvements for the organisation. Not only that, but individuals will also benefit from being prepared rather than facing the additional stress of fighting their way through a problem without either preparation, training or any understanding of what is expected of them. They will need to adapt, as we all do, in stages and with a degree of comfort and developed familiarity with what is required of them in challenging situations and circumstances.

Incremental change v sudden disruptions

Incremental change by its very nature happens gradually and can perhaps lull an organisation into a false sense of security in that it feels that it is able to deal with problems that develop over more prolonged and extended durations. This self-delusion can be dangerous, as incremental change can bring significant issues to the organisation that underestimates it. Even with slowly developing problems, the impact can be significant and immediate. Again, the organisation will have options to take and ways that it can approach a problem or developing incremental issue, and there are tactics and strategies that can also be applied to ensure that even incremental change can be effectively interdicted and rapidly managed.

Horizon scanning is the idea that we are looking beyond what is directly in front of us and considering what may be coming next. There is a whole industry around forecasting and considering what organisations should be thinking about in one year, the next decade or even the next century. However, what is critical is to be able to identify what the next developments may be, and how far away they may be in time, distance and effort for the organisation to think about. Horizon scanning therefore requires the organisation to spend significant amounts of time and effort on diligent intelligence gathering, surveying the landscape for potential issues and codifying in some way so that they can at least have an idea about what comes next.[12]

Monitoring. Monitoring is important for thinking ahead. However, it does need to inform and trigger some form of response. Here is a pertinent example. Climate change is a huge issue now – just about the top priority for all of us it seems. Doing something about it has taken a little longer to gain momentum than it should. For example, in 2011 climate change was at the top of the WEF's list of global risks by likelihood and impact combined. Although political and business leaders have discussed its importance and overtly taken steps for change, the continuing focus on unresolved issues may indicate that the attention paid to the risks as presented is lacking. WEF (2011)[13] observed that there tends to be a focus on events (perhaps a good example of that type of event would be COVID-19) rather than chronic risks that gestate and deepen over time (climate change). In effect, it seems that humans are more disposed towards reacting to global risks as they appear – vindicating their immediate action with immediate demonstrable benefits. In politics this type of activity may have helped election chances in the past; in business it may have shown that organisations can demonstrably act. Whether the

---

[12] Interesting blog here:
https://foresightprojects.blog.gov.uk/2018/03/08/the-ten-commandments-of-horizon-scanning/.

[13] World Economic Forum, (2011), Global Risks Report, Davos: WEF.

resurgent concern about climate change is a reality or a political smokescreen, inactivity has contributed to its acceleration; we need to act on what we monitor.

Avoid the 'boiling frog'. The boiling frog is not a theory, it is more of a fable. The idea goes that some murky experiment aimed to boil a frog to see if it would recognise the risks and jump out of a slowly heating pot. The idea behind it can provide an interesting illustration of the pitfalls behind becoming comfortable or complacent about risk. Staw, Sandelands and Dutton used the term 'threat rigidity' to discuss how individuals and organisations identify and deal with threats, risks and their materialisation, and the roles of stress and perception in responding. They stated:

> *"[...] depending on the source of threat, response rigidities can serve to either reduce or intensify the threat. The net results, of course, can be either a functional adaptation to the environment or a maladaptive cycle of threat rigidity effects."*[14]

That was 1981, so was a long time ago. However, I would contend that this observation remains apposite in the second quarter of the twenty-first century, and will do so at the same stage in the twenty-second century. In basic terms, by doing less than we should, we can make things worse, and if we do less than we should in response to that, the risks

---

[14] Staw, B.M., Sandelands, L.E. and Dutton, J.E., (1981), Threat Rigidity Effects in Organizational Behavior: A Multilevel Analysis, *Administrative Science Quarterly*, 26 (4), p.501.

develop and deepen further. Check what is going on around you now. Do you see it?

Sudden disruptions

The organisation that can manage sudden disruptions, by all logic, should not be in a position where it decides to take a course of action at the very last moment. In an ideal world, where the speed and pace of a problem surprises the organisation; if an organisation understands itself and the impacts that may arise, then it should be able to plan effectively. The capability should not be to plan rapidly, but to respond rapidly – two very different things. Naturally, the course of events will rarely be smooth or benign.

Disruptions may or may not be planned for; and it is preferable if planning has taken place. But they are most likely to be unexpected in that even if planned for to some extent, there will be a limited ability to forecast exactly when the disruption may arise and to what extent it will impact across the organisation. If it transpires that the impact is less than anticipated, then that clearly will be the desired outcome. However, it could be that the impact is or may develop into something that is much worse than initially thought; in which case the organisation does need to be able to demonstrate rapidity in response. Naturally, *sudden* disruptions will be undesirable for the organisation, and their speed, pace and impact will be something that the organisation needs to respond to rapidly to avoid a deepening risk. Sometimes there will be a case that the organisation itself, and likely the people within it, will not be able or willing to engage rapidly with fast moving disruptive events. The key to effective response is to demonstrate and build in agility in thinking and planning. That will be the differentiator between the resilient organisation and that which is unable to maintain its viability through significant rapid change.

We should also consider that disruptive events will be external in general – but not always. Although many disruptive events are generated from outside the organisation, there will be an equal number that will generate because of activities that the organisation itself has carried out or because of errors or omissions in internal processes. These will be no less damaging. Therefore, the organisation will need to develop some form of fluidity in its approach to managing variable options. There may be a need and capability to change focus from what is going on externally to what is happening internally and perhaps back again. In cases where there is significant activity both in the external and internal organisational structures, there is even more need to be able to combine decisiveness and speed with that necessary agility and capability. Internal or external – there is a difference between those that are in our control to manage – normally internal – and those that are much more difficult to control. External issues may be much more difficult to manage as there will naturally be issues and challenges that will arise because of events, decisions and actions taken that do not involve our organisation. Because these issues are out of our control, then the only management and mitigation that the organisation can reliably put in place is against that of the impacts.

It is also highly important to consider the fact that a sudden onset disruption does not mean that the disruption will be short-lived. The speed and pace of onset may mean that the problems require rapid response and some 'quick fixes'. However, the temporary may well become the permanent, and organisations should recognise this. Plans and contingencies will need to ensure that the natural wish to revert to normality does not override the key need to manage issues in the longer term. That reversion may be slow and gradual. However, failing to recognise that time may need to be taken, and that the pace may be slower than preferred, may bring further negative impacts.

Survive and prosper

To be resilient, the organisational aim should be to move through and beyond the challenges that we have discussed so far, and to ensure that it is able to return to, or even better, improve upon its capabilities before the event took place. Weathering the storm is not enough, and the organisation that wishes to maintain its viability must also consider that it will need to be able to *demonstrate* its agility, and its resilience, so that it can be seen to be a trustworthy, dependable, investment prospect. In general, the organisational aim will be to ensure that it can deal with an incident that arises, while maintaining the aim of the business or organisation. Although it may be that the tactical and operational aims will need to be adjusted in response to issues that arise, it is important to ensure that, in general, the strategy of the organisation remains on course and as planned.

Throughout any challenging or disruptive event, the organisation will need to do more than simply work through the problem and ensure that it has considered continuity to meet or exceed previous levels of capability. Outperforming competition and maintaining competitive edge and market share will be at the core of any business strategy. Other organisations will have different aims and objectives, but nonetheless, overall survival depends on organisational capability being focused on the need to do well; and ultimately to do better.

Essential to the ability to survive and thrive is also the need to ensure that people are supported. Crisis and disruptive incidents do show that people matter; and the organisation that wishes to survive change will be able to support and maintain the well-being of its people when challenges arise. More on that will come as we progress in our resilient thinking.

Shock absorption

Given that the forces applied on an organisation will not necessarily come from one direction, and that they may repeat or consolidate, we need to think of resilience as something that has longevity rather than as a short-term reactive process. Essentially, organisational resilience is about shock absorption rather than 'bouncing back'. There will be minor and major obstacles, changes and developments that will challenge the organisation, and will require it to flex and adapt a little, and occasionally quite a lot. Bouncing back is probably best analogised by a rubber ball hitting a surface and rebounding, losing energy along the way, uncontrolled and unpredictable in its direction and velocity as it rebounds. Shock absorption is best analogised by the suspension system built into every vehicle. What we tend to call 'shock absorbers' are in fact 'dampers' designed to soften impact and shock. They fit within a coiled spring that is designed to put the wheels back into contact with the road. The system is stabilised by various struts, bracers and rods, all of which are designed to maintain the direction of travel, and each with their own 'bushes' that are designed to further absorb shocks.

Shock absorption is not about a single component but a designed, coherent system of integrated components that allow smooth progress in changing circumstances while remaining unchanged themselves. Over time, these components degrade or need to be refined or redesigned as, for example, new technologies or performance needs dictate. The analogy with organisational resilience remains pertinent as these principles and requirements apply beyond simple mechanical structures. Most importantly, we should try to understand that shock absorption requires systems, and therefore has some inherent complexity, rather than the seductive simplicity of rebounding.

VUCA

VUCA is an acronym first used by the US Army in 1987 based on the works of Bennis and Nanus (1985)[15]. It considers that we live and exist in a world of Volatility, Uncertainty, Complexity and Ambiguity. All these aspects of our context and environment will implicitly bring issues for the resilient thinker to face. What this means is that the world around us is constantly changing and dynamic. Therefore, our assumption must be that a resilient organisation needs to be able to understand and cope with, and therefore operate affectively in, the VUCA world. We can look at any number of different examples of change that arise; Taleb's[16] so-called 'Black Swans' and any other unexpected or difficult challenges that we may not have all

---

[15] Bennis, W. G., Nanus, B., (1985), *Leaders: The Strategies for Taking Charge*, United States: HarperCollins.

[16] Taleb, NN., (2007), *The Black Swan: The Impact of the Highly Improbable*, London: Allen Lane.

the answers to when they arise or when we first hear of them. However, this should not stop the organisation in its tracks. All the VUCA elements, it can be argued, are by-products of human activity in a constantly changing environment. Therefore, what we do know is that people in any environment will be unpredictable, will change and will respond to stimulus so that they may change direction. This, in turn, means that, inconveniently we may not quite reach the answers we need when we need them. The resilient organisation is the one that fully understands this and can develop a degree of comfort in its ways of operating in VUCA environments. And if we cannot be comfortable, we should at least be capable.

Naturally, and theoretically, it is much easier to talk about this ability to operate in the VUCA environment than it is to deliver a capability. However, the important aspect of this is for the organisation and its people to understand that there is a dynamic world in which it needs to operate with multiple inputs from multiple separate microenvironments, which will have direct and indirect impact upon it and that those impacts and the causes of them will constantly change. Sometimes these may metamorphose into something similar, and sometimes into something unpredicted and completely different. This being the case, it is important that our organisations and their leaders understand that we cannot forecast and define all aspects of probability in risk before they arise; and that we must consider impact to be the key driver when seeking resilience in the VUCA world. It is worth the time, for the serious resilience specialist, to consider and study aspects of VUCA, as these shape our strategic, tactical and operational contexts. As we know, we need to understand our context if our organisations are to maintain their position, competitiveness and capabilities.

Figure 11: The VUCA world – What's in yours?

The influences that shape our own capabilities can, and do, change and shift. We are not all affected by all aspects of what surrounds us. However, our context is unpredictable and can confound our best efforts to control it either as individuals or organisations.

Functions and components – And conflict

It is of note that in the definition we have used for organisational resilience, there is no stipulation of the various elements and components that comprise it. In effect, although some of these disparate elements will be complementary, others will be in conflict, and this will cause problems for the organisation as it attempts to bring together a collective and coherent response to difficult problems. Also, there will be situations where a crisis, for example, does not involve a security response. The accomplished organisation will be able to consider which of the optimal responses are best used in the event of an incident arising. These will be different depending on circumstance and on the capabilities of those involved in dealing with the problem. However, in general, organisations should plan for involvement in all relative areas; and understand that silo and stovepipe activity does not preclude the inclusion of one activity or group of activities at the expense of another. It is important to ensure that internal organisation and composition do not prejudice or disadvantage the corporate response when attempting to deal with issues that arise either in the short or long term.

It is also important to consider the fact that while the terms that we use to cover the range of prevention and response functions provide a significant set of capabilities, these may not be overtly used within an organisation. This may be most evident in those organisations that have a more measured approach to incidents rather than standing up or developing what may be or feel like an emergency response. That feeling or impression of 'it's an emergency' may well be something that some organisations want to avoid. Also, we should consider that none of these issues or specific requirements may arise on a large scale if the issue is something that develops over a long time and is relatively low impact. Not every problem will be a full-blown emergency. Because of this, it is important that those who develop or wish to develop capabilities and skills in organisational resilience can take a broad view of the organisation rather than operating in stove pipes or silos. Although there will always be a need for distinct and separate activities, either managed in the matrix or a hierarchical way – or any other way for that matter – there will also be a need to ensure that there is a holistic role taken by all these elements within the organisation.

Figure 12: A wide range of activities and functions in the resilient organisation

They may or may not be in conflict; it is desirable that they are not. Some may be engaged, and some may not, and silo activity can be an attribute of any single activity, group of them or all of them.

In the next part of the discussion, as we consider criticality, we will also look at the idea of the organisational resilience function as a holistic system, and a process and series of functions at all levels that incorporates and brings together not only these specialisms but also the wider capabilities of the organisation to give a fully inclusive, capable, adaptable and agile, resilient organisation.

Criticality in organisations

At this stage in our thinking we are now moving to an idea of how organisations identify what may be the areas that are important to them when developing their response approach. The response may be to a disruptive event and require the maintenance of organisational resilience; but equally it may be a part of general, normal, routine, strategic and operational activities.

Every organisation has core functions, and from those come a whole range of dependent functions, feeder functions and peripheral activities that may need to be prioritised in terms of resource and allocation of effort at various levels. This requirement will be true not only in times of stress, but also in routine operations when the organisation is deciding how it manages itself, how it achieves its aims, how it manages its approach towards being viable and competitive in the long term, and how it is able to increase, decrease and reallocate efforts in relation to the demands placed upon it.

We are now considering criticality. That is, the assessment and understanding of what is most important to the organisation, and what may be less crucial at a particular time or stage in either its normal routine activity or in relation to a crisis. To begin, and bearing in mind that we are talking about the idea of maintaining the capability of the organisation in a resilient context, we should identify what we may consider the *criticality* to mean. Criticality is most definitely not about the idea that something is dangerous, but is adequately encompassed in this (my) definition:

"The importance and priority for protection and continuity of a resource, process, function, person or product to an organisation's continued viability."

Simply put, we are asking what is important to the organisation, and how it is thinking about the priorities for aspects of the organisational capability to be protected or maintained in the event of a particular problem or issue arising. This is not something that can be considered effectively once an issue has hit the organisation, rather, it is something that the organisation will have allocated time, thought and planning to before the event itself. The consideration of criticality should belong within risk assessments, where the calculation – if that is the word – of a particular risk and its impact will consider how important the area being considered is to the organisation. This does require careful thought, as there is a need to make sure that the capabilities of the organisation are not compromised, and that there has been thought and effort put into thinking about the problems involved. But, of course, that is the norm in resilient thinking.

The identification of criticality cannot be a 'tick-box' exercise by definition, as an assessment of what is important for organisational resilience needs active thought. It is also important during a risk analysis and impact assessment process to understand that there is a negative influence and thus negative effect that can be caused by perception and personal preference within an organisation as to what exactly comprises criticality. Therefore, this essential element of organisational capability necessitates careful thought, discussion, consultation and mapping to ensure that the important and correct areas are assessed as priorities for criticality, and that those that may be less critical are also appropriately ranked and managed. Perhaps for the short or even long term, those might be put on the 'back burner'.

People, for example, as the cliche goes; 'our most important asset', are usually actually just that. It has taken the COVID-19 pandemic for organisations to realise that the importance of employees is critical to resilience. What we have seen happening is the return of understanding that without engaged people, organisations; even aspects of society will change for the worse. The demands of people do need to be met in terms of how they operate, and how work-life balance, technology enabled or not, needs to be accommodated. This idea had been lost for some time, if it ever existed at all, but is now something that has moved out of the management and human resource textbooks into something that is real and of prime importance to organisations. Although previously people management may have been something more akin to a line in a policy or a phrase in a strategic brochure, rather than something of focused and deliberate organisational thinking, this has now changed. In fact, it is becoming the key aspect or organisational approaches to strategy, business and resilience. In that regard, it is important to understand the criticality of effective people for organisational viability and resilience.

For many organisations, reputation preservation is a key and critical element of their activity, function and strategic viability. A loss of reputation for whatever reason can have significant effects on an organisation's competitiveness and attractiveness to clients, stakeholders and investors. Therefore, most business organisations will protect their reputation at all costs. This is sensible, and appropriate in most cases. It may be that the organisation feels that reputation is *the* most important aspect of the strategic elements that it wishes to protect and therefore deems it to be the most highly critical. This does make a degree of sense in that any of the areas that are deemed critical, if they do fail, will probably be directly linked to impact upon reputation. However, reputation is not the only critical aspect of an organisation, and it is fed by most others, which will need to be critical also. Nevertheless, for many organisations, the impact of reputation can have the most significant if not terminal effect on income and profitability if not handled correctly.

While thinking about criticality, we also need to consider the importance of implied and 'dropdown' intangibles and tangibles. Behind every headline and statement in a risk assessment, and behind every calculation of impact, there needs to be a further degree of analysis and capability assessment. This will need to be in relation to what is behind and supporting the achievement of that level of capability and continuity, and therefore maintaining the critical elements. In other words, we need to be able to consider every single contributory factor that will either help or hinder our ability to maintain resilience in relation to a critical factor. This will require the organisation and its people to think very carefully, to be inclusive from strategic to operational level of those who contribute to the organisational capability; and to consider best cases, worst cases and options that come from the actions that we take. Dropdowns can be significant, and they have multiple aspects that need to be considered from the start.

For example, if we go back to considering people and their criticality to the organisation, there will be many other aspects that will need to be considered to support thinking about who we need, when and what they need to do.

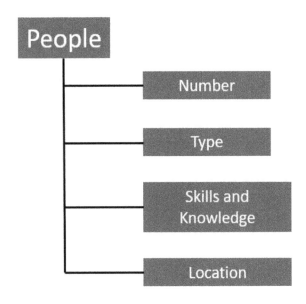

Figure 13: People

The considerations that we will need to think about will vary widely across the organisation; and, for example, when we talk about type, skills and knowledge, we will need to consider specific roles, and sometimes even the temperament of individuals, as well as how many we need for a particular role. We then become more focused on qualitative assessment rather than quantitative. It does not matter so much how many people we put into dealing with a particular problem, but rather their qualities, capabilities, attitudes, knowledge and skills, and their ability to operate under pressure. The criticality of the right type of people is more important than the amount of people we may have in a particular role or activity.

Criticality is not a simple assessment to make, and there needs to be a significant and detailed amount of applied thinking that goes into not only what is critical, but also what makes it so.

Systems

The importance of the capability for organisations to be able to optimise interactions and co-dependency within frameworks, requires the development of systems that can work effectively across levels and output requirements. In discussing systems, the idea that the various interactions and processes do need to be applied was considered through *Systems Theory* as proposed by Ludwig von Bertalanffy in 1969. His ideas were summarised by Heylighen and Joslyn in 1992[17]:

> *"He emphasized that real systems are open to, and interact with, their environments, and that they can acquire qualitatively new properties through emergence, resulting in continual evolution. Rather than reducing an entity (e.g., the human body) to the properties of its parts or elements (e.g., organs or cells), systems theory focuses on the arrangement of and relations between the parts which connect them into a whole (cf. holism). This organisation determines a system, which is independent of the concrete substance of the elements (e.g., particles, cells, transistors, people, etc). Thus, the same concepts and principles of organisation underlie the different*

---

[17] Heylighen, F. and Joslyn, C., (1992), *What is Systems Theory?* Cambridge Dictionary of Philosophy.

disciplines (physics, biology, technology, sociology, etc.), providing a basis for their unification. Systems concepts include system-environment boundary, input, output, process, state, hierarchy, goal-directedness and information."

If we consider the application of the theories put forward by von Bertalanffy, the idea of 'unity of science' is an interesting one that we can apply effectively towards the specific requirements concerning the development of resilience, its sub-activities and resilient thinking. Effectively, we are considering that a system can be applied in structure to any organisation. If we treat an organisation as a system, we are considering not only the simple and uni-dimensional idea of an organisation as one that conducts a particular business-orientated activity, but something that has a complex set of hierarchies and interactions across multiple functions. These functions unify within a system (or subsystems) and drive that organisation towards improved capability and of course wider security and resilience.

If we can make that conceptual leap, then we are also able to perhaps think about various other contributing types of theory that allow a visualisation of how we can design and implement much more effective and future-ready resilience structures that are able to anticipate, respond to and recover from the various types of problems and issues that face us not only now but in the future. The understanding of coherence and systems is structurally matched with clear ideas about not only what the interdependencies may be, but also how critical they may be for the organisation.

What is also useful to consider is the idea that further theories and ideas exist, which allow us to focus on centralised and dispersed interdependent structures, capabilities, systems and subsystems that power the organisation. They also allow us to think about building and developing *externality* in our ability to develop resilience. Such externality is not only the probably more traditional view of looking outwards from the organisation and seeing the effects of our own actions; but equally important it is considering the potentials, inputs, threats, risks and subsequent impacts from various external influencing areas that have the effect of changing not only how we are able to manage ourselves, but, in fact, how our systems may work. This links directly to *"system-environment boundary, input, output, process, state, hierarchy, goal-directedness and information"* as previously quoted from Heylighen and Joslyn.

What organisations should consider, analyse and act upon is the idea that the organisation itself is something that is not a series of lines and diagrams drawn on paper, but something that is much more organic and able to react, learn and grow (and sometimes shrink) in relation to the externalities that it faces.

Figure 14: Hierarchies

In the wider context, the hierarchical norms as indicated here need to be able to flex and change to meet internal and external changing and refreshing dynamics. The inability to do so will leave the organisation behind those that are able to be more flexible and resilient. Straight lines of command and control upwards and downwards will not always or naturally be the best option for resilience management.

The organisational concept can develop into something that is less of a traditional hierarchy and something more aligned to a neural network with interactive components that work in response to triggers and incentives, inputs and outputs. This should provide further actionable outputs for the organisation to meet its objectives. In the context of the much more dynamic and fluid operating context that appears to be facing most organisations as we move towards the second half of the twenty-first century, the equally fluid organic approach to organisational resilience then becomes something more of a cultural or organisational intangible rather than a driver that changes the physical structure (certainly in terms of first order change)[18] of organisations that we are studying. And even with a hierarchy drawn out on a page, that fluidity may still be able to be applied.

The approach can then be that, to develop systems approaches, there does not need to be a strategy to change the way that an organisation operates its structures (in fact, the imposition of a system on other structured frameworks may bring negative impact). However, if we perceive and understand the 'biomechanics' of the organisation, what nourishes, adds to and detracts from it as a responsive and growing entity, then we can think more clearly about how we can develop its capability in the most effective way. The behaviours, capacities, capabilities and knowledge of the organisation itself – as with any organic entity – will influence how it engages with its environment.

In considering systems, how they can interact and their overall impact upon each other, it is worth understanding that we can work inwards from space into every aspect of our lives as they are lived. Nations, societies, organisations, businesses, relationships and interactions all rely to a certain extent on systems. The inherent interdependencies are further reduced and refined into lower levels where teams, components, management structures, networks,

---

[18] First-order change works within an existing structure and view of the world. You could view it as tinkering with the system – doing more or less of something, making an existing process better or more accurate and making incremental changes. With first-order change, the *ends* of the system remain the same – it's the *means* of producing those results that change. What you seek, what you avoid, the way you see the world and your values remain the same. *https://coachingleaders.co.uk/first-order-change/*.

communications and control inputs are all operating in a co-dependent interconnected helical system.

Organisational Strategy
Helix

**Organisational Resilience
Helix**

**Connected by People, Product
and Process Functions**

Figure 15: 'Double helix' structure

With this 'double helix' structure; the functions and actions within the organisation can and will link directly to core elements of the organisational 'DNA'. The organisational strategy and organisational resilience helixes allow these strands to be linked throughout any process, action or response.

By looking at and thinking about an interconnected less 'organogram' structure, we may be able to visualise our systems differently. We should aim to visualise systems and interactions and the match, if any, between forward thinking resilience development and the fluidity of systems within organisations. The idea is that the organisation is informed by resilience expertise and response capability that not only understands what the threats may be, but also what the capabilities of the organisation as a system are. Furthermore, by understanding that the organisation *can* work in this way, we become comfortable with fluidity in response to problems.

Importantly, as learning outcomes, we are looking for awareness building. To what extent does organisational thinking really consider the depth that is required to enable it to be appropriately organised and equipped to understand the capabilities that it has, but also the capabilities that it needs to be able to maintain its resilience? The development challenge is that we need to be able to think much more widely in terms of organisational capability and resilience than has been the case for less capable managers and practitioners in the past (and still quite a few in the present). It is fair to say that the challenges facing specialists as we address massively advancing technology and communication advances are unprecedented. Equally, the challenges facing those who work and operate in resilience disciplines are much more extensive than those that may have been faced by others in the past. There is, therefore, a requirement to develop knowledge, understanding, capability and confidence in those who are looking to develop organisational resilience beyond the two-dimensional processes that have been sufficient in the past to deal with appropriately two-dimensional risks. The challenge to the resilient thinker is to engage with the inevitable need to develop.

Our focus, in reality, will not be nearly as much on the drawing of lines and diagrams concerning the necessary and required structures and systems. Much more importantly, it will be on deep people-centred activity that is essential for the organisation to develop in appropriate ways and in the face of this technological change that is currently facing us through the fourth industrial revolution. What we must consider within the system is not only the structures and capabilities, but also the human interaction that is essential for the organisation. Not only to work in appropriate ways to manage resilience, but also to be able to develop a capability in which human beings are able to operate effectively. This needs to be achieved while not compromising or reducing the effectiveness of resilience, and maintaining the required capability in the face of developing and dynamic risks and threats.

The overlay of humanity upon the much simpler ideas concerning structural layout is something that is critical to the development of this organisational and organic understanding process. It is not only that we have systems to develop that can be subject to both technological approaches and the highly developed electronic and information networks that support them. Also, we should have an equally well-developed people-centred focus that is able to ensure that we are comfortable and capable working with much more intelligent and knowledgeable network systems. Increasingly, and with AI and the multiverse becoming prevalent and able to operate without our input, our approach needs to depend upon our viewpoints of their effectiveness and impacts in relation to ourselves and our organisations.

Time

When considering the criticality of a particular asset to an organisation, the key influence on its prioritisation will need to be the amount of time without it that the organisation can continue to operate. The duration of an incident needs to be understood, and the organisation needs to be able to decide and specify how many and what assets need to be in place to facilitate its return to normal operations within a specified timescale. This is a facet of business continuity planning that uses such terminology as 'recovery time objectives', and considers that an organisation should have in place specific time-bound objectives for certain levels of recovery to be met. Organisational resilience is not purely a business continuity issue, and any form of terminology can be used to ensure that the organisation understands that the time aspect of any function and a duration assessment is essential for consideration and prioritisation. However, whatever terminology we decide to use, we should remember that the clock is always ticking and that unattended risks do not age well.

As a disruptive event situation continues to develop, the pressure of time will naturally increase upon the organisation. The more time that passes without it being able to respond effectively and its recovery time objectives not being met, implies that the organisation becomes less effective. In effect, when thinking about VUCA environments, and the demands for organisations to be able to demonstrate that they are responding to incidents, the pressure increases. The speed of digitally enabled news and information reporting, and time aspects of organisational capability and resilience need to be overriding. This overriding requirement is often regarded as more important than the quality of capability; in other words, it is tempting to gravitate towards the 'quick fix' solution.

However, although time is infinite, the ability of the organisation to cheat it is not. The expectations of the organisation will be significant, and those who wish to do it further harm will take advantage of the opportunity to exploit its time failures. In general, the assessment of time's importance in measured minutes, hours or days is simply one aspect of the overall assessment of criticality to the organisation. More important, is the ability to ensure that the organisation as a system understands that time is a critical factor, as well as the key contributor to the criticality of a particular function. Time and its importance should not be underestimated, and should always be in the planning and activity of response to risk impacts.

Phases of response and recovery

In close alignment to the issues around criticality, we also need to consider the fact that when unchecked, critical issues can more rapidly lead to further developments. Not only that, but we can also be in situations where unanticipated issues outstrip our ability to manage their effect upon critical elements of our organisational resilience or even organisational structure. The stark differences between anticipated and unanticipated responses can be seen in Figures 16 and 17 below, where in the first case, unanticipated issues can be seen to develop over time (T) along the lower axis, while the level of criticality or impact on criticality (L) can be seen along the vertical axis.

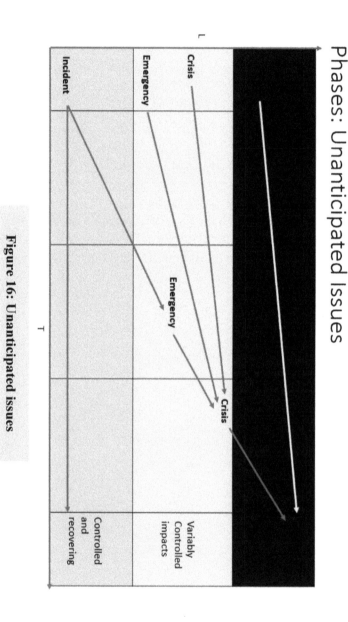

Figure 16: Unanticipated issues

Unanticipated issues can develop rapidly from the start point on the left, and as time passes will continue to escalate.

Intervention will be needed to stop that development reaching highly damaging levels. If we can keep pace with an unanticipated incident, we have the potential to keep it in the 'controlled and recovering zone'. Any other zone can be problematic.

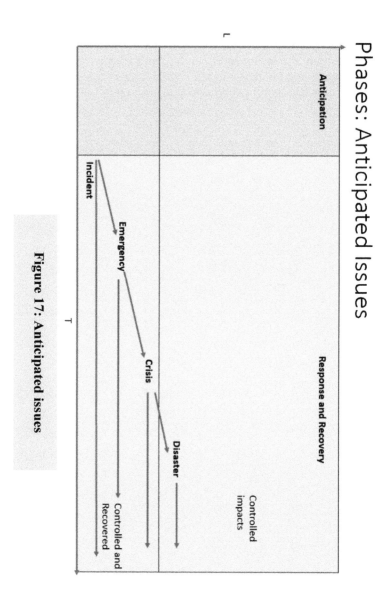

Figure 17: Anticipated issues

3: Organisational resilience – Principles and ideas

Anticipation should allow incidents to be contained, as we know that the issue will arise.

The application of the intervention is more important than simply planning for it. However, even if we do not know the exact typology of an incident or even the detail of how we may need to respond, we can understand and orientate ourselves for acting. That will make a difference.

Whatever the warning time may be for a particular incident, there are attributes that appear to some extent or another within each phase. The capability should be such that we are able to respond appropriately, recognising that these phase attributes exist and configuring ourselves appropriately to deal with them. This means that by recognising the phases and their attributes, we should be able to prepare and manage with minimised, or at least manageable, panic.

Phase attributes

- *Anticipation*: Clearly, what we need to achieve is to be able to anticipate as much as possible what may happen, although this may not be as possible as we would like. Although we will be able to anticipate that something may happen to us, we will be less equipped to be able to anticipate exactly what the attributes of that issue might be. Therefore, it is important to ensure that we have an anticipatory capability within the organisation. We need to be careful that we do not focus too much on forecasting the exact detail if we cannot do so. This is probably going to be wasteful of time and effort when we need to consider, more importantly, the impact, and therefore the response that we need to make. In its purest form, anticipation will be such that we are thinking about what the impact may be – regardless of the exact nature of the problem itself and its cause.

- **Response**: Response to an incident will need to be timely and effective. What we need to consider, again, is the fact that when we are given hardly any or no warning about the incident that may develop into something much worse, then we may be compelled to decide the exact nature of our response in less detail. However, we do need to be able to respond. The anticipation process that we have talked about should allow us to consider that at least we have people and resources in place to be able to respond effectively to a variety of scenarios. Whether our allocation of resources to that scenario is more or less than we anticipate, we will not know until the incident begins to unfold. However, what we will need to be able to do is to maintain that response for as long as it takes to get us through the problem at hand. Therefore, it is important to ensure that we consider response not as a one-time, short-term activity, but as something that may be long and protracted, and require additional resource and capability development as the incident evolves. That said, a rapid, effective response may put us in a position where we are able to deal with the problem and close it down at the early stage.
- **Recovery**: Recovering from a problem, incident or crisis, may not necessarily mean that it is something

that begins to take place *after* we have responded. In effect, we should have our eye on the requirement to be able to recover as soon as we are aware that we have been affected. This should be a clear element of organisational planning, with recovery activities in place alongside the response activity. This can be challenging; the main reason for this is that the organisation may well be focusing heavily on response, and recovery may be something down the line. Also, as with all the aspects that we have considered so far, we need to think about the next issue on our list, resource; we simply may not have enough people, materials and money to be able to respond effectively. We certainly may not be able to run response and recovery concurrently with limited resources.

• ***Resources:*** Involve people, material, those resources that are provided to us by externals and stakeholders, and time and knowledge. It is useful to assume that we need to think carefully about the allocation of resources long before we come to the point where we need them. It is probably a significant guarantee that if we leave the planning and allocation of resources too late, then we will not have them in the right place at the right time to do the job that we want them to do. Therefore, planning for resources is key and essential to the effective response capability whether the phase is long or short in terms of warning. The difficulty, of course, will also be the fact that resources are difficult to come by when the organisation is not under threat or has not felt that it will be. Therefore, the case for the allocation of resources needs to be justified – probably through a business case. Equally important is to influence through demonstrating and proving the need. Briefings, exercising and prompting top management within the organisation to understand impact through risk assessment and risk registers will all assist in this. The skill requirement for the consultant is to ensure that the organisation understands that resilience requires resources for critical functions.

- *Resilience*: Just a reminder. Resilience is often overlooked within organisations, and it is critical that they understand that it is not something that can be planned and delivered ad hoc. It should be considered as something to be developed and built before an incident takes place. Also, it is essential to understand that as an incident unfolds, there will be a need for people, structures, processes and functions to also be resilient. They will need to be able to allow the organisation to flex, vary approaches and recover from various ongoing issues that may arise as the problem develops – and respond accordingly. This resilience will require the organisation and its people to be aware of incidents and their complications and consequences as they take place, hopefully anticipating them, and being able to respond in the most appropriate and timely way. The potential for failure can be significant if the organisation does not carefully consider the resilience of itself and its people when under extreme pressure. Failing to do this can be problematic and lead to failure in the short, medium and long term. Of course you know this, *but do they?*

- *Capability*: There needs to be capability. It is important to note that capability is not a written plan, it is the developed ability of the organisation through top management strategy and organisational preparedness, down through all levels of management, or across all levels of management if you prefer, and then to the operational levels. This capability cannot be taken for granted, and must be part of a long-term developed and validated activity that is part of a plan. The comprehensive nature of a plan to prepare for incidents that are anticipated or unanticipated is something that may be overlooked in the race to put in place a written document. Developing capability requires the identification of appropriate people, it requires them to be taught, trained and built – in confidence and knowledge. They then need to be tested, and the plans validated, as they will be used by them. If this does not happen, the allocation of resources, the plan and any other strong sounding response will be weak, as it will not have been prepared or tested. If it is weak, it will likely fail.

- *Positivity*: The positive approach to dealing with a particular problem is that the organisation needs to understand that there will be an outcome. A positive approach, a proactive approach and one that pushes the organisation forward rather than folding when setbacks arrive is essential. In tandem with the development of capability, this ensures that the organisation can manage problems effectively. The organisation should aim to develop a culture whereby its teams at all levels are confident in their own capability and can rely on the organisation to support them when the potential for failure is high.

* *Adaptability*: Similarly, although specialisms are required throughout any type of activity, whether that be routine or in the face of a problem or issue that is either anticipated or unanticipated, there is also a need for organisational team members to be adaptable to change. Not only does this mean being able to carry out other peoples' roles – or at least support them – but it also requires adaptability in thinking and acting upon issues as they arise. At the core of any adaptable response will always be the need to maintain focus on what the organisation is aiming to achieve, and although the nuances of that may vary, it should remain the core of the organisational effort. However, it is important to understand that within that parameter, our people should be able to focus on the ability to change, adapt and deal with obstacles that may not be in their immediate area of responsibility and will take them out of their comfort zone. A lack of this ability to take an adaptive and flexible approach to problems as they arise will no doubt constrain the effectiveness of the response.

- *Learning applied*: Lessons will be learned, and it is not necessarily a fact that those lessons will be learned after the event. Organisations will need to ensure that they are able to learn as they go, especially if the problems that are being faced begin to develop into something more critical and damaging. The organisation needs to understand that its response will be based upon microlearning, in the face of problems and issues as they impact. Failing to take that approach will be significant in terms of problem and effect. The lessons may be rapid and painful, and may force the organisation towards actions that it would prefer not to take. However, repeating the same mistakes throughout the development of a particular type of problem or issue will only have negative effects for the organisation and bring compounded problems.

- *Maintenance*: Regardless of whether the issue is short and sharp, or longer and more protracted, we must maintain our focus on supporting our people and ensuring that they are able to cope with what may be traumatic, dislocating effects and events that will challenge them both mentally and physically. We must ensure that we have welfare processes in place to support our people. We must have the capability to ensure that we are able to offer support, guidance, encouragement and thanks to people who are going what will normally be above and beyond what they expect, and certainly what they will have in their job description. When this is the case, the development of a maintenance approach will ensure that the organisation and its people have the best possible chance of remaining capable for the longest possible time, and will have the ability to think about how they may develop longevity and long-term capability.

- *Decompression*: When the event has ended, and when most of the response process has ended and recovery is complete, or at least well underway, there will be a time for relaxation and reflection. It is important to allow the organisation to take a breath and recover from what may have been a significant issue for them to manage. There are other issues to consider. In the most damaging types of incidents, the workplace itself may have changed significantly. Capabilities and shortfalls will have been exposed not only in resources but also in individuals. And this may change the organisational dynamic considerably. There will either be confidence shown in senior management or a degree of dissatisfaction with the way in which a particular aspect – or the worst case the whole issue – was handled. Allowing space to think, recover, reflect and understand provides a real opportunity to get the best out of a damaged and disrupted organisation and its people.

Impact analysis and response

Managing impacts is integral to and fundamental for effective organisational resilience. Each organisation will have its unique structure, it will have its capabilities and it will have its response planned. However, any threat that contacts it will have an impact. As we have mentioned previously, it is important to understand that the impact may come from outside the organisation, and the impact as it presents itself will be beyond our control. What will be within our control will be the anticipation of the impacts and what they will be, and what we can do about an impact. We need to maintain the clarity of view that for the organisation, the cause is less interesting than the effect. For example, a personnel shortage could be caused by a breakdown in the transport system, a failure on the Internet or a pandemic, all of them are different in terms of their attributes, causes and the way they may develop. However, the impact will be the same for all; we have a loss of workforce. The difference will be in how the organisation responds.

Recognition of potential impacts involves a deep understanding of the organisation, its capabilities and its strategies. We need to be able to ensure that we can understand exactly what may happen within our organisation if we lose a particular capability within a particular timescale, and what we need to do to be able to manage that impact in any number of different scenarios or cases. Again, this is something that requires us to think about how we train and develop our people so that they can anticipate not only the impacts, but think about how far we need to go to be able to deal with them.

Impact management may not be sequential; multiple and spreading impacts can develop far away from the initial point of contact with the organisation. We know that there will be any number of 'drop down' issues that cause problems for the organisation, and although the levels of impact will vary, they will still be impacts and will need to be managed at the appropriate level. It is important also to consider that even small impacts, if left unchecked and unmanaged, will become impacts with much more consequence for the organisation, extending much more widely than we would like them to. All the attributes that we need to consider within the organisation and have listed above will come into play in dealing with impacts, and recognising that they are not just an impact at one point but could be long term with widespread further impacts.

Preparedness

Plans are least effective when they are deficient in self-analysis, and reflection is missing or incomplete. Organisations may deceive themselves about their preparedness for, and response to, incipient crises for reasons that may seem valid but may also bring a risk of negative impact. The deception may well be inadvertent: within the organisation itself there may be truth spoken; however, the very dynamics of the organisation may not allow for recognition and communication of gaps, problems and constraints. Again, whether struggling with the downside effects of '*groupthink*', or concern about blame culture, plans that ease the mind and soothe the organisational ego rather than solve the problem can be deceptive and problematic. Preparedness should be built on solid foundations rather than easy assumptions; and the upheavals of the past four years, and particularly in relation to the global pandemic, have shown that it is all too easy to talk about a problem without resolving it rather than preparing for its impacts.

When preparing for unwanted events it is simply human to assume in all forms of risk management that the horizon-scanning, forward-looking, 'Black Swan' identifying actions have been planned and thus we are prepared. We may deceive ourselves with models and frameworks, and a subsequent belief that our excellent foresight and forecasting will see us through. Recently, this planning myth has revealed fault lines, and probably much more widely than we would like to admit. COVID-19 has shown that plans do not work as we would like, because as human beings we allow our conceits to overcome our knowledge. Predicting the future and its nuances is a panacea but an impossibility; when we cannot position our organisation and its understanding of risk effectively, we are in no position to face the risks with any degree of effectiveness or capability. If we accept that, as PwC stated in their Global Crisis Survey (2019)[19], crisis preparedness brings competitive advantage, then preparedness should be a reality now rather than an intangible concept written into an unworkable plan. PwC said that: *"It's not if. It's when: No one is immune."* At a time when 'immunity' is something that is much more in our consciousness, we need to understand – as with a virus – we can take steps to prepare; we most certainly should not watch and wait.

Effective preparedness with a clear head and understanding that we cannot manage out every nuance of every eventuality is key to success. And as we enter the new understanding of resilience that COVID-19 has catalysed; we can see quite clearly that although everything has a cost; the most damaging long-term cost can be a lack of preparedness. For the resilient organisation, clear

---

[19] PwC Crisis Preparedness as the next competitive advantage: Learning from 4,500 crises, *https://www.pwc.com/ee/et/publications/pub/pwc-global-crisis-survey-2019.pdf.*

assessment based upon judgement, history, experience, models, learning and foresight is part of preparedness but not all. A longer-term planning assumption is that the organisation will be able to orientate itself to mitigate effects and to anticipate where the opportunities for growth on the other side of the problem may lie. Growth in a time of confusion and change is not a *non sequitur*, and in the commercial context, only those organisations that know themselves, their operating context, and are prepared to learn and engage with change, will survive and thrive.

The preparedness that we do build needs to be resilient in itself. There are many variations on the sentiment first attributed to Helmuth von Moltke; *"[...] no plan of operations extends with any certainty beyond the first contact with the main hostile force."* But we need plans nonetheless – and as General George Patton stated, *"A good plan violently executed now is better than a perfect plan executed next week."* Both ideas are predicated on the fact that something is better than nothing; and that 'something' needs to be based on knowledge and understanding; which, in turn, gives the preparedness necessary to engage with the problem. It is doubtful that despite their qualified statements regarding planning, either general would have been comfortable in pressing on without maximal preparedness in place. Thinking too hard about what may initiate the problem is less of an issue than understanding that there are vulnerabilities and targets; that someone or something is exploiting or bypassing those vulnerabilities; and may well get through. If the target is reached, then the thought and effort expended on deterrence is wasted, when we could and should be thinking about impact. Preparedness is more about dealing with that target penetration rather than cutting off the problem at source.

Therefore, organisations would do well to think about their preparedness. Primarily, the ability to think innovatively without fear of ridicule or constraint is critical for the development of preparedness thinking. We should be wary of ruling out ideas while 'ruling in' what has served us in the past. The 'constructive error culture' espoused by Rami and Gould[20] discusses the advantages of blame-free thought and is a useful component of preparedness thinking. This preparedness thinking should also focus on what is *learned* rather than what we think we know already.

COVID-19 has taught us many lessons; the need to learn among them. The idea of organisations as learning entities, as espoused by Senge[21] and by me,[22] rather than reactive, defensive groups of separate, somehow linked subgroupings, sometimes working at odds, should be attractive to those looking for new resilience capability. If we treat an organisation as a system, we are considering not only a single-dimensional idea of an organisation as one that conducts a particular business orientated activity. We also need to think of the organisation as something that has a complex set of hierarchies and interactions across multiple functions, unifying within a system and

---

[20] Rami, U., & Gould, C., (2016), From a "culture of blame" to an encouraged "learning from failure culture", *Business Perspectives and Research*, 4(2), 161–168.

[21] Senge, P., (1990), The Fifth Discipline: The Art and Practice of the Learning Organization, London: Century Business.

[22] Wood, P., (2016), "Organizations and Management: Inherent Resilience Inabilities" in *Security and Risk Management: Critical Reflections and International Perspectives*, London: CSFS Publishing.

subsystems, and driving that organisation towards improved capability and, of course, resilience.

Barriers and accelerators of capability

When faced with any type of problem, the organisation that is managing to develop organisational resilience will also need to understand that there will be barriers in the way. No response will be 'plain sailing', and all will require not only the understanding that the issues will change and develop from outside of the organisation, but also that there will be problems and issues developing within teams; competitors and challenges within the organisation who are either unable or unwilling to deal with the problems that may arise. Understanding what undermines the capability is crucial, and will require some significant self-analysis and honesty within the organisation to not only identify what the problems are, but to deal with them in a timely and effective way.

It is important to consider what allows the capability and enhances it in the first place. Have we got an effective management team, are all our various levels of management and activity fully enabled, trained and capable not only in their normal routine roles but also in their ability to manage a problem that may arise? If they are not, then the organisation does not have a capability in the first place. However, if we assume that we have that capability in place, we also need to understand how to maintain it. If, for example, we have a well-defined 'matrix' system where our teams are empowered to carry out a particular organisational response, and we revert very rapidly to a hierarchical system in the case of an incident, is that going to mean that the organisation can work as effectively as planned? It may be, of course, that there is benefit in moving to a hierarchical, even autocratic, structure in the case of the significant focus that an incident may bring on points of failure. It may also reflect the lack of confidence of senior management in its people and processes. However, the key point to remember here is that we must consider and understand this and therefore anticipate it before we are faced with a problem. A failure to do so will mean that we are challenged beyond capability almost immediately. Also, if we have committed to a particular management and operating process, it will be difficult to pull back from that once we are faced with the developing incident. Again, inherent flexibility and adaptability emerges as a key resilience trait.

Organisational understanding can evade many within the organisation as they focus on their own aspects of work. This does not mean that we all need to know everyone else's job, but we do need to know what our organisation does, what it means, what its aims are and what it is planning to do. We also need to understand who may be a barrier or point of failure in a particular type of incident. In the midst of a crisis or problem is not the time to manage a poor performer, and we need to understand within our organisation where our potential issues may be with our people long before they arise. Again, this is about the resilient organisation understanding what it means to be resilient. Preparation and the development of capability are crucial, and involve the unpalatable as well as easier options in dealing with our people and confronting and anticipating where the barriers may be before they are put up.

Personal capabilities and capacities are important to consider. If we look at the points that we have raised so far in terms of organisational and individual capability, resource and knowledge, we need to ensure that we have understood how far we can push our people when we need to. We will be taking our people outside of their comfort zone, we will be asking them to make difficult, challenging and perhaps life-changing decisions. We must be confident that we are able to do that. COVID-19 has shown that we have perhaps underestimated this important element of our organisational preparation, and the lesson learned has been that we should consider very carefully what the impacts of a particular type of problem may be, and how we may deal with them going forward. For example, if we think about the arguments for and against vaccination and adherence to both sides of the for and against argument, how did organisations put in place a policy for working through a significant crisis when a selection of the workforce could not be compelled to fully prepare itself? More importantly, having recognised that this is a problem, how could the inclusive, understanding organisation manage the issue? This difficult and challenging thought and decision process is as much part of resilience planning as any other.

Consequence perception changes – Changed environment?

New normalities: The outcome of a crisis or event will have challenged any organisation, even those that consider themselves to be prepared and resilient. It is important to ensure that the organisation itself understands that its shape when it went into the problem will have changed in some way. We have mentioned the decompression element; there will be people who leave the organisation, there will be a requirement to consider how the organisational structure, and in the worst case, the organisation, may lose its appetite for a particular type of business activity or operating in a particular location or business sector. When this is the case, the organisation will need to consider how it develops and manages its new normalities and perhaps its new structure. It will also, of course, need to understand that its planning will need to adjust to ensure that it reflects this new normal state. The changed organisation will need to consider how it puts in place and implements different practices. Also, any change to it may lead to different threats, risks and impacts; as a changed profile for the organisation will lead to new challenges. Change to the organisation may expose new vulnerabilities or areas for targeting by adversaries.

In extreme cases, a new world view may offer opportunity for a reborn organisation. The cynical and pragmatic approach will be that in most cases the organisation will review what happened and be thankful that it recovered, without making any significant changes. But, it is also important to understand that the organisation may well wish to make changes to ensure that there are opportunities exploited and that opportunities missed during the crisis or incident are learned from.

Impacts are inevitable – it is the organisation's response that will define it and set it apart from lesser organisations that are less resilient, and therefore less competitive and less prepared. The main denominator will inevitably be less about the structure or plans, and more about humans and their ability to adapt and deal with impacts effectively. The aim of organisational resilience is straightforward – to achieve the ability to work through problems of varying magnitudes. Such resilience is not forged in fire; it is built by effective teams and responsible, non-hierarchical leaders who understand the challenges that they may face and the primary importance of the people, not the paperwork/plans and processes, should the need to step up arise. While talking about this in the emotive terms of 'crisis' and 'emergency' response is exciting – diligence in leadership will bring the results.

Business fit

So far, we have been looking at the way that your business and you as an individual can start to think your way into some degree of resilience against what could happen. You can help yourself by considering, thinking, mulling things over, and taking an adaptive and flexible approach to what could come next. The fact that you're reading this probably indicates that you have some level of interest in the subject matter and that you want to ensure that through adopting the resilient-thinking approach you will be able to improve the survivability of your organisation, and help it conclude, whereby, if something does happen, you will be able to respond and recover to meaningful levels.

That will be good for you, as well as fantastic for the business. If there is a real problem or issue and you are the person who steered it through to success, then, you, as well as your organisation, will reap the benefits. You will have anticipated the problem, you'll have considered the threat and the risks, you'll have looked at your organisation and its processes, you'll have conducted the checklist BIA, you'll have ensured that your plans are in place, and you'll have managed those plans to ensure that, because of your thorough preparation, you've led your organisation winningly through to the end result. In effect, you will have reached the nirvana of resilience, and will be envied and admired as a paragon of capability.

In the real world where you must operate in line with the organisation's requirements on a routine basis, it means that you must balance the day-to-day needs of the organisation against your legitimate and mandated wishes to put in place measures to ensure that the business can maintain its viability. The prime factor to understand quite clearly is that, although you are keen to ensure that the principles of resilience, continuity and protection of assets are applied within your organisation, not everybody else sees it that way. It is more than likely that you will be within a significant minority in your organisation. Those of you who have been working in this sector for some time will, no doubt, have had bitter experience of resistance, ignorance and downright apathy when dealing with people who do not value your inputs and expertise. We will come back to the issue of how people like us are perceived, and how resilience is perceived, later; but here's a clue about where we are heading: it isn't all the fault of the observer.

And, at this point, we should probably remind ourselves of something that is quite fundamental. You need to make sure that whatever resilience measures you put in place are designed to ensure that the business can function, operate, and, in the final analysis, retain its profitability, market share and competitive edge. That's why your organisation is in business in the first place, and that's why you're employed as a cog in the machine to ensure that the business will go on. Now, you would think, because you're reading this and you're interested, that this resilience thing is a high priority for your organisation.

The fact is that, with few exceptions, it will only become a real worry when things start to go wrong. Between now and then, the truth of the matter is quite straightforward: most businesses pay lip service in some degree to the issues of resilience, be they security, continuity, crisis management or any combination of these. Thinking about your organisation right now, are you able to say: 'Yes, we have a full resilience organisation; Yes, we have a full crisis communications management and delivery programme; Yes, we have a fully equipped crisis management room; Yes, we have a fully planned and implemented awareness and succession planning programme to ensure that we do not have personnel gaps and deficiencies in the event of an adverse effect impacting upon the business?' If you've managed to answer all of those in the positive, then perhaps you have reached a high degree of effectiveness and preparation.

But now back to reality! As with most businesses, you will find that you have a potentially resilient organisation that could be developed further, you have a document that mentions the resilience management and delivery programme, you have a room that is used for something else routinely, but which, as an afterthought, can be turned into a crisis management room at a pinch, only a proportion of people know what's going on and what to do, and your HR department has not really planned to ensure that you have personnel resilience. I think COVID-19 demonstrated the potential of that weakness. If you are really unlucky you may have discovered that most of these apply to you. But do not despair, there are some positives to think about. All the deficiencies in planning and corporate will to survive, the ability to understand and look ahead to the issues that might arise and the other various potential planning gaps that might appear, can be overcome by influencing human traits and behaviours – probably at relatively low cost. However, often it is a more prosaic and mundane issue of allocated finance that can be at the core of the issue; usually, sadly and understandably, money or the lack of it will stifle or limit your planning abilities.

Money matters

Here is a simple equation: proportionately less money spent on resilience equals proportionately increased impact and effect! And like everything else for the resilient thinker, there are ways to ensure that the budget that is available can be manipulated and stretched to ensure that it can accommodate these important issues and ways to manage priorities to support the fact that resilience is quite important. This is where you need to draw upon your initiative, knowledge and business capability. You do not need to be a resilience expert to understand that if you do nothing, bad things can happen. What's even worse, if you're not prepared to spend anything, or, even worse than that, if you're not capable of demonstrating cost/risk benefit, then you may have real problems in ensuring that you have a viable business-linked resilience process in place.

Conversely, you can spend a lot of money on ill-informed and misjudged, resilience programmes that have not been properly thought out and are not risk and impact commensurate. Overspending on the wrong things can provide you with a false sense of security and make you think that you have resilience when none exists. So, it is important to understand. I'll repeat that: it is important to *understand*, rather than simply to put in place protection, response and recovery at full cost, or simply at high cost – in fact, at any cost – without ensuring that the benefits are going to outweigh the expenditure. If you think about it in terms of business finance, what organisation in its right mind is going to waste its money and invest time and effort in something that cannot give demonstrable financial benefit? If you cannot provide real, demonstrable financial benefit from the measures that you put in place, then there is no benefit. If there is no benefit, then your business will not adopt the recommendations. Any way you look at it, you will not be protected, and you will not be able to ensure any form of resilience that is commensurate with, and incorporated into, your business or organisation's activity.

You need to combine your interpersonal skills, your knowledge and your understanding of your organisation, and an understanding of what you can actually achieve financially and in terms of operations, without disruption to the organisation itself. From that point, you can then begin to properly consider how you can make things work. One of the maxims that you need to understand and apply is that resilience will cost money – that is inevitable. How much money you choose to spend is a matter for you and your organisation, its budgets and its aspirations, as well as for its willingness to ensure that it remains viable.

However, one of the absolute stone-cold guarantees is that, although resilience does involve expenditure, failure in most cases will cost more. What we really need to do is to apply the resilient-thinking concept to ensuring that we understand what we need to understand; that we are aware of the consequences of inaction and failure; and that we have balanced the risks, the costs and the potential benefits in various combinations and at various levels, which will then provide us with the ability to produce informed outcomes that will help the business to stay alive and to stay functioning seamlessly. And remember, that's what you are there for. It's also good to remember that this is not only about money, profit and loss. It is about people, their safety and security in every sense, their livelihood and their motivation to stay with you. And if you do not invest in your people, one way or another you will lose them.

The structures of resilience

But let's stay positive. If we can assume that your organisation has 'grasped the nettle', wants to spend and invest, and wishes to put in place some kind of resilience organisation that works, then in most cases you are going to need to ensure that you have a structure in place in terms of personnel and capability to actively plan and to manage any disruptions, loss of assets or other negative impact activities to successful conclusions. Once again, this is where you, the thinking resilience expert, have the capability to shine and to earn your salary, maybe even your promotion.

To put in place the correct structure, you need to ensure that you understand what the structure is going to support and that what you are trying to achieve can be achieved by the structure that you want to put in place. It sounds simple, but perhaps it may be more difficult than you think. Of course, in a business with two people it is quite difficult to put in place a fully top-down, bottom-up, matrix or kaizen[23] structure that allows you to manage to a conclusion everything that you need to cover in the event of disruption. Or is it? If you only have two people, then you have pretty direct lines of communication and a deep understanding of who is responsible for what. Under normal circumstances in a small business where people work closely together, this understanding is a major strength. What you may lose in the ability to manage without half of your workforce, you more than make up for in the development of cross-functional skills and a shared vision of where the organisation needs to be. So, there are benefits and deficits. Wouldn't it be

---

[23] Kaizen is a Japanese business management term for a process of continuous improvement that involves all levels of the organisation.

marvellous to transfer that capability to all organisations, regardless of size?

Let's turn our attention to the massive multinational corporation. This will be a multiple-level organisation with specific and well-planned organisational processes in place. There is probably a well-developed organisational culture with multiple departments, globally dispersed, carrying out different types of (perhaps unconnected) activities, all of which are contributing to the mother ship's bottom line. Organisations like this tend to be inherently strong in that they are well-financed, have well-developed and protected reputations, and have the ability to employ at the highest level possible in terms of capability. Organisations like this need to ensure that they are competing at the top level in what is a very competitive world for them.

However, there are, of course, many vulnerabilities in an organisation like this by virtue of the fact that its size is a weakness. Multifunctional, multilocation and multimission organisations must try to retain focus on what they are trying to achieve at the same time as ensuring that they have the maximum possible spread of activity and capability across the maximum possible geographical range. To achieve this, carefully planned management structures are put in place to ensure that capability can be maintained, and that there are always sufficient resources within the organisation to be able to ensure continuity, and thus to maintain viability, and hence profitability.

In fact, the way in which an organisation orients itself towards the ability to plan for resilience depends absolutely upon the organisation and where it is going, and, most importantly, on the people who are involved in it. Organisations are worth very little if they do not play to their strengths and utilise the resources that they have in both normal routine and emergency management operations. You may also want to think about the idea that, although you can come across two organisations that have the same number of people, the same overall types of responsibility and the same general mission as each other, it does not follow that they will be equally successful when they are tested. And here's a parallel: think about two armies at war. You can have two battalions facing each other, both with infantry, artillery, aircraft and the full range of support and resources to allow them to fight each other into oblivion. There are not many examples in history of two battalions coming up against each other and then calling it a draw because they are equally matched. Why? Because, although they may well be organised along the same lines and generally have the same kind of technology to wage war, it is the exploitation of their strengths and acknowledgement of their weaknesses, and an understanding of where pressure can successfully be applied to the opposition, which allow one side or the other to prevail. And the lines between prevailing and failing can be very fine indeed.

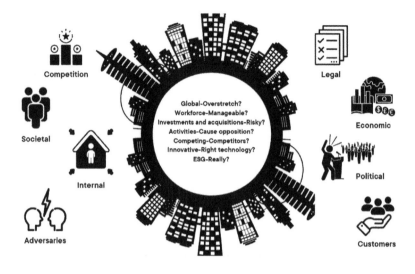

Figure 18: Organisational differentiators

The very activities that your organisation carries out to differentiate itself from its contemporaries and competitors mean that it is exposed to risk. If you are required to go out into the world and conduct business, then you need to break cover to let people know what you're doing and plan to do in the future. Some of this risk exposure will be voluntary and some will be mandated or forced upon you, but that does not really matter.

Importantly, if there are risk areas that are exposed, then they will be exploited. You can accept and manage risks to mitigate effects and impacts, but the more areas of weakness you have, the easier it is for them to be exploited.

Behind the headings in the diagram above, and in all cases, the management and involvement of people is the major issue. Are they aware, involved, briefed, capable and motivated, for example? You may have planned for every eventuality, but, if your people strategies and implementation are flawed, then you may have a bumpy ride.

If two organisations are very similar, and the difference is in the way that they are configured in terms of people, then it must be the human element that makes a difference between the two. If we take this a little bit further, time spent on configuring detailed organisations can be time well spent; there is nothing wrong with spending time and effort on planning your organisation line diagram and flow chart. However, it is more important to spend time on ensuring that your organisation and structure are resilient in terms of real people rather than flow charts and line diagrams. COVID-19 has shown this. You can give people planning tools, but, if they do not understand them, they're useless. You can have a hierarchy in place, but, if it does not meet the challenges of an event that demands a resilient organisation, then that hierarchy will be useless. If you haven't addressed your key points of failure and considered how you're going to work round, over, under, above or through particular incidents, then your organisation is useless. What we are saying here is that you must have an organisation that is configured to effectively manage resilience in place. You would be stupid if you didn't. But – and it is a big, major, show-stopping 'but' – if the organisation you put in place isn't properly planned, business-matched, realistic and workable, built on people rather than on concepts, it is worth nothing at all, whatsoever.

If you read books on organisational behaviour and management, you will come across all kinds of terminology and theories concerning the best organisation for the best-optimised business activity. We have hierarchies and we have matrix management, we have things such as kaizen. All are good in their place. Many of you reading this will be familiar with terminology, such as strategic, tactical and operational management – translated into 'gold, silver and bronze'. These are easy-to-remember, visual models that allow you to easily situate in people's minds what the hierarchy is and who tells what to whom at what level. Very useful, very important and something that should not be ignored. The point is, you can have as many of these as you like, or any combination, but if the quality below the surface is not adequate or appropriate, then even the best structures will fail. If people do not understand their place in the organisation, the best structures will fail. If the organisation itself really does not believe or hasn't applied any real thought towards the organisation, and has not trained its people properly, then the structure will fail. It is strongly recommended that you consider putting in place an organisational structure that is designed to meet resilience problems. You should be able to look at what your organisation does, who is responsible, what your outputs are, what you need to maintain this as far as resilience is concerned and what you need to protect. If you know your organisation as you should, that should only take you a very short time indeed.

What should be taking your time is applying the thought processes to how you make that line diagram work in reality. Drawing pictures, pyramids, flow charts and line diagrams is fantastic, and it all looks good in company documents. Documents are worthless without planning that can be translated into reality and people who can make that translation happen. The value of people who work in systems for effective resilience is crucial to understand, and even more crucial to communicate.

DID YOU KNOW?

It was reported in 2021 in a survey of US businesses that 31% of them failed to innovate during the COVID-19 pandemic.

You can read about it here:

https://sifted.eu/articles/innovation-failure-pandemic/.

Thoughts on plans and people

This book is about being a thinking and effective planner, so let's pause now and consider planning efficacy and the importance of people a little more. Because you have considered this carefully for your organisation, haven't you? In the ideal world, you're considering a plan that is going to allow you to come through the fire and get to the other side in better shape than you were before it all began. Minimum losses, everybody's happy and we can get on with our lives. That would be nice; however, we do need to continue to think about the world of reality. Plans are never enough. In fact, most plans are weak, poorly thought out, not rooted in reality and are probably unworkable on the day they are signed off. Are you thinking now: 'we have got plans; we spent a lot of time on them and they cover every major risk – we are ready?' But what would be really useful for you to do now is to go through a self-critical thinking process. First of all, put your hands on your plans right now. (If you're reading this book in bed, you're exempt.) If you're able to do that, congratulations – you're probably in the top 1 percent of the business population. So, look on your bookshelf or in your filing cabinet. Found it yet? Well, if you have, you're probably now in the top 35 percent of the business population.

Here comes the reality check: the remaining 64 percent of us are now searching around the office, broom cupboard or stack of files in the corner of the room for the hard-copy documents that are going to save the organisation. 'Aha!' I hear you say, 'we have got all of our stuff on the system.' OK then, go find it. Are you there yet? If you are, what have you found? Is it legible, is it current, which version do you have? In other words, do you have the instantly accessible, up-to-date, totally infallible resilience plan for your organisation to hand right now either in soft or hard copy? Probably not; don't forget, no power means no soft copy.

Here we are in the world of reality, where what we think we must work to in order for an organisation to stay resilient may not be exactly where we want it to be, and in the shape it needs to be in. Whose fault is that? And you can stop looking around because it's yours. If you have a place within the organisation, especially at executive, managerial, operational or functional management level, then you need to have some understanding of the currency and capabilities of your plans. We hear all these clichés about them needing to be living documents, current and reflecting an agile organisation. They may be clichés, but clichés are normally there for a reason; and the reason is that they are said often. If something is said often then it has a good chance of being true. So, if what you have in place does not match these clichés, then what you have in place is probably not worth very much. If you've got your planning significantly wrong, what you have in place may actually be a liability.

You could have written your own organisational suicide note.

This is what commonly happens with plans. Someone within the organisation (and we can emphasise the some *one* rather than a group of people) always seems to be singled out as the owner and manager of a particular plan. It may be a specific role, as part of the primary job, but often it is some kind of secondary activity. This is common but builds in an inherent weakness. In resilience, we normally consider the issues of layered protection, strength, in-depth succession planning and personnel continuity. But often we start with an inherent weakness, in that we put all our responsibility into small areas and load individuals who may well not be capable. Actually, people as an entity are a complete problem for resilience-aspiring organisations. People are your best asset; you are responsible for them, and they will make your plans a reality – but they can ruin everything!

People as a problem

We mentioned at the beginning that the problem with people is that they are individuals with opinions, aspirations and issues. We are all human and all of us to some degree are lazy; some are stupid, all are self-centred, and we all have our own motivations and opinions. We may be highly motivated towards the organisational mission, or we may not give two hoots. At any given time we may be tired, disinterested, distracted, bored, intimidated or recalcitrant. And you are the person responsible for ensuring that the whole organisation is interested in complying with and applying the plans and procedures that you have put in place. And those are the tame ones. What about the angry, aggressive, drunk, drugged, criminal and malicious members of your teams? Unless you work in a monastery or a convent (and maybe in some of them – who knows) you will have a proportion of your workforce who are working against rather than with the business. It is an important aspect of business planning to understand that you cannot plan in isolation, and your plans will change as soon as they are read because they will be interpreted. Here's an example for you:

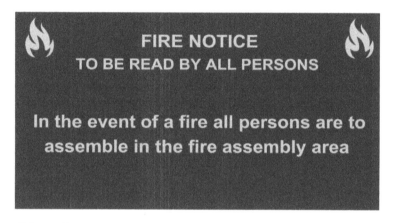

Figure 19: Fire sign

So, how much of that can be misinterpreted or misunderstood – or even deliberately ignored?

- Fire – where in the building is applicable? Everywhere?
- All persons? Do all persons know that they should respond? Contractors, visitors, intruders?
- Assemble? What does that mean and what if there is only one person – can one person assemble?

- Are? Is that an order, or a statement of fact, or an assumption?
- Assembly area? Which one? Where is it?

And that's just one sentence. If you consider that there may be thousands of sentences in your painstakingly written plans, policies, procedures, etc. how wide do you think the scope for failure may be? The problems and issues related to the inability to communicate, both on behalf of the sender and receiver, are important – in fact critical – areas for us to consider. Reflecting on your own organisational communications; are they correct, are they complete, are they understood? If not, this important aspect of your organisational capability needs to be addressed. Interpretation of messages – especially those that offer direction rather than suggestions – may lead to any combination of responses.

Looking in the right direction

There has been quite a debate for quite some time about the efficacy of management in resilience organisations. Some people think that things are fine as they are; nothing wrong with that if it works for them. Some people think that modern management is effectively dysfunctional, and that it has failed to keep pace with the development of technical innovations and society-changers, such as inclusive, consultative leadership and the new behaviours that it brings. There are others who think that organisational processes should be subject to constant and detailed theoretical debate about improvement, refinement and reorientation. Careers have been built on this and fortunes have been made. There are thousands of theories, texts, white papers, websites, advice bureaux, companies and social media 'influencers' and 'thought leaders' that make their profits by telling you how to develop management processes. I do not think that there is necessarily anything wrong with that; it needs to be done and someone needs to do it. But the focus does need to be on taking an appropriate direction to ensure that objectives can be identified, targeted and met.

To begin to look in the right direction for effective management – and remember that we are talking about resilience-oriented processes here – you really need to consider what is in place at the moment and where you need to get to. You need to think about where your workforce's mindset is; what they are doing; what their hopes, dreams and aspirations are; and where it all fits in with your requirement to provide whatever output you need to deliver. To become effective, you may want to consider forgetting all the theories about management, unless you can see that they apply directly to you and what you are trying to achieve. It's probably about time also that we stopped using buzzwords and obfuscation and got to the point.

Why do we call things that people need to live their lives 'hygiene factors'? The answer is because it sounds esoteric, and it means something to those who have studied it. For the rest of us it means washing our hands after we have been to the bathroom. So, let's consider looking in the right direction and thinking about realities, rather than scoring points off each other with fancy buzzwords and ideas. Behind every item of jargon and every management theory with a funny name there is someone who is trying to look smarter than you are. And that's all great if you want to live in that world. However, if you want to be effective, efficient and responsive, and recover effectively from what can hit you in the face, cut out the salad dressing and get on with the planning. Direct vision, unadulterated by interference and distraction, will put you on the road to successful results.

Try this: the next time you attend a meeting or a conference and you start listening to those who are talking the loudest and pushing their views and personal agendas toward you, apply a simple check. Every five minutes, or after every agenda item, ask yourself this question: What has just been achieved? Will you be able to write 'decision made/lesson learned/action taken/progress made'? If you cannot write any of those or something similar, then everything that has been done during that meeting, conference or speech has effectively wasted your time. You could have been doing something else; you could have had a day off – at least by having a rest you would have been fresher at work instead of having your brain melted by yet more wasted talk.

We can sometimes be confounded so much by our human traits and behaviours and the need to score points off each other; the need to look good and the need to show that we are cleverer than everyone else that we can sometimes forget the fundamental things. And it is important to remember here with a good deal of clarity: when things go wrong and when problems arise, you do not have the time or luxury to score points, to try to look good or to demonstrate that you are smart. You will need to cut to the core of what needs to be done quickly and decisively, and to do that you will have to think clearly and in a focused way.

The best way to approach your planning is to concentrate hard on maintaining your organisational capability, and to forget about all these additional influences and human traits that will come to bear during normal routine processes and will be rapidly and scarily highlighted as weaknesses when the pressure is on. If you can do this, and if it all goes well, then you'll be able to sit back, and everyone will see how great you are. Job done. By looking in the right direction and avoiding the distractions, you will become an effective, efficient and highly capable resilience professional, contributing to your organisation and helping it to be truly resilient. And, of course, it will all be attributable to you, so well done!

Persuasion and sales

Of course, it won't! It's not just about you; it's also about everyone else within the organisation: your stakeholders, your partners, your customers, your clients and even your family. You must ensure that everyone that you have contact with in the context of this business-supporting activity can help you to achieve what you need to. You need to be able to let people know that what you are doing is valuable, that it is required and that it is actually mandated in some cases. It may be easier to persuade your customers and clients that this is the case, rather than the people in your internal organisation. So you need to consider how you persuade and sell your activity to the organisation: how do you make them see that what you are doing is critically important for the business's survival and for their own long-term benefit?

If you go to one of your colleagues in your office who is not directly involved in resilience and related activities and say to them, 'What will happen if your computer goes down?', they will probably come straight back to you with: 'I'll speak to the IT department and get a replacement.' As you are reading this book, you are probably a resilience professional anyway, and I am not going to go into detail here on the 1,001 reasons why it is not as simple as that; you should know that anyway. But, importantly, remember that the person you are speaking to is not a resilience professional and probably does not understand for a second the fact that it's not just about the hardware.

Here's a thought about awareness: how many people driving around in their cars today in your city, or town or on your street have checked their spare tyre within the past 12 months? We could probably confidently say that it will be less than ten percent of them. So, what happens when they get a flat tyre? They aren't ready – it's just not something that they think about at all, even though in most cases they will be pretty dependent upon their vehicle. And if I said to you, "Get into your car, go out late at night into the most 'dangerous' part of your town and then stand in the street waiting for something to happen," would you do it? Of course you wouldn't. But what if you are driving in that part of town late at night and you get a flat tyre, and, just to make it extra interesting, your mobile phone is not working or the battery is dead. You're in exactly the same situation, and you got there because you didn't think it could happen to you. Regardless of intent, regardless of whether you put yourself in that situation deliberately, by omission or ignorance, the outcome is the same – you are up to your neck in it.

It's important to not try to appear like the big, scary person who is giving all the big, scary warnings to people who do not know any better. You will simply be perceived as a scaremonger or a smartass, and one of those people who have nothing better to do than to be pedantic about irrelevant operational points – and nobody pays any attention to them. You need to try to persuade people that they should be prepared, and that they should think of resilience not as something that should be at the forefront of their thoughts, but as something that they should prepare for and something they should think about. You need to be able to explain the benefits of being ready and being prepared. You need to be able to explain to people, not through warnings and threats, but by telling them how their lives will be better and less difficult if they make a little effort beforehand.

Think of yourself as a salesperson, someone who is trying to tell people what the benefits will be of buying your product, rather than not buying it. If you think about what salespeople do in every single situation, they are telling you about how your life will be enhanced if you buy their product: how it will make you rich, make you look good, how it will make things easier. No salesperson ever emphasises the negatives or downsides of what they are trying to put across to their customers. They understand the limitations of their own products and will privately acknowledge them. Tell your organisation that if they buy into resilience, the organisation will continue to grow, it will thrive, it will be a better organisation to work for and overall it will be a fantastic life-enhancing experience. If the by-product of putting in place effective resilience is that people must work a little harder and be a little more fastidious in putting their plans together in support of what you are trying to do, they'll be able to work out the limitations for themselves. If that's the case, you will also need to think about continuing your sales pitch constantly and maintaining buying and awareness throughout your working life.

Summary

The principles of organisational resilience are that the organisation needs to be able to develop a range of attributes for it to be able to manage its way through challenges that it would face in both routine and non-routine situations. The potential for volatility requirements to manage a series of dynamic and constantly changing events means that organisations need to be well orientated towards anticipation, response to, and recovery from, the impacts.

The organisation needs to build its capabilities such it is effectively configured to be able to meet the challenges that it may face; and its people also need to be able to understand specialist requirements and response capability that must be in place. Impacts need to be clearly understood, and we should also understand that communication is a clear and necessary requirement for organisational effectiveness. That communication will depend for its effectiveness on the quality of what is transmitted, as much as how it is received.

In the next chapter, we consider some challenges in a little more detail, and think about some home truths we need to address.

Here are your resilient thinker think points from this chapter:

1. Reflecting on your own organisation, or one that you are familiar with, to what extent do you feel that it is holistically resilient?

2. How prepared is your organisation for the impacts of incremental change and sudden disruptions?

3. When you think about the capabilities and limitations of the organisation in meeting the challenges discussed in this chapter, what are their causes?

4. To what extent do you feel that an introspective focus (concentrating on your organisation itself) has a positive or negative effect on its resilience?

5. In thinking about the overall effectiveness of your organisation in the resilience context, where can you identify the fault lines? Conversely, where can you identify the good practices?

CHAPTER 4: THE SPAGHETTI BOWL OF RESILIENCE

> *"Oh what a tangled web we weave."*
> **Sir Walter Scott**

Resilience and resilient thinking are straightforward on paper; easy to write and learn about, and easy to visualise as components in a coherent and well-oiled machine. However, there are challenges with organisations, and those who are charged with managing and building resilience, if negative but natural human traits are able to get in the way. Every sector has its own properties and nuances. In resilience, there are a range of challenges that arise from various directions and that can be difficult to overcome. The 'spaghetti bowl' that we refer to in this chapter is a representation of something that is tangled and confused. The idea is that to those who want to make sense of the entanglements and confusion there are obstructions in the way – some accidental and some quite purposefully placed there. Fundamentally, we are considering why we make resilience more of a challenge than it should be; and why those who put obstacles in the way to others might want to be that way.

The secret art

Having reflected on the state of the world and where it may be heading and taking us, and having thought about the change that has happened and accelerated us into previously unexperienced territory, we can perhaps agree that we live in 'interesting times'. It is illustrative that as much as ever, not only is the world difficult and dangerous to live in, but it is also cut-throat and competitive. Whatever the size of an organisation, all face threats, hazards, risks and adversaries that have the potential to affect either the bottom line or make a negative from any positives.

Reflecting on the challenging nature of the problems it purports to address, the resilience industry is no less a warzone than any other, and competition and jockeying for position and credence are understandably common. What is interesting to me is that resilience professionals and practitioners – business continuity, security and safety managers, for example – although they often look on each other with a degree of disdain, are more often than not cut from the same cloth. Let's see if you recognise this profile: white, male, middle-aged, ex-police or military, officious and practising their own 'secret art'. These types, who have now been joined by cyber and associated specialists, seem to be quite adept at building a false mystique around simple principles. Cyber specialists actually seem to have this as a fine art, with whole communities talking to each other in self-affirming cyber-speak and developing that mask of elitism that they may feel sets them apart. They actually call cyber security 'security'; as though there are no other types or typologies across a huge spectrum of security disciplines.

The building of a façade of specialist capability self-affirming groups is exclusive, and that means that it is not inclusive. That seems to be where many human beings like to sit, with the attributes of Irving Janis's *Groupthinkers* being prevalent and reducing effectiveness, yet again.

Although this clustering of the like-minded for comfort does go on, and despite the challenges that we have discussed so far, it is interesting to observe that there has been a significant step change in the inclusion of wider thinking about resilience within organisations at all levels. The move away from exclusive silo thinking, such as that between emergency planners, crisis and business continuity practitioners, into something that reflects more of the ideal of organisational resilience as a coherent function, is encouraging. Less encouraging perhaps is the adoption of additional buzzwords into the overall resilience picture. No sooner had organisational resilience become something that was garnering wider attention, someone came up with 'operational resilience'. There is actually no real difference between the two, and for me, the only addition to the whole overall resilience landscape – an understanding of it – is that we have yet another terminology in place and being used. This development of 'emperor's new clothes' terms for already accepted and in use functions, is not, in my view, forward thinking in action.

Perhaps it is more in line with the laudable approach to developing new concepts and thinking, although adding a new coat of paint to an existing structure is less about change than re-presentation of the same thing. It does also narrow a niche and allow more opportunity for those at its core rather than for those looking in from the outside.

Similarly, we have additional thinking around psychological and mental resilience – which should be naturally highlighted by, for example, COVID-19. The increased awareness of well-being and our ability to work in stressful environments engendered by everything from home and financial worries to the feeling of inadequacy when our social media profile does not match that of someone else, absolutely merits attention. However, again it can defocus some thinkers from their need to concentrate on what they are trying to protect against. Ideally, of course, and perhaps something to aspire to, the absorption of an inclusion of the psychological and well-being elements of personal resilience are something that should be fully part of resilience thinking.

One thing is certain, when translating our plans into reality, COVID-19 has taught us that we must consider how our people will react, and what the effect of dealing with very challenging circumstances can have on our ability to respond to and continue operations and functions. Perhaps we can think about how we build in an additional and embedded capability for our resilience thinking so that this crucial part of our overall resistance to negative impacts can become integrated and integral.

Another resilience facet that has come into play is that of societal resilience and that driven by government agencies in the face of the challenges that we consider – but at a strategic level. So far, it seems that in the UK, in particular, this approach is really about being able to put in place and develop a more coherent response capability to various types of negative events, such as flooding and natural disaster management, by bringing together emergency services and 'local resilience forums' (which are neither local, staffed by people who understand resilience or forums – they exclude outsiders) to deal with them. It is probably aspirational and beyond the capability of governments and their public services to be able to blend together such capability, especially with the generally poor track record of being able to develop a coherent response to many significant events in the past. Trying to develop agility in inflexible hierarchies of comfort is not necessarily a rewarding or fruitful venture.

Naturally, any such planning that is ring fenced within national organisations and agencies will suffer from the usual issues of silo, self-importance and intra-departmental competition; and that will probably be to their detriment. There is no doubt that the tendency of governments and local governments that work within them, to overcomplicate and follow hierarchical systems to develop capabilities, will and does have a negative impact on their overall ability to effectively manage significant and complex challenges.

I'll go a little further here into the 'we know best' mindset that taints so much organisational thinking, especially within our public services and at least in the UK. Countering terrorism and security threats, for example, is a major issue and something that places increasing demands on our public services. However, there seems to be an absolute paranoia about bringing the very significant expertise, knowledge and *thinking* that is needed to counter adversaries (who can also think) into the national capability. Policing and national security in particular have a very incestuous approach to all of this; with appointments at all levels being made – even designed to include and fit retiring and career-changing police officers. Policing alone is not security, nor is it resilience, nor is it the paragon of counterterrorism capability. However, it does seem to be a route into building a mirror of policing into our national resilience response. They are not the same thing.

Being given access to intelligence does not necessarily develop capability; having responded to a terrorist attack does not build counterterrorism expertise. Being in government does not automatically confer the expertise to build a counterterrorism strategy. But the ability to engage through the impenetrable layer of counterterrorism security advisers and other appointed 'experts' is limited. We can hear the advice, see the presentations, read the limited information that is released and follow the guidance, but it is superficial. Is the overall aim to maintain jobs for the boys and girls alongside trying their best to improve capability with a limited toolkit? Probably – and is it helpful for our national security and resilience? I'd suggest not as much as it could be.

All of this tends to paint a complicated picture of what organisational resilience and resilience thinking can and should be. Although it is true that there are many strands to resilience, it does not need to be overcomplicated. There is a lot to do when an incident occurs, and anticipation before it happens. However, the whole thing does not have to be difficult. And the resilience 'professional', who jealously guards plans and supporting information and revels in the *'I know something you do not'* approach, is, quite frankly, a waste of money and time; a progressive, competitive successful organisation deserves better than that. Even more so, wider society should demand that. Resilience, when characterised by complicated systems, procedures and terminology, is a refuge for the 'Sir Humphreys'[24] of this world.

---

[24] Sir Humphrey was a senior adviser to the Prime Minister in the TV comedy shows *Yes, Minister* and *Yes, Prime Minister*. His great forte was to hide the true meaning or intent of a statement or action behind a smokescreen of long words and red tape. Sounds familiar?

4: The spaghetti bowl of resilience

We should try to pull the rug from under the feet of the 'Humphreys' and try to establish some assumptions about resilience and its components. It's probably quite fundamental that from this point we at least understand in our own minds what the various elements of resilience actually are, because once we know what we're talking about then perhaps we can go ahead and figure out how to go about saving the business. It's a useful exercise to try to unravel the spaghetti bowl of resilience and straighten out the tangles.

Given the dynamic, fluid and competitive strategic, operational and tactical environments that they inhabit, modern organisations must operate in the context, and against a background of problems, events and trends. These, and any aspect of them, have the potential to develop into significant safety, security and continuity threats. These threats, some of which may have been in existence for a considerable time, and others, which have been the more recent result of either malicious human intent or omissions, have the potential to combine and to link together, and to have a consolidated impact that could be far more serious and far-reaching than if they were to occur in isolation, either temporally or geographically. We have experienced it with pandemics, toilet roll shortages and meaningless panic buying of fuel. We have also experienced the rapid impact of increasing global costs on commodities such as oil and gas. Whether they arrive sequentially or cumulatively, these impacts are extremely damaging.

Organisations, big or small, public or privately owned and run, must be able to deal effectively with the range of potential threats that can materialise into impactful risks and cause 'business' failure. The organisation must learn to become resilient – to protect itself, to absorb and adapt to shocks, and survive and capitalise on any opportunities that may arise. Frankly, those that cannot achieve that happy state will fail sooner or later. And the failure does not need to be total. Partial failure and degradation of capability will have an impact on our workforce and on our wider stakeholders and perhaps investors. When confidence and trust in an organisation is lost, it is very difficult to rebuild; and that can have even more impact on its ability to continue to progress.

Moreover, this is a multilevel issue. Not only can threats have adverse effects on individual organisations, groups of businesses and other enterprise organisations, but also, they can become risks with an impact at local, national and international strategic levels.

Further down the line, consequential or later impacts of risks have the potential to spread beyond initial points of protection failure and even to change in effect as they move onwards and develop from where they hit originally. Therefore, it is important to recognise and act upon such threats before they become too difficult to manage, control and mitigate. Small fires can become raging infernos if all the conditions for growth are there. There is a clear, demonstrated and demonstrable need to intervene and to manage the challenges to a satisfactory conclusion. This may take time, and will certainly take effort, but it is a fundamental essential.

We should also consider another layer of complexity – we ourselves may well become the source of negative impacts upon our environment and stakeholders. It is important as we move ahead in thinking about organisational resilience that we really make the effort to understand, through analysis, our own positive and negative attributes. We need to be able to see with clarity and balance what our actions mean not only for ourselves but for others. Our own organisations may well be properly open, self-critical and honest about our failings. However, if our external stakeholders do not see how we are mitigating for their benefit, their approach to our organisation and our relationship may change for the worse.

Challenges and silos

Naturally, although resilience should be all-encompassing for a business, specialists, in particular, have a crucial role to play in limiting the effects of risk upon their organisations. A considered and forward-looking resilience management process, with realistic and flexible mitigation planning, will provide an organisation with the ability to evaluate risks and to put in place effective countermeasures and associated processes and procedures. However, in a results-oriented environment where the focus rests on maintaining profitability, this can be a challenging process. If managers are overly focused on pure response processes and in putting in place measures that are localised and reactive, they may miss what lies over the horizon. And, although it is understandable to deal with local losses in the 'here and now', if managers fail to engage with, or to consider the effects of, current or forthcoming threats, because they consider them to be outside their area of concern, then there is a risk of vulnerability to partially self-inflicted failures.

The difficulty is first of all in getting the attention of those who are able to assist us in developing resilience within organisations. (Not enough time, not enough resource, not enough interest.) It is also important to be able to put across the idea that they are not assisting 'us' in our resilience work but that we are working collaboratively with them and within the organisation to ensure that *they* survive and thrive rather than simply going through yet another pointless distraction from their main focus in their daily work. The fact of the matter is that for most of the mainstream employees within an organisation they will expect you to do the planning, they will expect you to tell them what to do and they will want to blame you when it all fails to work effectively.

If, however, you have been able to put together a planning and implementation process that is based upon collaborative and consultative thinking, then it is a fair consideration and assumption that your joint planning is a chance to be much more effective. In our results-orientated organisation, it is an essential requirement for the organisation itself to understand that all of its results may be in jeopardy if it does not contribute to the ability of the organisation to protect itself against the impacts of adverse events. The manifestation of human behaviours, which we will talk about later, is something to consider when seeking to overcome and penetrate the internal borders within organisations that will get in the way of effective resilient thinking. Overcoming the challenges that these behaviours are set in our way is, in my view, just as important as having in place any number of written plans that will not stand in the face of their first test.

Within any planning 'suite' or set of components (resilience-related or not) there will be various elements that have traditionally been the responsibility of separate departments or managers. Silo management has managed to keep apart activities that should perhaps be merged or, at least, complement one another. And this, in turn, may have a consequent detrimental effect on response capability, particularly if there are 'gaps' in coverage, either by omission or in ignorance. Omission and ignorance are dangerous for resilience professionals and practitioners; as we go along, we will discuss how we can apply thought and action to reduce omissions and avoid the pitfalls of ignorance.

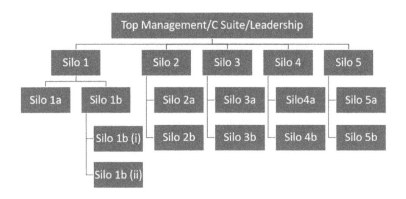

Figure 20: Simple silos

Elements of the organisation working in their own particular areas of activity where interaction with other silos may be necessary but limited for various reasons.

Silos tend to have tough walls and porous roofs, as it is important to be able to talk to top management and get that all-important direction and communication going. It helps with promotions. And they can go on and on – with smaller – but just as damaging – sub-silos merrily working in isolation, while assuming that it brings strong performance.

In Figure 20, Silos 1 to 5 – and there can be many more – represent the various organisational functions. For example:

- Silo 1 – Finance
- Silo 2 – Operations
- Silo 3 – Human resources
- Silo 4 – IT
- Silo 5 – Security

In silo organisations, each separate area concentrates on its own world of activity, and the points of interaction that often matter the most to them are those with the people at the top of the organisation. This is understandable, as in traditional hierarchies that is how things work. However, the problems caused by an introspective approach, such as this, can be significant. To make the organisation coherent and to reduce overlaps, overspends, misunderstanding and miscalculations, the components of the organisation should consult and consider links and areas of potential duplication or failure. And silos are very difficult to break, this is because of another aspect of organisational behaviour, where separate groupings within organisations establish themselves based upon their own sense of purpose, common skill sets and a sense of importance in relation to the organisational mission.

All of these can be, and are, positive aspects of organisational capability and team development, especially with mission focus at the core of performance demands. However, the strength that silos bring also means that such structures can be exclusive of thinking that does not match their own, and therefore can lead to continuing progress down what may be the wrong routes. Although we will investigate more detailed examinations of human behaviours and their influences at a later stage, some attributes of silos are worth considering early in our progress towards resilient thinking.

People compete for status, recognition and advancement. This can blind them to the more strategic requirements of the organisation; obstructive and uncooperative behaviour can result. This behaviour, in turn, may lead to the development of friction at best and gaps in the resilience process at worst. In the context of maintaining effectiveness, the very ambition that most people have can stifle and hinder their organisational capability. In silos, that ambitious and competitive approach may mean that those within then lose sight of the potential damage to the organisation and its interests caused by their own desire to win.

Managers and their departments and functions should strive to excel; that is a fair and normal expectation. This can sometimes be counterproductive or at least wasteful of effort, as activities have the potential to be duplicated across organisations in the pursuit of larger goals without interdepartmental consultation and communication. The problem is that, in a similar way to the ambition focus that we have just mentioned, the push towards silo-excellence rather than organisational and blended capability can be blind and counterproductive. Like the concept of the 'secret art', and the exclusion of those who may have the answers we need, this can be damaging and negative in impact.

Culturally, and because of their structure, many organisations discuss teams and 'buy-in' without communicating to their employees, not only their own strategies but also what the organisation expects from them. What can seem to be a good idea in the lofty corridors of power can lose some of its lustre when it is faced with a lack of acceptance by workforces. The processes relating to making things work in an organisation are also related to the imposition of unilateral decisions in one way only – the two concepts are incompatible. Levering people out of their comfortable and familiar silos – where they may be invested with kudos and power – will never be an easy, simple or straightforward option. I have worked in organisations where large amounts of precious financial resource have been expended on consultants to devise ways of changing culture and every time there has been no change. Why? Because people are cultures and people don't want your good ideas – they want their own.

Because of all these example behaviours, often, not always, but definitely often, silo working can be a negative element of organisations. To avoid this, many progressive organisations recognise the fact that blended and dynamic operational requirements (and risks) should lead to a blended and dynamic response; and the more forward-thinking of them have attempted or have managed to reconstruct their existing silos and associated behavioural and organisational norms into integrated functions. Such planning will incorporate all functions in a merged manner to provide not only business efficiencies, but also a concerted and reliable response, and ensure business survival. However, this is not something that can be achieved rapidly as it will fall under the emotive banner of 'change management'. Change, as we all know, is in general something of which we humans tend to be wary. We expand on the impacts and effects of change management later when looking at organisational behaviour. Suffice to say at this point; developing and implementing new organisational approaches has its challenges.

In relation to silos, there is potential for the negatives to outweigh any perceived positive aspects or attributes. In a resilience context, there is an absolute need to optimise silo effectiveness by identifying where the areas of incoherency, mismatch and potential protection and resilience failure may arise, and by acting to ensure that the subsequent risks are minimised to acceptable levels. Avoiding and countering the fixed mindsets that keep silo thinkers happy and comfortable (we'll come to checklisters later), is crucially important for the development of effective, flexible and dynamic protection, which in itself is essential to meet the equally flexible and dynamic threats, risks and impacts that we face. It is also important to consider for the moment that any disadvantages that may come from silo mindsets and practices may well be magnified when stress is applied – and resilience challenges will bring many types and manifestations of stress.

The other types of silos that are worth our consideration are those based on our social types, our groups and our preferences about who we work with. As we tend to focus on our organisational and functional silos (that is thinking about how our work defines us), we perhaps do not realise that we put ourselves and our colleagues into silos. We include or exclude people because they are or are not like us, because we are not on the same generational or cultural view as our colleagues. Sometimes this is deliberate – and sometimes we do this inadvertently through our pre-loads, our biases and our prejudices. It is worth confronting and facing this as part of our thinking about what causes our resilience capability to tick.

When we look at the representation of those of different gender, race or even religion within our organisations we need to know that we should do better. We need to do better because we need the very best people to be able to make our organisations resilient rather than those who have dominated resilience activities over the years. The signs are encouraging, with formal representation of those who have not been represented across organisations and businesses in general, although in some areas, such as security, males still seem to dominate. White males even more so, at least in management. This will change, it is inevitable, but we should not and must not forget that talents that are needed to face the world of resilience must reflect that world in order to truly understand it. Only by truly understanding it will be able to ensure that we are effective, resilient and able to meet changes and challenges effectively. A fully defensive organisation with barriers around it will inevitably be constrained and lose a degree of flexibility – and in a dynamic, VUCA environment, flexibility and understanding will give a key advantage. The days of white-haired, white-skinned and suit-wearing resilience leaders are hopefully numbered; for the future to be anything else would be organisational suicide.

To resist or deny the change that is coming and is already happening is, in effect, a thoroughly silo way of thinking. Enclosed focus on preferred outcomes without thinking about what is happening outside of the area of interest or responsibility and self-affirming our own beliefs leads to nothing and nowhere. Excluding brains, talent and knowledge that outshine our own – however they look and however they sound – is a natural human trait. But it is neither right nor productive, and its days are numbered.

Thoughts on resilience planning

Despite the multiple approaches to resilience, the multiple understandings and levels of understanding about what it is, the vast majority of us probably agree that planning is important. Effective planning is even more important. As far as my understanding goes, I think of resilience planning as being ready and prepared for something to happen, and as then having thought about and prepared ideas for response and recovery. I have carefully included the 'ideas' element because I believe that rigid plans can confine responses and offer excuses for inaction. Ideas for absorbing anticipated impacts, not probabilities, are what we need to develop. But to be effective, the plans must be built collaboratively and through consultation, and so cannot just sit in the minds of a select few. It is also a good thing to consider putting your carefully sculpted final thoughts into some kind of recorded document – electronic or even on paper – and then ensuring that what you've spent so much time and effort on is provided to the people who need it for them to check, verify and accept. That means that they will then be able to use it, which will then make it useful. A good and well-developed plan will not be seen as yours, but theirs.

Effecting plans that bring about resilience requires people who have the plans, and are included in them, to actually read them. This can be quite a challenge, and we will talk about this (and the contributions of wider organisational people in general) a little later. Naturally, not everyone affected by the plan will have been involved in its development. Therefore, and going a stage further, even if they have read your fantastic plans, the next thing we need to think about is ensuring that they understand them, and making sure that the plans can be made to work at pace and be thoroughly effective in the event of something bad happening.

Although plans should be comprehensive and have encompassed eventualities; it may not be evident in its final form where the blockages and challenges – human, process or other – have been factored in. *They must be factored in.* If you do not think this way – or assume and plan in isolation (processes and actions do not follow automatically from others or link to them in some organisations) – then all you have is a loose combination of some components of a notional process. These components need to be brought together closely, and it is important to ensure that any gaps between them are filled, meaning that there will be no opportunity for any undesired event to cause you any deeper trouble than you may have already. The concepts of the team player and of buy-in rather than direction as being effective organisational management enablers, are totally appropriate here. The caveat and difficulty may be that despite your positive approach and consultation and inclusion, your colleagues may not be interested or have been 'voluntold' to participate and assist. If that is the case for you, then you may well be continuing along a route with you driving, but with many passengers.

If you want to get people to understand, it may help to develop some clarity. You can call what you do risk management, continuity planning, incident management, disaster recovery, contingency planning, crisis management – whatever you like; feel free. It does not really matter what you call 'it', as long as you and your people understand it and what it means to you – and them. It is a lot more difficult to unravel the spaghetti bowl of resilience when you do not really understand what the ingredients are. There are some fundamental problems with resilience management, and I have seen the symptoms and causes in people with uniformed backgrounds, people who have never worn a uniform, all genders and types. Sometimes, poor managers allow such problems to develop; but that does not help the resilience objective.

It seems to me that there are a lot of people who try to keep the ingredients of resilience secret or try to confuse issues with different and little-known flavourings. There are a lot of people who, again and again, reuse the same recipe that was particularly well received on just one occasion. Some even try the ready-meal microwave short cut, or order in a takeaway. It may be worth thinking about the idea that, as with all recipes, the best ones have the simplest ingredients, but need care and a little expertise in preparation to impress the consumer. Very importantly it is worth investing in thinking about what suits the tastes of the consumer, and whether the whole thing is palatable. This does not mean that they dictate what is in there; but they need to be able to taste the benefits.

Moving away from the food metaphors, but to underline the idea, it's my opinion that the secret of good planning and, therefore, a good response, is simplicity. If you can get to the root of the problems that you may face, and can then devise simple but effective responses and recovery options, then it is a good bet that these options will be effective. Being complicated just for the sake of it will benefit nobody; in fact it will probably make most of your colleagues lose interest, and have wider and deeper negative effects.

Effective resilience planning needs a skilful blend of specialist knowledge, consultation, information sharing, persuasion, communication and pragmatism. The end product is that there is an ability to deal with anticipated and unanticipated issues with the least possible complication. Importantly, do not be a 'type', and do not profess to be an all-round top-secret expert. You're probably not; I'm certainly not and I do not know anyone who really is. You will have to work at this and learn every day for as long as it is your responsibility. Challenge those who do this, call out their behaviours, and set aside their non-workable and clunky plans.

Parts of the whole

In reaching this point, we have ascertained that it is in the organisational resilient thinker's best interests to devise and build plans that are inclusive, can be understood and acted upon. Effective planning should concentrate on a clear process frame that can be flexed to manage dynamic impacts and will allow any incident or risk to reach a successful resolution. Thus, flexibility in management will complement and enhance effective planning. By combining the various elements well, effective management aims to allow an organisation to maintain functionality, and it should be sustainable and realistic. Organisations should use any and all varied and appropriate methods at their disposal to plan and deal with incidents.

One problem that I have often encountered – and we have mentioned terminology adoption already – is that we can be less clear than we should be about what is involved. Resilience planning and measures should incorporate all of the risk, incident, emergency, crisis, business continuity and disaster recovery functions – all on their merits and as contributors to improving organisational capability through and beyond times of stress. Not only that, but resilience planning also needs to incorporate a very clear understanding of the human element, as without that, plans will not be able to take effect within the organisation. Again, COVID-19 showed this – it took an underestimated threat to fully expose the impact of human preference on organisational resilience. We must remember that lesson.

It is probable that there are some people who may disagree with this, who will think that we should separate everything out and that all the component parts of resilience should be different and dealt with separately. In reality, and with an enlightened view to support it, effective planning will aim to provide a studied and informed blend of the various component elements, ensuring that we have an agile and appropriate anticipation, response and recovery process. Organisational resilience is not solely – not even – about fighting fires and dealing with crisis. It is worthwhile remembering here that some problems may not happen quickly, they may develop over a long period of time. In fact, you might not even see them coming. And as we will discuss further (as evidenced by our generally weak societal and governmental resilience responses), even when we do see them coming, we still seem to lack the capability to respond effectively. As resilient thinkers we must change that deficit in our organisational and individual capabilities; they are killing us. Therefore, the agility of thought that we are talking about and the ability to navigate comfortably and confidently between the various component elements becomes even more important. Sitting by and letting our limitations in thinking and lack of flexible thought overcome our need to plan and implement organisational resilience capability is for losers. Literally.

Spectators who are prepared to allow things to happen and develop around, over, behind and despite them, will find themselves looking uselessly at events that will rapidly become uncontrollable. It is one of the big and repeated lessons from history and the global problems that we are facing right now as you read this that, without fail, prevarication and late intervention lead to bad things becoming worse. COVID-19, the Russia/Ukraine war, Islamist terrorism and the Fukushima meltdown in Japan could have been prevented in the most part. Inertia and the other traits that show a *lack* of resilient thinking allowed them all to gestate and build when they could have been mitigated. We should assume a principle that history can and will repeat itself for eternity. If you are responsible for putting in place intervention, protection, prevention and resilience, if you fail to meet your responsibility, pain and sorrow will be heading in your direction. And your legacy will be no better than that of those who allowed these issues to develop unchecked over time.

Hopefully now it is becoming obvious that, with the aim of providing resilience for the organisation, resilience planning should follow a process that should, ultimately, lead to a satisfactory outcome rather than a half-completed sticking plaster response. Ideally, the organisation will need to recover operational capability very quickly to a level commensurate with or even higher than that before an incident. In practice, this will rarely be achieved and, therefore, the organisation must be prepared to recover to pre-planned levels by pre-planned times or decision points. And it follows that the resilience process must apply across all levels of the operation and across all functions. Therefore, there is the ensuing challenge. Resilience planning is not the sole responsibility of an individual or single department, but a function of all stakeholders in the organisation who must plan and respond in a cohesive and co-ordinated manner to what may be multiple levels of risk impact. It is extremely important to organisational success and resilience that there is a clear connection between those who mandate the resilience requirement, those within the organisation and its stakeholder groups who build the capability and cohesion between the disparate elements. If that cannot be achieved, then the organisation is like an octopus trying to eat soup with a fork. It kind of knows what it wants and has some capability to achieve it; but there are probably smarter aims and methods to get there.

Making the parts coherent

The aim of 'resilience' is to ensure that your area of interest and its contributing assets maintain continuity. It has component parts, and all have elements of nuance and specificity. However, they all have areas of similarity and complementary functions. The main focus should be to ensure that they do adhere to each other – even if we cannot blend them – so that the incongruities can be managed and controlled for organisational benefit.

For any successful combination of components, especially one required to cover a diverse and dynamic business operation that needs to move in a single direction towards a unified aim, there will always be a need for those components to join and to 'stick' to each other. Different types of components may not fit together easily, and therefore any planning function that requires them to work together should be very carefully considered and managed. Plans may be required to be applied at multiple and varied levels within any structure, at different times and speeds; and the planning task must capture and include the activities and functions that can work discretely and in combination. This will contribute greatly to the alignment of plan components and to the eventual successful adhesion at their points of contact and convergence.

By combining, connecting and joining the various elements, effective planning should aim to allow an organisation to maintain continuity and to protect assets from loss with the fewest possible potential points of weakness and failure. Just as water finds the hole in a hosepipe or a bucket, a problem or issue will find its way to the gaps and omissions in uncoordinated plans and silo organisations. When the gap or omission has been located and an interaction with it has taken place, the organisation will find itself in *reactive mitigation* mode, which is generally more costly, stressful and exhausting in every way than prevention through effective planning and preparation.

This idea will hit resistance. You may hear some functions saying that protection of assets is security's role; if you are planning for continuity of operations and processes in support of products and services, then you will need to protect the assets. You won't be putting fences around things, but you will be building processes and measures to reduce impacts – that is protection. In emergency management, every measure that you take is there to protect assets, people and infrastructure, and to ensure that there is continuity in communities, societies and regions that may be affected. That may be continuity of food supply or medical support, but it is all continuity.

We must concede that there are necessarily specialisations, specific focuses, and training and education requirements for all of these activities. They may become active at different stages and times. However, we must not concede that they are mutually exclusive and that one is a more valid or 'better' process than another, because that is just not the case. Take a look at the plethora of institutes, institutions and interest groups that exist globally and that follow the separatist agenda. All are fighting for space and the agendas that will build their brand kudos and the personal ambitions of their lead players.

Look at government agencies – cross-cutting each other and fighting for primacy at budget time. All are hierarchies where such battles for attention, budget, promotion, recommendation and recognition for our own area of interest are built in and endemic. Those behaviours might work in areas where there is protection and support for them, and where accountability is normally given 'top cover', in that we can always blame the top levels. In wider society, it is not about the colour of your uniform or the relative value of your department to the government – it is about being able to deliver on responsibility. Diverting attention and effort into favoured areas is not what makes resilience work. Have a look at some of the decisions that are made by the organisations I have mentioned, and you will see that the shortcomings are very plain to see. Self-service, obfuscation, jobs for the boys, 'it's the way we do things', exclusion of outsiders, entitlement, defence of mistakes and denial of responsibility. All seen in resilience sub-disciplines daily – and all counterproductive failings.

The business context

Expanding on some of the ideas that we have been discussing allows us to begin thinking about how we make resilient thinking an attribute rather than an afterthought. We have considered the tangled and confused nature of resilience components and the silo mentality that can cause untold problems. But let's begin to root these ideas in reality – we need to ensure that we can allow our organisations to do what they need to do. We must put in place protection against threats and risks and their impacts, cross-functional and trans-organisational planning, and the necessary cohesion between management and planning efforts. To protect the organisation, we must put any planned measures in place while also considering the operational and business context, and the need to maintain output of products and services. The process and success of planning depends to a large extent on the nature of business, its critical factors of production and competitive advantage, external and internal forces, security and information management, human capital and training, risk management strategy and business continuity plans – all embedded in the overall corporate strategy.

In short, the planner cannot produce a plan for management and recovery without a detailed analysis of what may be affected, and to what levels, in line with business imperatives. Thus, planning should ensure and include consultation at all levels with stakeholders in order to ensure that appropriate actions are carried out at the right time to deal with events, and to ensure that the most valuable and valued assets are properly and wholly protected. The perception of 'valued and valuable' will often be subjective; the views of everyone involved will always vary and this can cloud judgement, blunt compatibility and ruin effectiveness.

The plan to anticipate, manage and mitigate the impacts of events must also be prioritised in consultation with the business. It is natural for every organisational function to assume that it is the most important, whereas there are various 'core' and 'supporting' functions that will require differing priority of treatment in accordance with their criticality to the organisation. Fundamentally, planning must determine what is most important to protect and in what timescale it needs to be recovered to functionality – but in accordance with overall organisational need. This crucial and underpinning tenet lies at the root of effective protection, response and recovery planning.

It may be argued that there is not only merit, but an absolute requirement, for any strategy that aims to deliver resilience within an organisation to be absolutely aligned to the overall organisational strategy. However, the approach considered and the level of understanding that is reached will depend upon the perspective of the individual towards the importance and criticality of resilience planning itself to the maintenance of organisational products and services. Any deviation or failure of capability in this regard, may be caused by the organisation's inability to recognise the importance of resilience as a strategic enabler, or it may alternatively be the product of an assessed lack of need. Does the organisation itself, regardless of its understanding of resilience (or lack of understanding), feel that there is a need for an additional capability over and above that which is part of the organisational management process? Enablement of strategy and its successful implementation within an organisation; and thus its long-term support to organisational objectives, will depend upon the degree of acceptance and the perceived entitlement of resilience to be a component of the organisational process. If, for reasons that are either clear or unclear, there is no strategic requirement to implement, then the lack of entitlement will, of course, ensure that the overall resilience of the organisation is reduced.

The willingness of organisations to take this risk; to continue organisational activity without considering the full effect and impact of the lack of resilience capability, is perhaps more common than may be supposed. It is not unusual for organisations to fail to strategise effectively for resilience. Equally, it is not unusual for organisations to completely misunderstand the fact that what we are trying to achieve is maintenance and continuity of operations.

The dissipation of strategy into the further enabling sub functions, objectives and capabilities, requires further examination, analysis and study. At what point does the overall strategy for the organisation become one that can be construed as a resilience orientated or informed approach? Also, at what point does the development of resilience strategy have an upwards and lateral influence upon that overall strategy? There is also the consideration of compatibility between the two, and the requirement to bridge between a function that will, by necessity (or at least implication), have a direct influence upon the organisation's maintenance of products and the flow towards outputs.

There have been many studies on the issue of threat and risk perception, and of organisational and individual approaches in terms of culture and view. Organisations see themselves in a certain way and profile themselves in terms of approach and attitude. There will be a significant difference between a large, perhaps multinational organisation that is subject to governance, and has clear and defined organisational structures and objectives, and a less governed organisation that may be founded on a more relaxed set of cultural rules and norms. In either case, the application of a rigid set of 'resilience' rules may be quite difficult to apply in one situation rather than the other.

If resilience, for example, is perceived to be compliance and governance rather than an enabling function, then perhaps the less compliant organisation; ergo the one that requires to be freer and 'enabled', is the one that will offer the most resistance. If there is an assumption that this may be true for some or all organisations, the adaptation of the framework activities that are common to the majority of guidance and standard structures can be difficult to orientate across differing perceptions and viewpoints or approaches. Are we able to think laterally, and should we?

There is also a need to consider the focus, or lack of focus, in terms of perception of the importance of internal and external actors upon an organisation's ability to realise its own strategies. The effective resilience management system will have encompassed internal and external activity. However, that is mainly a guiding principle, and in your own examination of the true resilience 'picture', you may discover that in some organisations there is a mistaken perception that there is very little, or conversely and perhaps equally mistakenly, a great deal of external influence exerted upon them. This influence may be financial, or the result of supply and logistic interdependencies, or the draw from the consumption end of the supply chain that dictates the orientation of a particular strategic route that the organisation may wish to follow. If organisations over-emphasise and over-analyse the importance of external scrutiny on them, and re-orientate themselves to meet their perception about what that scrutiny means; there is potential for the external influence to act as an over-influential driver for resilience planning and implementation. Conversely, it may be that in some organisations the perception of the importance of these elements may be more nebulous than in others, and as a result there will be potential for failure to initiate the correct and appropriate activities and strategies; in fact to support effective business and organisational activity against this background.

An underlying message is that perception is one of the key areas to be considered when assessing the effectiveness or otherwise of appropriate resilience management systems. The assumption should perhaps be that the organisation will need to at some stage consider its perception of itself and externalities, and therefore build in processes that are able to recognise not only perception bias, but also how perception *may need to change* in order to ensure that resilience can be effective.

Of course, a developed understanding of resilience and of the requirements for managing impacts clearly indicates that it is applicable across all activities within any organisation, regardless of whether the coverage is required for infrastructure and systems, or for succession planning and the maintenance of personnel continuity. However, the ability of organisations and their personnel to fully understand and face the integrated requirement for resilience will inevitably be compromised by their understanding of its applicability to all of its systems. The test of understanding is often during BIA activity, when organisational components that are not normally orientated towards resilience will normally be required to consider and analyse in detail their critical functions and the impacts upon them of undesired or unannounced events. Even for those who have been involved in BIA activity, it can often be a significant problem initially to gain any indication of the level of understanding of not only the impact but the consequential effects in wider terms. For those who are not involved in these processes, the lack of understanding may skew the organisational viewpoint significantly.

This issue in itself leads onto a further issue, which is one that has multiple facets within an organisation. The parochial view of individuals and groupings within organisations – an extension of the silo thought process – can have a considerable and damaging effect. Whether the focus is on a specific element or component of the organisational process, or another area of concern, there are some very childlike human traits that influence our ability to particularly focus upon that which may affect us in the long term. Importantly, although we may recognise many of these traits as indicative of issues that crop up daily, of course when we are dealing with a dynamic threat or risk situation, the effects of such parochialism can be significantly compounded. We will consider personality traits in more detail when we cover organisational behaviours; but it is important to maintain our focus on the idea that in organisations that are run by humans, human behaviours and characteristics will drive us to success or failure.

Summary

Having taken a detailed look at organisation resilience and reiterated the core challenges, we can see that there are many assets to consider, and many ways in which we need to approach resilience in order to ensure that it will work effectively in the face of significant challenges. In the entanglement of human beings, their priorities, prejudices and propensity to exclude what they do not want to include, we can perhaps see that the challenges 'on paper' become much more difficult when the human factor is included. It is really important to understand that human behaviour in general is not malicious, especially in those who are working within our organisations. Also, it is probably not the most effective approach to harmonious working if we seek to stamp out every aspect of human preference and behaviour. Even if we could, it would not be sensible or effective to do so.

The importance and necessity within our organisations is that we must ensure that we are able to recognise where these human traits and issues may arise and bring obstacles. When the challenges that face the organisation tip over from something that is a minor obstruction or roadblock into an incident, event or emergency, then we are looking at systemic problems that we need to manage and overcome in the short and probably long term. If we can't achieve that, then we may be tipping over into crisis mode, where the causes may not be so much an external issue as something that we self-generate through our own inability to manage resilience at points of initiation.

Crisis management needs very specific recognition of the issues that it raises and of the specialist's need to do things well. In the next chapter, we will look at aspects of crisis management while considering the challenges we face on an ongoing basis from dealing with ourselves and others as normal, sentient human beings, with all the advantages and issues that we bring.

Here are your resilient thinker think points from this chapter:

1. Where do you think the various departments or components of your organisation are structured and staffed well, or not so well, for resilience?

2. To what extent do you think there is coherence in thinking and action within the organisation:

   a. In normal circumstances
   b. When challenged by an event, incident, or crisis?

3. How do you think that any resulting deficiencies in the organisation are understood and incorporated into organisational strategies and plans?

4. Within your organisation what is the understanding of resilience? To what extent is it understood to be about personal health and wellbeing? Is it understood as we have discussed in this chapter?

5. Within the organisation, if you could identify three action points for developing resilience, what would they be? You should bear in mind the lessons learned from any significant resilience challenges (e.g. pandemic).

CHAPTER 5: CRISIS

Crisis is the focus in this part of our discussion of resilient thinking. The ideas that are involved in managing crises are as diverse and numerous as the types of issue that can arise, develop and worsen without intervention. Personally, I believe that 'crisis' is an overused and misunderstood term. Therefore, before we go any further, it is useful to begin with some form of definition so that we can begin with a working idea about what is involved and what needs to be thought about. Here are two definitions:

"An organisational crisis (1) threatens high-priority values of the organisation, (2) presents a restricted amount of time in which a response can be made, and (3) is unexpected or unanticipated by the organisation." (Hermann 1963)[25]

"A crisis is a disruption that physically affects a system as a whole and threatens its basic assumptions, its

---

[25] Hermann, C. F., (1963), Some Consequences of Crisis Which Limit the Viability of Organizations, *Administrative Science Quarterly* 8. 61–82.

subjective sense of self, its existential core." (Pauchant & Mitroff 1992)[26]

An Internet search will reveal that there are many variations and variants of definitions. However, I believe that these two provide a sound basis for what an organisation should be aware of when thinking about a crisis and its effects; and at this point, it is also worth thinking about the obsession that organisations quite naturally have with reputational damage in a crisis. We should also take into consideration how the 'comms people' see a crisis ending. Here is a crucial layer added to our previous definitions as covered by the Institute for PR (2007):[27]

"The crisis response is what management does and says after the crisis hits. Public relations play a critical role in the crisis response by helping to develop the messages that are sent to various publics. A great deal of research has examined the crisis response. That research has been divided into two sections: (1) the initial crisis response and (2) reputation repair and behavioral intentions."

This definition emphasises the idea that effective and supported coverage of a crisis is needed. Naturally, this coverage is linked to the routine need for crisis

---

[26] Pauchant, T. & Mitroff, I. I., (1992), *Transforming the Crisis-Prone Organization. Preventing Individual, Organizational, and Environmental Tragedies*, San Francisco: Jossey-Bas.
[27] Institute for PR, (2007), Crisis Management and Communications | Institute for Public Relations. [online] Institute for Public Relations.

communication and messaging as a critical element of organisational capability and response. In considering crises, in the immediately connected information age, how organisations are perceived to manage a crisis can be seen to be equally, if not more, important than the response itself. Communications are rapid, methods and routes for dissemination are expanding on what seems to be a daily basis. With that in mind, it needs to be considered as a vital contributor.

The nature of the problem, risk, issue or threat can be interpreted in a particular way and then influenced before it begins to have any direct impact upon us. Therefore, there will be these external drivers for change within an organisation or part of it, reflecting its characteristics, which mean that a crisis, as it develops, may differ from the problem that arose initially. If we consider the influence of social media, the mainstream media and the general speed of information flow, we can see that how we respond to the development of a particular problem primarily needs to keep pace with the interpretation that is being placed upon it. Also, we ourselves need to be able to communicate and effectively interpret to ensure that our own capability to protect ourselves and respond effectively matches the nature of the risk or threat itself. So, we need to be informed and to inform.

Putting this into context, we need to think back and remember that there has been a significant shift in the interconnected world; powered by social media, from the acceptance of organisations' (business, governments) authority and credibility. The Internet is a powerful weapon in the battle for persuasion and effect. 'What we say, goes' or 'trust us' are no longer accepted responses to accusations and suspicion. Individuals and groups have been empowered by the ability to garner support and empathy through their ability to circumvent traditional media channels of communication and to question, challenge and debate. Global split-second communication has allowed an ability to blur traditional boundaries of culture, belief and national loyalties, and provides a fertile ground for differing, legitimate and malicious views to be expressed and actions taken.

Moreover, the existence of large organisations that must communicate their responses to crises, provides a useful target for those who wish to take aim. There is much to consider as the communicating global community begins to discover its capabilities and potential to exploit interconnectivity and technology. Digital technology has enabled a new form of critical and adversarial community that feels it is neither influenced by nor is accountable to traditional views and attitudes, and certainly will not accept what we say without question. What we say as well as what we do about a crisis, contributes to the whole. This is being expedited by the way that we now behave and think in an information-led society, where borders are now irrelevant as far as communication and international relationship construction is concerned. The ability to persuade stakeholders has never been so important, so fundamental.

On the other side of the coin, 'crisis communications' is not the pivotal element. Businesses are built on this trope – that PR is critical to alleviate a crisis. It may well do that, but it will not resolve one. Crisis communications or 'what we say about what we are doing' is important; but is not *the* fundamental. The basis of good crisis management (as a component of a wider resilience capability) is to actually do something, do it well and reduce the impacts. Crisis communications can be interpreted as a symptom of organisational fear about repercussions – impacts in their own way – but are not as important as many like to think.

COVID-19, our perennial case study, wasn't a communications crisis; the mixed and confused messages and resultant policies and approaches came from a lack of planning to deal with a pandemic. The 2022 cost of living crisis was not a communication problem, but was the result of multiple impacts converging. Some of these because of poor planning and policies, others because of risk homeostasis, others because of greed. In a crisis like that, where costs for basic provisions are prohibitively high, words won't keep us warm or feed our families.

In our world everyone is watching, expecting answers and resolution, and needs to feel reassured that something or someone is going to help to ease their concerns. This happens in any crisis. The thing is that we can tell people what we are going to do, we can reassure, we can promise and we can say that everything or some things are in hand. How much of these statements are palliatives and platitudes is probably proportional to the difficulty in resolving the crisis. And in all crises, the difficult challenges tend to be the most critical for individual and organisational survival.

Resolving a crisis is not necessarily about what we say, it is about what we do. Crisis planning needs to be tested against impacts and damage and not solely a reputation management communications checklist. The loudest voice in so many organisations when a problem arises, and the one everyone looks to for comfort and messages to send, will most likely be the PR/comms specialist. This may be an important aspect, but will not necessarily lead to resolution.

Thinking about crisis

Moving on from the PR and comms 'spin' requirement, we should now consider the real issue: how to avoid the deepening and worsening of a crisis and its impacts. Many, but not all, crises begin with something smaller that we could perhaps term as an event or incident. To understand how to respond to an incident and to avoid its development into a crisis with damaging effect, it is most important to reflect and think about not only its attributes but also how the response might work. The problem that we face is not only in understanding the crisis, but in understanding what we can and will do about it.

Do you think that a crisis management process is something that can be delineated clearly and generically? This is a useful question to raise and ask yourself so that you can understand the parameters, similarities and differences between varying types of events. Incident, emergency, crisis, disaster or catastrophic event are interchangeable terms for some; however, they do represent differing attributes and levels of severity or impact. Developing our thinking further – based upon your own analysis and experience, what do you feel are the characteristics of crises and emergencies, for example, that make them different from each other? They are different and thinking about that will inform your wider thinking and allow you to use the outcomes to inform your understanding so that you can describe and explain to others at all levels of an organisation what their real meaning may be. And, when we think about the power of communication, we also need to understand that effective response to a crisis needs our people to clearly understand what a crisis means.

It is useful also – as with all aspects of management – to consider what hampers and what enables effective crisis management strategisation. What are your views on the applicability of organisational crisis and emergency strategies when interfacing with both internal and external stakeholders? Crucially, the interpretation and perception of a crisis and its impact on the organisation will depend on varying influences, as will the organisational response.

We have talked about silos previously and we will come on to organisational behaviour in the next chapter. However, for crisis management and strategies, where do you consider the obstacles and barriers to successful implementation might be? What are the strategic approaches that organisations can take to enable themselves to overcome obstacles? In terms of hierarchical process and the relative importance of various strategies, is crisis management a more pressing and therefore valuable and important component of the resilient organisation than others? If the organisation does not consider that to be the case, then there are potentially many difficulties not only in planning for crisis response, but also for translating that plan from theory into action. But does every problem mean that a crisis is here right now? And where can we intervene to manage them down?

Crisis in context

As with all aspects of the resilient organisation, and our aspiration to be and become resilient thinkers, how might we develop our own understanding into that action? Who and what are most important, and who needs to manage it all? Organisations do not sit in splendid isolation, and it is important to understand that crisis management not only sits in the context of its organisation, but also within a wider set of 'resilience' sub-disciplines; and it is instructive to assess the applicability and focus of each. All aim to anticipate the potential for threats to materialise, although business continuity, crisis and emergency management and disaster recovery should focus or place weight on effective impact management. Security, for example, will tend to focus more on risk, and its probability of occurrence, and will attempt to prevent risk from leading to loss or damage. Other disciplines will focus less on prevention and be orientated towards response and recovery. It is important to ensure that this is clear to the organisation, and it is important to focus on what is most meaningful.

Although all have the objective of contributing to organisational resilience, the functions are complementary and separable. Security requires barriers and preventative processes to be implemented, which will be designed to operate with balance of protection and inconvenience to the organisation. Crisis management, and indeed the other disciplines, should not be concerned with putting up barriers to the external risks, but with organisationally embedded management and systems that maintain capability, even when preventative procedures and risk management have *failed*. Having made that distinction, it is useful also to note that crisis management itself will necessarily involve the blocking and prevention of further crisis issues. That is, ensuring that the crisis does not worsen and deepen. And essentially, as always with resilient thinking, the attributes of a learning individual and organisation as well as a responsive one will need to be developed.

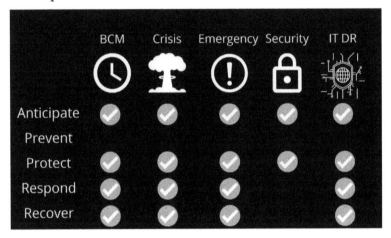

Figure 21: The subtle differences between the resilience 'sub-disciplines'

It is important that organisations understand and can allocate resource, time and planning effort to each of these while maintaining efficiencies in approach and resourcing.

In a discussion concerning critical infrastructure interdependencies following a presentation that I gave on the Frontier Risks Security Risk Management and Consultancy programme; we began to explore in some detail the issues around organisational capability in the face of blended threats, overlapping risks and hybrid warfare. The issue of concern and discussion was really that organisations tend to have problems dealing with multiple inputs, especially those that challenge them to think about impacts too much; and that they pay for the dubious experience of having to do that thinking. In the old days, before intertwined and layered technology completely took over society and its fundamentals, risks were still probably thought of as sequential, compartmentalised and manageable. Even though to an extent Figure 21 shows that the disciplines (and the way the risks are managed through each) may differ, they are most definitely complementary. They may also be more complex than they appear at first glance.

As we have already determined, risks and threats to organisations have changed, and the new nature of business means that they have become more synergised and holistic. In other words, they join, grow, expand and change. An issue may not constitute a specific threat. The action or inaction of a particular element or contributor to a wider risk does not necessarily mean that it is threatening. However, the consequences of the actions that are taken or not taken can develop into impacts either over time or more worryingly (and often), in a very short period – perhaps leading to crisis. The additional concern is that whether those risks and threats are identified or not; there may be other influences that either accelerate or slow down the development of the crisis event either by design or by accident; or even by the juxtaposition or joining of an element with another. This will constitute a change; or metamorphosis, and this metamorphosis will not only be in terms of the structure of the problem itself; but naturally of the effects and impacts that will come from it. So, a crisis is not a 'thing'. It is a convergence of 'things' that other 'things' can change. These, in turn, change the emphasis, effect and outcomes from a crisis direction.

Crises will not do what we want them to do and crisis management can very rapidly become crisis defence. There are also accelerators and inhibitors to risk development. What about PESTEL effects?

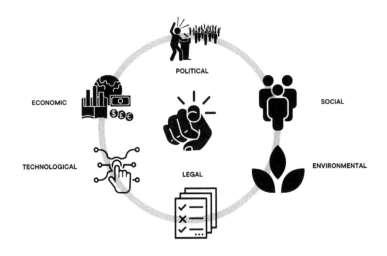

Figure 22: PESTEL environmental analysis

This is perhaps the most used of these types of models (and most misused). It does not incorporate the important 'O' for Organisation; perhaps because of a perception that the organisation is an internal focus for the equally misused 'SWOT' analysis. The organisation affects and is affected by its external environment (replace the central circle content with the word 'Organisation' and it changes the acronym but clarifies the concept).

There are various acronyms like this that explain the external operating environment for organisations. The elements of our capability can also be affected by the environment within which they are engendered or flourish. Political action or inaction will have some effect upon the development or decrease of the effect. On a global scale, economic issues are clearly fundamental to our interactions and to the organisational and business interactions that we follow to ensure that we can maintain organisational viability. Our vulnerabilities do not sit in isolation; and they do not necessarily generate their own pace; and effect-acceleration may be forced upon them by the environment in which they sit. The connections between all of them are important factors to involve in our thinking and planning.

Where a crisis may arise is another challenge. 'Black Swan' (Taleb, 2007) like issues can add to the problems we face: in essence, we are looking at the idea that there are some absolute unknowns in terms of threat and risk about which we have no understanding or ability to respond effectively. Reasonably and rationally, it would be a fair assumption to make that there are less of these unknown problems to deal with. However, there will always be cases where an unprecedented form of threat or risk may strike us. In talking to people about these issues, it is quite difficult to define what may come next; it is even more difficult to define whether they want to consider the issue at all. The use of the term is widespread, while the challenge for organisations is in understanding that there are still challenges that are unknown and unprecedented. For many organisations and specialists, the issue may be that although they use the term, they may not understand what a Black

Swan is. Ask anyone with an interest or involvement in resilience and they will have an answer for you. Some may even know where the term originated. The problem is that most will not have read the book that sells the term as a concept. I've seen and heard many people 'Swansplaining'; with everything from airliner crashes to pandemics, recessions to terrorist attacks being 'Swanwashed' with the term because they may have caught us out a little.

Conversely, the attributes that may accelerate the effects and impacts of a particular crisis may also slow it down. In terms of communication, there may be a situation whereby the lack of communication or understanding and interpretation of a particular problem can allow it to gestate and develop. If little action is taken to manage it, and its effects continue to be felt more widely than at the point of origin, the issues may rapidly move beyond organisational response capability. Simply put, we may just simply fail to see what is in front of us, or our interpretation and bias may not allow us to see the true nature of the problem. That will be significant. In another sense, effective and rapid communication about the nature of a particular crisis that may be developing, using effective communication channels and to those who have the ability, and capability, to handle a particular problem, may mean that the acceleration and growth of a particular issue will and probably can be stemmed before the effects are felt.

Just as PESTEL can work to increase and develop the effects of a particular problem or issue; it can also work to contain an event and its impact. There are interventions that take place on a routine and on a reactive basis that will allow the impacts to be contained and shrunk; and we should be aware that even though we may not know the nature of an issue, there will be a global toolbox of responses and environmental attributes that will serve to inhibit the impacts of crisis development.

Does a metamorphosis of the nature of a crisis alter others, and does the removal or collapse of a risk affect the balance elsewhere? The idea that a risk will remain stable for any period may reflect a propensity to 'box' and 'frame' areas of issue – such as in risk registers and analysis; and will not reflect the dynamics of change and of the now increasing rapidity of change because of, for example, PESTEL dynamics. The result will be a different landscape and background – with a changed shape and risk profile, and potentially inferred or implied changes to what we as organisations are prepared for. Does this mean then that a risk register and profile that is based on prediction or assessment of probability will be outstripped and rendered obsolete (and therefore ineffective) by the new patterns?

What we can therefore discern is a significant difference in the risk landscape; the picture presented to us once the changes have happened. Reflecting the true dynamism of emerging crisis development, we will have a different set of issues to address and consider. Links that were real, visualised, predicted or implied may no longer be there. Connections and inferences will be lost – and new relationships between the crisis risks may emerge.

A crisis case study – RMS Titanic

Figure 23: A synergistic risk overcoming planned capability – RMS Titanic

The story of RMS Titanic is well known and is a fine example of how a lack of understanding of combined or holistic risk can circumvent what the organisation may feel is a 'watertight' plan. The Titanic was a revolutionary design with a compartmentalised hull – the watertight compartments were designed to render the ship unsinkable, as up to six of them could be filled with water before the vessel became unable to maintain the necessary stability to stay afloat. That was the plan and intention. The ship had been designed in benign circumstances and without complete thinking about potential problems. In that benign planning environment, Titanic was considered unsinkable.

Titanic was designed to resist holing and even torpedoing – with no single threat or weapon able to cause enough damage to sink it. The ship's keel was built to be robust and

5: Crisis

durable. Not even a huge iceberg was considered a threat. Perhaps icebergs were not considered at all. If it was considered, the benefit of hindsight probably tells us that the thinking was that an iceberg may make a large hole, but the number of watertight compartments in the design would keep it afloat.

Titanic's iceberg was not hit head on – it scraped along the starboard side of the ship, which was travelling at 23 knots. The resultant impact did not gouge a hole but caused the rivets to fail and steel plates of the keel to split apart, allowing water to fill the compartments and nosing the ship down until it sank. This was a synergistic risk made real. An iceberg on its own would have been manageable. However, the crisis was caused by the fact that the iceberg was not spotted until it was too late to take fully effective evasive action. The decision to avoid the iceberg meant that the glancing impact did not hole the ship but burst its 'skin'. If the ship had not tried to change course at the last moment and exposed its starboard side to the iceberg, it would likely have hit it head on. That would have been along the lines of the expected type of impact for the ship. If there had been no response to the sighting of the iceberg, the outcome may well have been different.

A I think everybody knows, thanks to the magic of Hollywood, the impact was fatal, as the design and emergency plans were for the threat to be manageable and not for a combination of coalescing risk factors to synergise as they did. That compounded these risk factors into something that the planning had considered unlikely; but more probably had not been considered at all. The lesson for effective crisis management is clear; identify as many scenarios as possible and avoid simplifying plans for that

240

which we would like to happen, rather than considering the options, challenges and changes that may influence the outcome. Our optimism, thinking, biases and inability to predict negatives at the expense of shoe horning in positives, can bring far worse outcomes than we might wish.

Crisis influences

The dynamism and dynamics of a crisis are subject to multiple and variable influences. Some are attributable to the crisis itself (and its associated risk contributors), while others will be, in part, because of the organisation's interaction with the crisis and subsequent responses. There are many influences on the effectiveness of crisis response, and it is worth thinking about some of them now.

Firstly, we should consider balance and imbalance in activity and thinking. The influences on organisational capability to be able to manage a particular type of crisis include the balancing of an activity in the environment in which it operates. At some point, the organisation will be able to understand and cope with operational, tactical and strategic crisis development that it feels it is able to control; or at least keep pace with in a stable balanced environment. However, at other times, activity and external environment dynamics will feel unbalanced, and may put excessive pressure on society and sectors more widely, not just our organisations. The effective organisation will first understand that there will be balanced and imbalanced situations, and that it will need to develop strategies beforehand – and be prepared to change its strategies and operational response based upon not only how the balance is encountered initially, but also how it may develop in response to other stimuli. The uncertainty of imbalance is an aspect of crisis development that should be considered by all organisations that need to prepare an appropriate response.

What is going on around us will change our ability to respond. Global, national, regional, local activities and situations will have an impact on the development of a particular type of crisis. For example, we may respond to a global crisis in a particular way to be able to demonstrate compliance or some form of corporate response (if we are a corporate organisation). However, that may have repercussions around more local levels. If, for example, a manufacturing organisation that operates globally responds to a global recession by changing its profile and manufacturing basis, there may be a more regional and local impact on the workforce and reputation that may be significantly critical for the organisation. It is important, therefore, for organisations to recognise that there will always be a consequential impact from large-scale global events, even though they may take a significant amount of time to filter down to local levels. The time taken for this is not necessarily guaranteed, and a global issue can very rapidly impact at local levels. It is important that no aspect of crisis development is taken for granted or assumed to follow a specific pattern.

Every aspect of our lives and our existence is susceptible to crisis development on some scale. What may affect one organisation as a crisis may or may not impact others in the same way or to the same level of severity. There will be situations where even very close neighbours, either geographically, or in the same business or industrial sector, will not have an even level of impact among them. Some organisations will manage better than others, others will not have the in-built resilience that will be required to ensure that they are able to navigate effectively through a crisis. Every organisation is different, and one size does not fit all. The importance of difference should not be underestimated, and as a resilient thinker, crisis or other specialist or consultant who is looking to advise an organisation, it is important that templates and 'boilerplate' solutions are not overly relied upon to apply to all. Not only that, but every crisis will be different, and thinking and planning will need to take that into account.

When considering the amount of effort to put into crisis planning, try to think of something that isn't susceptible to crisis. This will be a difficult challenge, as it is usually the case that an incident or issue that is not managed will compound into a crisis if not addressed. Crises do not necessarily need to be large in scale – the loss of a small amount of income can be a crisis for a low-income organisation or family, for example. Large or small; the generally applicable rule of thumb can be that the compounding of issues can be rapid and impactful. The main learning point here is that no organisation or individual is exempt from being affected by a crisis.

What may be controllable and uncontrollable? The influence on how we respond to a particular problem may well be prejudiced significantly depending on whether we perceive it to be controllable or uncontrollable. We may decide that it is something that we are unable to effectively challenge and deal with, or that we may be able to mitigate rapidly. Conversely, this may not be the case, and we may find that the whole problem is something that can develop into a crisis beyond our control in either case. That being so, our perception of a particular crisis will not necessarily influence the outcome in anyway. It is useful to be mindful of the fact that crises can develop despite any efforts that we make. If we do not or cannot recognise this – rather than us having a perception of control, they will outstrip our capabilities to manage. Perception is not a reliable guide of the gravity of a crisis or its duration, and certainly, it will be no indication as to the severity of impact; it is too subjective and influenced by our own biases and experiences.

Short, medium and long term. Linked to the idea of perception influencing our thinking about how controllable or uncontrollable a crisis may be, our perception of its duration or possible duration. Also, while embroiled in a crisis, our perception of its actual duration can be problematic. There is a significant difference between the three of them, as they will bring resultant and specific challenges for organisations and individuals. Short-term issues may not even develop into a crisis at all, and therefore may be quite inconsequential. On the other hand, they could be impact-intense and extremely damaging. Similarly, a long-term issue may be significant or not. However, it may allow the organisation the time and space to adapt and develop mitigation, and may even lead to adaptive recovery; where the organisation is able to work its way out of the crisis. The duration of a crisis therefore has no explicit or reliable link to its eventual impact and cost to the organisation.

Spectate, participate or be affected. There are multiple ways in which we as individuals and organisations can respond to a crisis or an incident that may develop into one. It may or may not be a conscious decision to either look on and do very little, to attempt to intervene in some way or to stand by and allow ourselves to be affected. This is where we again need to consider what has been termed 'risk stasis' or 'homeostasis'.[28] Individuals and organisations may find any number of reasons and excuses for failing to act or respond to a developing problem. The issues and influences will vary; however, in the main they will be rooted in a human issue; which may involve anything from a fear of consequence to an inability to understand or apply ourselves to dealing with the issue. Whatever the reason or cause for the inability or unwillingness to act appropriately, the implications can be highly significant for the organisation.

Identify the slow-, medium- and fast-burning issues; these will need to be prioritised effectively, efficiently and at a pace appropriate to the 'rate of burn'. The importance of understanding that this rate is not necessarily controllable by our organisation is also something to consider. Also, the organisational preference may not necessarily be that for a particular type of pace or development rate, this will inevitably be out of our hands. Therefore, we need to consider how we may be able to manage impacts of differing development rates. The 'rated burner' will also depend on the complexity of the incident that may develop into a crisis over a particular period. Consideration should be made about how developments may accelerate a particular problem or crisis, and therefore the rate at which we need to respond. One of the common concerns will be the ability of the organisation to keep pace with the speed

---

[28] Wilde, G. J. S., (1998), Risk homeostasis theory: An overview, *Injury Prevention*, 4, 89–91.

of development of the problem that is it before it, and to develop the complexity of response that is needed to be able to match the complexity of the problem itself. This returns us to the idea of flexibility in thought rather than a rigid and framework process that does not allow the organisation the ability to move and respond to the challenges that face it.

Organisations fundamentally need to anticipate a complete range of potential, developing and differing crisis impacts across the whole organisation. This is something that is generally considered to have been developed within organisations within risk registers and impact assessments. However, it is probable that there will be a significant number of the total risk registers in organisations worldwide that are that either incomplete or have been used as a 'tick-box' exercise to meet a governance requirement that is not effectively audited.

By shoehorning the unpredictable into frameworks, models and processes of our design, we may create an illusion of control that is not reflected in the dynamism of reality and its intended or accidental consequences. When thinking about the potential for threats to impact upon organisations, we can return to what Staw et al. (1981, 502)[29] termed *threat-rigidity;* where *"a threat results in changes both to the information and control processes of a system and ... a system's behaviour is predicted to become less varied or flexible".* Although this study is 30-plus years old, there is

---

[29] Staw, B.M., Sandelands, L.E. and Dutton, J.E., (1981), Threat Rigidity Effects in Organizational Behavior: A Multilevel Analysis, *Administrative Science Quarterly*, 26 (4).

still room for some recognition that the threat-rigidity behaviours endure in many organisations. Recognising that organisations do respond in such ways, Barnett and Pratt (2000, 77)[30] later advocated and proposed a focus away from rigidity to flexibility and asked *"[...] why and when may crises generate flexibility (change) vs rigidity (fixedness) in organisations?"*

For the future, as AI and machine learning continue to develop and will go on to dominate many aspects of workplace management, we will need to ensure that anticipatory and governance processes are not designed out of the organisation. The ability to undertake not only logical approaches to various input issues but also intuitive and flexible responses, is something that will be a requirement for any effective automated system that is designed to look at scenarios and develop responses. If we have assumed that crises are unpredictable in some ways and predictable in others, then there will clearly be a requirement, at least in the short term, for organisations to ensure that algorithms and automation have a controllable and auditable role within the organisation. Also, effective anticipation, management and response to problems that may arise based upon human knowledge and capability, will be appropriate for crisis management, capability and response. In the future, and not too far away, we can anticipate full automation of crisis response processes.

---

[30] Barnett, CK and Pratt, MG, (2000), 'From threat-rigidity to flexibility - Toward a learning model of autogenic crisis in organizations', *Journal of Organizational Change Management*, Vol. 13 Iss: 1, pp.74–88.

However, developing organisational trust in them may take some time.

Organisations need to respond to non-direct impacts. The natural response for many in the organisation will be the need to assess and to give themselves as much time as possible to be able to consider what actions may need to be taken. While prioritising speed and pace of response, we need to consider that there will be impacts not only that we can see and feel, but also those that are outside of our immediate area of influence and response capability. There may also be expected impacts that we will have planned for, but perhaps we have yet to consider the full range of impacts that fall from them as consequences. The understanding of indirect and consequential impacts is something that needs to be considered very carefully within organisations.

This is a concern of organisational capability; however, in this part of our discussion, we are not only considering (in fact not even) the issue of rigidity and flexibility and associated advantages and disadvantages in the face of threats from the organisational structure point of view. We are primarily considering the issues related to linked and interconnected threats, as it is contended that the key to effective organisational configuration of response and recovery is not one of how we ourselves are structured, but how we have identified and mitigated the threats in the first place. Without discussion and analysis of the ability of threats and issues to combine and compound, to morph and change because of stimulus, interaction and external forces – any organisational configuration, rigid or not, will be inappropriate and unable to encompass the ability to effectively implement a response. The hypothesis of this discussion is that nothing happens in isolation, and that there is a generality of psychological approach that underestimates or misinterprets the need to understand and address the complications and issues that may arise.

The resilience web concept is one that works on the assumption that the cause and effect of an event or issue has ramifications and impacts elsewhere. As one would expect with any analogy to a 'web', this concept in relation to resilience (and crises) assumes the principle that there is a potential linkage between any, some or all the types of activity, function or influence that are illustrated in Figure 24. It should be noted here that the contents of the web are not exhaustive but are merely examples. They may act alone or may combine to cause or to deepen the effect of problems or issues on the organisation. In the context of a discussion of the resilience web, problems and issues that require a strategic response may happen in isolation or may be conjoined; and it is important to remember also that these do not just influence the central requirements of viability, functionality, growth and profitability, but also each other. In other words, what may happen within one of the areas covered in the headings in the diagram may deepen (or conversely improve) the situation caused by another.

Figure 24: The resilience web

A graphical representation only of the linkages between various
headline potential threat, risk and impact influences. Each
heading represents an issue that may link to and influence
another; conversely it may not. However, the crucial aspect is the
analysis and development of understanding of the connectivity
and consequence; and the potential impact on the organisation's
core functions.

For example – 'US Policy Changes': In the context of the
shape of global activity; we have been seeing in the twenty-
first century a realignment of power towards China, and
away from what we may consider to be the traditional
US/European dominance. If we consider the way the US
has changed internally and externally in recent years, there
has been a significant move from the 'global policing'
approach to a more insular, circumspect and perhaps
hesitant approach to involvement in the activities of other
nations. At least on the surface.

It is perhaps worth questioning the issues related to this – what fills the gap when there is a hiatus such as this? And where will this influence wider organisational and business capabilities and viability in the short and longer term? To what extent do policies and processes look ahead to the impacts of this change in isolation, and its effects alongside other resilience web headings shown here? Have our plans encompassed operating in challenging and unsettled environments, as we continue to progress through changes in global, and thus our own, societal structures? To what extent is the world of the second half of the twenty-first century (and its interconnections) dependent on this one single part of the web? Maybe, more crucially, how have the developing crises of the 2020s brought about, or will bring about, further crises? Is the continuing growth of China and expansionism in territorial and global commerce a crisis for the US to face down? The decision on that will change life for everyone in the next three quarters of the century.

This illustrative process forms a useful basis for us to be able to consider causes and to look at the potential for wider interconnections. It doesn't need to be a web, and could take any form (a flowchart or mind map could be used if preferred); however, the core activity of assessment, evaluation and critical analysis of the issues raised is the key and main function and focus of its use. It is useful also, before delving into further analysis and throughout, to bear in mind the following:

This is not a new or revolutionary activity; I would say that *any* resilience professional should be considering the underlying principles of wide awareness and analysis that aligns with a study of the resilience web. However, the reality of application of thought and evaluation necessary to fully investigate and interrogate these ideas is probably not reflected in most routine activities. If we consider that within the web there are many hidden 'nodes' of activity, we can perhaps think of the potential complexity.

In terms of what constitutes these individual nodes, well, that will vary. A node in itself may not constitute a specific threat. The action or inaction of a particular element or contributor to a node does not necessarily mean that it is threatening. However, the consequences of the actions that are taken or not taken can develop into impacts over time, or more worryingly, in a very short period of time. The additional concern is that whether those risks and threats are identified or not; there may be other influences that either accelerate or slow down the development of the particular node either by design or by accident; or even by the juxtaposition or joining of one node with another. This will constitute a change; or metamorphosis, and this metamorphosis will not only be in terms of the structure of the node itself; but naturally of the effects and impacts that will come from it.

Effectively, each node is connected in some way to something else, either directly or indirectly, and will have its own 'drop-down' list of attributes, causes, accelerators and inhibitors that will compound or diffuse their impacts or effectiveness. These may or may not be in response to other influences and issues – and will probably also confound any attempt to categorise or predict their course and development.

If the current weather patterns continue to change, evolve and have increased levels of severity, what will the overall effects be in terms of societal change? These questions are for forecasters and predictors to consider, and as we have already considered, there are many variables and imponderables that will make that a difficult issue for them. In terms of resilience, and in thinking about what individuals and organisations are able to consider for their own positioning in the future world, we should consider the possibilities for the future. Importantly, at no stage will we discuss what will happen; because we simply can neither control nor predict future events with accuracy and confidence. Hindsight and experience allow us to review and learn from our past; and the major lesson from the past is that although we may have an ability to shape and influence the future, we cannot make it.

If we think about a particular node; about a particular risk or situation that is in existence at any particular time, what are the issues that can cause these risks to increase, accelerate and have further significant impact? In terms of emerging risks or a developing crisis, there are clearly degrees of understanding or a lack of understanding that will cause a problem or potential risk to become a threat, and for it to become much more difficult to mitigate if we are not focusing clearly upon understanding the impact management process. But what we are talking about here are the attributes and influences on the node itself, and the ability for it to change in terms of its threat profile – and subsequent importance to our organisations – as this development and change process takes place. I have termed these 'accelerators'; we may not necessarily see the implied speed of development that the term offers as a connotation, and the development of any problems and risks that may arise over time may be slow rather than immediate.

However, accelerators will change the pace of risk and crisis development; let's consider some.

Communication and interpretation. When thinking about communication and interpretation, we are looking at the idea that whatever is presented to us, or maybe what we cannot see initially, can be identified and communicated about by others. Perhaps the nature of the particular problem, risk, issue or threat can be interpreted in a particular way and then influenced before it begins to have any direct impact upon us. Therefore, there will be these external drivers for change within a node, or to that node's characteristics, which mean that as presented to us it may differ from the problem that arose initially. If we consider the influence of social media, the general traditional media and the general speed of the information age, we can see that how we respond to the development of a particular problem firstly needs to keep pace with the interpretation that is being placed upon it, and the communication and interpretation, but also we need to be able to communicate and interpret effectively ourselves in order to ensure that our own capability to protect ourselves and respond effectively matches the nature of the risk or threat itself. So, we need to be informed and to inform; and that needs to be based on clarity of understanding.

Movement. Issues can move in time and space from their point of origin, if any of the other accelerators or inhibitors that we are talking about in this and the following discussion have an effect, then the actual change of location of a point of origin or the point of delivery of a particular problem can have a significant effect on us. We can take multiple examples – a good generic one is that conflict spreads when unchecked – and the subsequent displacement of people can have a significant long-term effect on a much grander scale. Clearly, we can see an example of this in the Middle East and Europe right now, and the seismic impacts of a changing and dynamic situation that will have an effect and impact on a local societal and organisational scale for many others, have yet to become clear. However, as an example of the inability to 'pin down' a particular problem or issue, there is probably none more current at the moment.

PESTEL effects. As we have already mentioned, there are various acronyms similar to this that explain the external operating environment for organisations. The nodes within our resilience network can also be affected by the environment within which they are engendered or flourish. Political action or inaction will have some effect upon the development or decrease of the effect of particular note. On a global scale, economic issues are clearly fundamental to our interactions and to the organisational and business interactions that we follow in order to ensure that we are able to maintain organisational viability. These are examples, I will not list all of the various breakdown elements of the acronym; but the PESTEL nodes do not sit in isolation; and also they do not necessarily generate their own pace and effect – acceleration may be forced upon them by the environment in which they sit.

'Watery' traits. There is a cliché, and a scientific fact, that water finds its own level. Water doesn't necessarily always follow the path of least resistance, but it will tend to seep out from areas that are not intact, and will usually find a way of dealing with any potential method of containment that is not carefully and coherently constructed. Our risk nodes can act in the same or similar way, in that their fluidity, and potentially a build-up of pressure caused by the threat itself or any combination of other accelerators, will mean that if there is a particular route for it to follow, or if it can seep into or envelop another risk node, it will do so. Clearly, this will become problematic, in that one node may fuse into and join up with another one and cause more than one problem.

'Smoky' traits. Smoke – you can't hold it in your hand, and you can't contain it too well. It also reacts readily and rapidly to other influences. Some of our nodes and their attributes will be difficult to identify rather than being simple and straightforward; and may influence all of the other accelerators because of that. Both watery and smoky traits are those that make it difficult to 'nail down' the exact nature and particular situation and a particular time of a problematic issue, and therefore our ability to predict and manage where they might go and how they can be compromised.

The overall aim of thinking like this is to put ourselves in a place where we are considering that although we are using metaphors to explain and provide some mental picture of what the emerging threats and risks may look like, the reality is that they are complicated and difficult to not only understand in some cases but also to interpret and contain. The speed of acceleration will vary, the strength of the impact will also vary with the acceleration effect that may be felt by the node itself. In other words, an emerging risk does not come fully formed, and will often not come to us at the point of impact in the same form as it began. Therefore, in attempting to predict what a particular emerging risk will look like, how are we able to accurately put in place preventative and protective measures when we do not know what the shape of that risk will be? How do we manage the causes of crisis?

On the other side of the coin, the attributes that may accelerate the effects and impacts of a particular node's properties, may also slow it down. So, in terms of communication, we can have a situation whereby the lack of communication or understanding and interpretation of a particular problem can allow it to just grow and develop, while we do very little about it, and its effects continue to be felt more widely than at the point of origin. Our interpretation of the seriousness of a particular issue, or our inability to recognise the fact that a problem or issue will translate into a particular type of risk or threat, may be significant. Simply put, we may just simply fail to see what is in front of us, or our interpretation and bias may not allow us to see that true nature. That will be significant. In another sense, effective and rapid communication about the nature of a particular threat or risk that may be developing, using effective communication channels and to those who have the ability, and capability, to handle a particular problem, may mean that the acceleration and growth of a particular issue or problem can be stemmed before the effects are felt.

In terms of nature and location, it is not always the case that a particular node has a global impact. There may be many cases where the impacts and effects of a particular problem are felt locally and continue to be confined to a local location without spreading. Clearly, in terms of nodes that are linked to and have implications for global financial markets, trading and interconnected global activity, this will not be the case. However, there may be some regional issues and problems that stay completely confined to a particular continent or region and do not go further than that. This can be a double-edged problem; first of all we may look on at a problem that we see as being inhibited – and may not recognise that there are some points that could change. Also, because we perhaps connect a particular type of problem or issue with a region or location, we do not feel that it will have an effect on us at all at any time in the future. That type of thinking may not bear fruit for us in the long term.

Just as PESTEL can work to increase and develop the effects of a particular problem or nodal issue; it can also work to contain an event and its impact. There are interventions that take place on a routine and on a reactive basis that will allow the impacts to be contained and shrunk; and we should be aware that even though we may not know the particular nature of an issue, there will be a global toolbox of responses and environmental attributes that will serve to inhibit the effect of the nodal development.

Wateriness and smokiness can also cause the effects and impacts of nodal attributes to be inhibited. Water can flow in many directions; but it can also be contained. And by putting in place strong containment and also developing responses whereby we can direct the flow of activities and impacts from particular problems or issues, then we are channelling the affects into the directions that we see fit. As far as smokiness is concerned, although by its nature it may be difficult to grasp and identify and even to contain, it may also be temporary in nature and be quickly defused by influences upon it.

Does the metamorphosis alter other nodes and does the removal or collapse of a node change the balance elsewhere? The idea that a node will remain stable for any period of time may reflect a propensity to 'box' and 'frame' areas of issue – such as in risk registers and analysis; and will not reflect the dynamics of change and of the now increasing rapidity of change because of, for example, PESTEL dynamics. So what we end up with is a different landscape and background – with a changed shape and risk profile, and potentially inferred or implied changes to what we as organisations are prepared for. Does this mean then that a risk register and profile that is based on prediction or assessment of probability will be outstripped and rendered obsolete (and therefore ineffective) by the new patterns we can see illustrated here? It's likely …

What we can therefore discern is a significant difference in the risk landscape; the picture presented to us once the changes have happened. Reflecting the true dynamism of emerging risk development, we have a different set of issues to address and consider. Links that were real, visualised, predicted or implied may no longer be there. Connections and inferences will be lost – and new relationships between the risks may emerge. In other words, none of this is standing still and, therefore, we cannot effectively predict our risk profile in its entirety at any one time.

Although better prepared organisations will be orientated towards the absorption and management of crisis impacts, there is merit in considering (even with such orientation embedded) how impacts can be deepened, how causes can interlink and how they may become subject to compounded, concentrated or dynamic effects that would not necessarily be evident at the point of initial cause. The fact that risks and impacts can be dynamic and interlinked is an issue; however, there is probably commensurate considerable and inherent risk in the mental and functional approaches that organisations may take to the categorisation of risks and impacts, and thus to their crisis readiness.

Ownership of problems. A crisis requires a response, and this means that organisations must be prepared to be able to engage with a particular type of problem and 'own it'. There will be multiple occasions, especially during a challenging and perhaps longer-term crisis, where organisational teams will be required to operate on their own intuition and without direct supervision, and will need to make decisions that will influence the overall outcome of the crisis. This means that they will need to engage with the problem and take responsibility. This can be problematic within organisations that do not have structures in place to allow an intuitive response to issues, and as we have mentioned are perhaps more hierarchical than optimal in more modern interconnected structures.

However, whichever way the organisation is structured, there will be situations when individuals will be required to step up and deal with problems. The challenge caused by this requirement to own problems should not be underestimated, and will perhaps be one of the most influential of the challenges facing leaders and teams as they attempt to work their way through problems and issues related to a crisis. This is particularly important to understand when we consider that the outcomes of a decision may in the worst cases lead to financial or other loss, including outcomes that affect human beings directly and adversely. This, therefore, calls for clarity of thinking, and levels of responsibility to be allocated and accepted well in advance of crisis situations arising. It is most useful to allocate responsibilities within plans, and ensure that those responsibilities are tested and trained through validation as part of that planning process. During the crisis is not the time to have a reorganisation of the response team; even worse, we do not want that team to break down or fail.

Negotiable crises are not an option. In general, although we can respond, take ownership and carry out all our mitigative actions, there will still be the need to understand that the organisation is not dealing with a crisis necessarily on its own terms. Once a crisis has begun to impact upon an organisation, then it will be in mitigation mode and looking to respond and recover as soon as possible with the best possible outcomes. However, we are required to consider that we are facing and responding to the challenges that are set before us rather than the challenges that we would like to be able to deal with according to our playbook. As we have considered that we cannot necessarily predict how a particular crisis may go, then we also need to understand that we cannot negotiate with the crisis, and that we are in a position where our responses will be driven by the direction in which the crisis may be heading. Mitigation must be planned to ensure that the organisation can respond as rapidly and precisely as possible. As with any negotiation, the outcome may involve significant compromise. The best possible outcome for the organisation is to ensure that the compromises are kept to a minimum and that the crisis is contained as much as possible. This may not be as simple as it seems when written on the page.

Management to closure is important for effective crisis management. It will be natural for the organisation to wish for the crisis to have come to an end as soon as possible. Every moment that a crisis is running, there will be the potential for loss and damage to the organisation, and therefore it is human nature to hope that the crisis will end rapidly. However, we need to understand that the crisis – particularly with its consequential impacts, may be ongoing for a significantly challenging period even beyond its visible endpoint. When this is the case, organisations should try to ensure that they are maintaining a form of crisis management capability, albeit in a different and perhaps 'lite' form. The capability should include not only continuation of the crisis response in the long term, but also an ability to initiate ramping up and reversion to full capability if required. This reduced crisis response capability may well be subsumed back into a normal operational structure, giving some degree of normality back to the organisation, but will necessarily need that lite structure to be able to revert to full capability and activate when needed. There will also need to be maintenance of access to organisational management for response and, if necessary, allocation of people and material resource to support changes.

The end of a crisis may not be consistent. What is closed for the organisation at what it perceives to be the centre of the crisis may not be so for stakeholders and their interests. Although stakeholders and interests may be complementary, they cannot be guaranteed to be a close match to those of the organisation. Therefore, if there is some form of agreement, service level agreement or commitment in any way offered or promised to a stakeholder, the organisation will need to be sure that it is able to address those requirements within its crisis management planning and response. All too often, organisations will naturally tend to look inwards and attempt to deal with their own problems without fully understanding the impact of problems that hit their stakeholders with equal or even more severity. This can have two types of effect.

First, there may be an immediate effect whereby the stakeholder is not able to operate, respond or participate in the way it might wish to during a crisis itself. In short, the organisation's stakeholder may be damaged, perhaps beyond recovery. However, the second type of effect may be even more serious, whereby the stakeholder reaches the end of the crisis on its own, or even on our, terms. There may be repercussions, especially if they feel that they have not been invested in or supported by our organisation. When this happens, then the relationship between the organisation and its stakeholders may be irreparable. If the stakeholder is not necessarily one who has a business stake within the operation or organisation, but is an observer or, for example, a pressure group, NGO or similar, then it may be that they will be seeking to exploit any response and recovery failings that the organisation may have shown. There must therefore be consistency in our planning to deal with inconsistent crisis attributes.

Levels of understanding

It can be very tempting for individuals and organisations to follow a particular route for response and recovery that mirrors either the organisation's own experience previously, or that of an external organisation. There may be a reliance upon consultants or others either within or outside the organisation to provide the crisis management expertise in relation to everything from response and recovery to media management, which is understandable when the services exist to help organisations to manage particular types of problem. However, it can be an over reliance on these types of organisations and supporting entities that can bring difficulties for the organisation itself. If there is a lack of capability and understanding within the organisation to manage the problem for itself, there is a significant risk of that organisation being unable to meet the challenges that it faces in good time. However, there are many influences on the way in which an organisation may prepare itself in terms of its development of understanding and the application of that understanding, to its ability to deal with the problems it faces as fully as possible.

Interpretation, standpoint, points of reference. The view that we take of a particular issue or situation will depend upon our interpretation of it and where it takes place aligned with our point of reference. This will, in turn, affect how we respond and recover; there may be significant differences in the responses to issues and problems between two or more very similar organisations, and the difference may simply be because of the way in which the organisation and its people at all levels perceive problems and options. Experienced crisis responders may be less prone to risk avoidance; analytical thinkers may be able to think their way around and out of a problem or issue. Points of reference may well include what has been experienced previously, or it may be related to knowledge and understanding. The points of reference may also be related to what has happened to another organisation – learning from other's experience – which is valid when considering how organisations may decide to interpret and enact their own response. The standpoint of the organisation may be a key element also. For example, an organisation with a particular strategic, political or ethical stance will make its crisis response decisions based upon, and aligned with, those aspects of its organisational 'DNA'.

Distant or close. If the incident that is potentially generating a crisis is felt to be at a considerable distance, either in reality (i.e. physically close), or virtually, then the organisation may take a specific type of approach to its response. There is a degree of natural human response influence that is related to the imminence of a particular problem or impact, and how it may affect individuals and organisations (distance equals safety). The organisation will need to understand that although something that may have an effect is potentially at some distance, the impacts may well surface and resurface much closer to us; and when this happens, the organisation will need to be able to respond effectively. This idea is perhaps best illustrated when we think of disasters that happen at geographical distance and in less-developed countries that have less influence on our national consciousness. The events that take place in say, Africa and Asia, are probably only of brief interest to most of the Western public. Governments and stakeholder organisations will have more interest and may respond; but our populations move on quickly as it is not their crisis.

Following on from the 'remote or close' thinking, whether the organisation feels that it is affected or not will have an impact upon its ability to respond effectively. The naive organisation will perhaps consider that those crises or incidents that are occurring a little more widely than in their own location are not going to directly affect them. Of course, this could bring very specific problems to the organisation, especially if the consequential impacts appear without warning. Therefore, it is important to understand that if there is something that is happening as a societal trend, such as a pandemic, a fuel shortage or even an upsurge in terrorism, then that will affect our organisation at some point. We must remember that although a crisis may not be directly impactful upon our structures, people will be affected, and their attitudes and commitment to the organisation may be challenged. If we consider the impact of COVID-19, and understand that there will be long-term implications for our workforce and our organisational capability, then we are better equipped to deal with those implications. The pandemic has caused an employment profile change that may become a crisis in some sectors. Importantly, the organisation that can see beyond the first-order impacts and consider the much more detailed and complicated second and wider impacts will be the one that is best prepared. The offset, of course, will be the need for the organisation to expend time, personnel and financial resource to ensure that it is prepared for these impacts. Unfortunately, this aspect of the crisis planning requirement can be a significant contributor to failure to plan.

Learned. A learning organisation is one that can develop and understand capability based upon experience – and apply it effectively. Martensen and Dahlgaard (1999)[31] provide a thorough overview of the various academic and theoretical models related to organisational learning. They summarise as follows:

> *"The ability to learn faster and be more creative than competitors can be important competitive advantages in the intensive competition of the future. People must continuously advance their knowledge and learning by transferring the knowledge from one person to another. We believe that this continuous tapping and transferring of knowledge and information across functional and divisional boundaries will expand everybody's knowledge, creativity and learning, and therefore be essential for successful innovation."* (1999, 890)

In the crisis context, the issue of innovation and thinking is probably less important than the need for the organisation to be able to apply what it has learned through the adoption of evidence-based thinking about the organisational enablers that can come from effective learning. Any organisation that is unable to learn either from its own or other organisational experiences, will find it difficult to be able to keep pace with the development of change and the fluctuating needs of society and the organisation itself. Learning and thinking tend to be the neglected elements of

---

[31] Martensen A. and Dahlgaard JJ, (1999), 'Strategy and planning for innovation management – supported by creative and learning organizations', *International Journal of Quality & Reliability Management*, Vol. 16 Iss 9 pp. 878–891.

organisational planning, at the expense of perceived need for speed and organisational preferences. The difference between those who will be prepared for the development of challenging crises and those who are less prepared, is that some thought will have been applied to successful planning. Learning is not about inaction but about informed action. Action without learning will tend towards having the properties of a 'blunt instrument'.

Interested parties and stakeholders have a say. No organisation operates in isolation. There will always be interested parties, stakeholders and others who have an interest in what the organisation does and the outcomes of its efforts. Clearly, there will be issues related to reputation, customer perception, client and stakeholder relations, etc. Without going into a long list of who may be involved, the important idea for the organisation to understand is that there will be consequences from decisions made. There will also be direct influences upon the decision process that may be outside of our control; the crisis itself has a say in what organisations do. Organisations should be able to understand that what they may wish to happen may not necessarily be what is allowed to happen. Therefore, there will be parameters that will be set for them, and these will be difficult or impossible to circumvent. The range of impacts is immense, depending on the crisis – from loss of corporate knowledge through loss of staff, to the imposition of law and regulation. From the spread of a volcanic ash or radiation cloud to that of a pandemic; power cuts to budget cuts. The complications that are out of our control are those that threaten to halt organisational capability.

Low and high consequence. With all these competing influences and distractions for the organisation, it can sometimes be difficult to select the correct decision and then act upon it effectively. It can be easier to work towards the management and delivery of 'quick fixes', which may give equally 'quick wins'. But, it is important to be aware that these may potentially be of lower consequence than other more challenging or even hidden issues that we may not see at the start of the problem occurring. When this is the case, we can be distracted from the area of immediate concern, and we can then be in a situation where we have put in place significant time and effort to resolve issues that either did not need to be resolved, or were a distraction in time and space. We should also be aware of the potential danger from silo thinking, where individuals or groups within an organisation will consider that the consequence of a particular crisis is more important in their area than in others. The assurance of management oversight to ensure that this silo approach is avoided may be necessary.

Standard responses

Standardised responses, 'playbooks' and other framework structures can be very useful for organisations to be able to allow them to move directly to manage problems following agreed and planned formats. They can give organisations the ability to have clear ideas about what they are doing and how they are going to do them, and they will allow them to train, test and validate frameworks in advance of a particular problem arising. The identification of specific types of problems or issues, and how they may best respond, gives points of reference, examples and models through which they can identify, for the organisation, how they will be able to manage a particular crisis or problem.

The frameworks and standardised responses will also be a useful method to be able to put in place planned approaches linked to governance or other regulatory or advisory frameworks. This, in turn, will allow them to build a capability for compliance and be able to offer that vital reassurance and assurance for stakeholders and governing authorities that they are, as organisations, fulfilling obligations in plans and organised capabilities.

Conversely, standardised responses to fluid problems can bring significant concerns. Plans can be useful to give us the ability to follow structures, but they can discourage thinking as the plan outline may be slavishly followed. This is not problematic until the point where the crisis develops into something that challenges the framework. Standardised responses can discourage innovative thinking and force organisational teams to blindly comply with frameworks and rely upon them to give parameters. This may be especially useful in an organisation where blame and consequence are challenges for teams and individuals; but less so when innovation and initiative are needed.

For some organisations, also, there can be a skewed 'learning organisation' trait where what has been learned is not necessarily or effectively applicable in a particular situation or challenging environment. What worked last time or what was used in previous employment may not necessarily be that which is going to be effective next time around. Preloaded thinking can have significant repercussions for crisis management capability.

Similarly, a common term used in some organisations (and often those that wish to profit from it, is 'good practice' or 'best practice'. Although there can be no doubt that there are multiple basic and baseline practices that can help all organisations, this does not mean that what is offered as good or best practice is necessarily widely applicable. Good or best practice will also be influenced by the message that the originator of such practice wishes to put across, and which service they may wish to offer. Crucially and critically, the circumstances, impacts, structures and aims of every organisation in every context will be different; and it is important to maintain an open mind when facing crises and related issues, rather than immediately going to best practice for all the answers.

It is instructive to consider that plans can fail easily because of the nuances that are influential on planning and implementation. There is no doubt that well-formulated, practised and validated plans can be highly effective in helping an organisation to meet its aims, especially in facing crises. However, there are potential setbacks from ineffective planning based upon various influences.

Often, the nature of planning within organisations, especially when dealing with crises, can fall upon a small number of individuals who will be thinking and operating in relation to the potential demands that will be placed upon them should a crisis strike. It may be that when a particular crisis planner is isolated from the core activity of the organisation in routine operations, they are 'outside the loop' of the business. Although they own the plan, there is a risk of them not being engaged with or consulted by the organisation as fully as they would like. More likely it will be that the organisation at large will not have the time or will to engage fully with crisis planning. Clearly, when the crisis has not happened or if there has not been recent experience of a crisis, the likelihood of this is higher. In such circumstances it may follow that plans are produced in isolation, and even the most coherent plans 'on paper' may have been developed to suit and align with the ideas of the creator, rather than of the organisation more widely.

If the drafted plan is not tested, then often this isolated planning approach will not be discovered until the crisis or problem strikes. Therefore, the crucial element of planning is to test and validate the plan by involving not only the design team but also the organisational elements that will be affected by the plan and the crisis. This is the essential core of any form of planning, and particularly for such high-stress environments as will be generated by a crisis. When plans are tested, the aim will be for them to take the organisation to successful resolution of incidents as they impact upon the organisation and preferably before. However, it is equally valuable for the plan's deficiencies to be highlighted in the testing phase to ensure that required changes can be made in the plan itself. Therefore, when the plan is tested, it is important for the organisation to ensure that it is mapping its performance against the plan, and looking for any deficiencies and errors that indicate either that the plan itself is not compatible with the challenges facing it, or that the challenges are not fully addressed.

When the testing of the plan has taken place, it is important to ensure that the organisation not only updates the plan itself, but also that it upskills its people if necessary. This will ensure that the next time the problem occurs, it is in a better position to be able to deal with the highlighted areas of deficiency. Again, this is something that is essential for the organisation to be able to implement and understand, so that it can operate effectively in the face of crisis. As a learning organisation, it will be essential for the organisation to be clear about what it is looking to achieve from the plan itself. Also, there will need to be the corporate and organisational will for the organisation to put in place any changes or updates rapidly.

Roles and capabilities of effective crisis responders

When considering the roles and capabilities of effective crisis responders, we are looking to develop and gain assurance that we have the full range of possibilities covered in terms of what we can do and what we should do to meet any challenges. This is something that can be overlooked before a crisis; and we should consider carefully what we need to do to improve preparedness to face a challenge. We should, therefore, also consider very carefully what attributes we need and what we need to put in place to ensure that our organisation is able to defend itself against the worst impacts of a crisis or a problem that is generating a crisis in the shorter, medium or long term.

Summary and conclusion

Crises challenge organisations in ways they do not want to be challenged. No organisation when it begins or sets itself up for business has a desire to work in crisis mode. However, the reality for us, is, as we know, much different. The range of crises that can affect us is immense, and the consequential impacts can break organisations and the individuals within them indiscriminately and with significant further impacts as a result. It is a need and duty for organisations to prepare themselves to deal with and manage crises.

A crisis may or may not be something akin to what we understand as an emergency. The crisis could be slow to develop, or it could happen very quickly; it could be widespread, or it could be very localised. The crisis may manifest itself as an issue that can be resolved by effective communication, or it may involve a whole organisational response in terms of, for example, changes to processes and actions to be able to navigate and work through the challenges that the crisis brings.

Recognising the cause of crisis is less important than understanding that there needs to be a response that leads to a satisfactory conclusion for more than just the organisation. There is also a need to recognise that there will be an impact on individuals as human beings that may well cause problems for organisations that they may not have anticipated when planning in isolation. Organisations need to learn, understand and be agile and innovative in their thinking and development of capabilities to meet the challenges that crises bring. Ultimately, crisis management is about an effective contribution across the organisation and the external environment in which it operates, to ensure that any potential damage is minimised, and that the organisation can continue to operate or even improve because of the crisis.

For those who wish to specialise in this field, there is a huge body of knowledge available that will provide insight into not only case studies but also the academic theories that have validated some of the behaviours and the efficacy or otherwise of responses and the reasons why. The informed crisis specialist will understand and aim to develop deeper knowledge of the reasons why crises happen and why they can be so damaging. Learning about crises involves investigation and objective assessment of what went wrong and what went well. The informed crisis specialist will be best placed to develop capability and advise organisations on the appropriate path to take when challenges arise.

Most importantly, organisations and crisis specialists would do well to consider that crises rarely develop without some form of trigger or warning, and that there are enough examples of effective and ineffective responses to show the way for optimal planning and response. Learning and understanding will give the best possible basis for effective organisational crisis management. Understanding the nuances of crisis management is an essential component in the resilient thinking toolbox.

Here are your resilient thinker think points from this chapter:

1. **Thinking about your organisation, what do you feel would be the most damaging type of crisis that it might face?**

2. **Having identified your crisis type, to what extent do you feel that the organisation has the agility to meet its demands?**

3. **To what extent do you think that the organisation has the capability to understand the intangible and interlinked long-term potential causes of crisis?**

4. **Within your organisation, how much emphasis is placed on a crisis being a PR or communications issue, rather than as a threat to organisational survival?**

5. **In assessing your organisational preparedness, how much interest in crisis response is shown at strategic, tactical and operational levels? Where have you identified the deficiencies?**

CHAPTER 6: ORGANISATIONAL BEHAVIOUR INFLUENCES

"People are our greatest asset."

Every HR person

The academic and practitioner study of organisational behaviour is extensive, and there has been, and continues to be, a great deal of research and discussion about how organisations and their people think and act; and what could be done to change thought and action. The study of culture and change sits at the centre of any approach to understanding organisations, and even when thinking about security and risk, it should be your focus. This means that, in the context of resilient thinking, you should seek to build on the understanding that you develop of general organisational behavioural impact. You should then be able to link that to its influence on the management of security, risk and resilience challenges. In this chapter we discuss and signpost thinking about wider organisational and personal behaviours; and our own 'overlay' should correlate with risk management issues. Any Internet search will result in an array of written and media resources that look at multiple aspects of behaviour, and it will be important for you to study and read widely to get the fullest and widest possible view of the subject. The key then is to link these well-established ideas and theories to your thinking about people and risks.

I think it is crucial for resilient thinkers to develop a clarity of understanding of the challenges that face our organisations and how we may be able to manage some of them (if not all) with some degree of effectiveness and capability. We should consider the preparation capability and capacity of organisations, culture and associated challenges, bias and prediction, and the shaping of organisational behaviour. Hopefully, thinking about this will mean that your understanding and knowledge of this evolving subject will be enhanced and developed; and allow you to approach organisational leadership and management with justified, evidenced thought and recommendation for actions to improve and develop capability.

What is most important to remember is that from the day that we are born, we are living and working within organisations. We all have ideas and memories, and of course involvement, in the cultures and behaviours we are discussing in this module – you will recognise the issues we discuss and that are based in theory – and they are real. Recognising behaviours in yourself or the organisations with which you interact, should help you to assimilate and rationalise the ideas and their meanings.

Organisational risk and impact preparedness

Even the most naive, unfocused or challenged organisations will be aware to some extent that there are risks and issues that may impact upon them as they go about their business. Regardless of whether they are public or private sector, whether they are commercially focused, or not for profit, all organisations should have that awareness. Clearly, there will be different levels of awareness within organisations, and some organisations, because of the nature of their business, will be more focused on risk management than others. However, if we can assume as some form of baseline that first of all the risks exist, and secondly that it follows that organisations that wish to survive or at least manage their way through a particular problem should have risk awareness, why is it that many organisations are less prepared in some cases than they should be? How can obvious risks, such as pandemics, weather events and economic crisis catch us unaware and unable?

Moreover, with the continuing and growing requirement for organisations to comply with regulation and governance in order to be able to operate not only effectively but legally, why do organisations still find it difficult to meet not only the governance requirements placed on them, but also to take what would be reasonably considered to be common sense approaches to the management and mitigation of risks? There is no lack of clear evidence that risks are 'out there', and there is no lack of evidence of the impact of those risks. This means that there is no requirement for very deep analysis to understand that there is a link between a threat or risk and the impact on an organisation, and even the most challenged or naive organisations should therefore be able to look at such examples and translate them into some form of learning or guidance. This should be of value both for themselves and their stakeholders; to be able to understand and develop some form of capability and response. However, it seems that almost daily, yet another organisation falls victim to a risk that may have happened to someone else, somewhere else, and therefore could have been reasonably prepared for and then mitigated.

It seems odd to me that organisations are unable to effectively anticipate the impact of risks and associated problems to themselves, and if we can identify at least some of the behavioural issues that contribute to this lack of preparedness, perhaps we can also consider and recommend some potential methods of improving outcomes for organisations. Why are organisations unprepared to implement appropriate responses and to develop the capability to be able to at least manage the following organisational and individual functions?

Why don't we recognise risk? What are the reasons for individuals and organisations to either fail to or ignore the risks that either are in plain sight or may be happening to someone else. And therefore give a sound indication that the impact could spread to our own organisation? Risks can come in many forms, and be highly visible or quite difficult to identify. However, it may not necessarily be a fact that the organisation is not able to discern what the risk may be, there may be a simpler explanation that the organisation does not want to see the risk or considers that the risk may be someone else's problem.

Why don't we prepare to act upon risk impacts? If a risk does impact upon organisations, why do organisations either take excessive time to act upon the risk impacts, or even fail completely to act upon them and therefore bring additional damage and impact to the organisation? How do organisations first of all fail to act, and secondly, if they do act, why do they fail to act appropriately? These are important questions, as organisations have a responsibility to themselves and to their stakeholders to be able to act appropriately. Not only that, but there are also governance and regulation requirements that organisations must follow.

Why can't we avoid repeat impacts? It can be quite frustrating and sometimes lead to significant penalties for organisations when they have been impacted previously and have failed to learn the lessons or refused to implement the necessary mitigating actions that could avoid further damage. What might be the reasons for this inability to learn lessons and ensure that the organisation is not further damaged by issues facing them?

At the root of all these issues is of course organisational behaviour. The various influences on organisational thinking and action can come from various and varying levels and directions, both internal and external to the organisation. The causes of inadequacy could be either blindness, failure in perception and direction, or the inability or unwillingness to make the necessary responses. Because organisational behaviour has been well covered in academic and business studies, we have many resources to draw on that we can apply to our thinking in this area, specifically, our considerations should always be anchoring our thinking towards the endpoint: *improving organisational behaviour such that we are able to effectively mitigate risk.*

The question is that, although there is considerable effort and thought applied to the ability to set frameworks and models; and to the development of structures and hierarchies to deliver a capability; are we, as human beings, able to configure ourselves to effectively meet the issues and deal with them? In the orientation of ourselves and our societies to be able to cope with the developments that we face, do we fall more upon the safety of visualisations and models, of supposed paradigms and ideal types, while failing to understand that we should develop in ourselves paradigms of behaviour and a consideration of ourselves as ideal types who are able to effectively match the development and impact of the threats and issues we face?

Why most organisations are unprepared

If we do assume that many if not most organisations are not fully prepared for the impacts of risks and non-desirable events happening to them, then we can begin to think about how the general ideas related to organisational behaviour may influence levels of preparation and capability. There are certain commonalities of thinking and action that may be prevalent to some degree within organisations, and that will have a definite influence on the overall organisational resilience capability. The academic approach to understanding behaviours tends to focus upon identifiable traits and exhibited behaviours that are easily and effectively researched within organisations and individuals, and then shaping some form of validating theory that allows further research to take place. From that, we can set forward analytical proposals and recommendations for improvements and addressing of any constraints – or highlighting any areas that can practically be developed for organisations and individuals to make improvement. Academic thinking and theorising are fine; but we also need to apply that thinking to reality.

The range of influences on the preparation of organisations, naturally, is significant. There will be multiple reasons for particular behaviours being exhibited, and for organisations to address problems, or conversely, to ignore them. We therefore need to consider that we cannot encapsulate and capture all of the contributing factors here. What we need to be able to do is identify issues that may contribute to either negative or positive effects on organisational outcomes. It is important to remind ourselves that in the most severe cases (and we do know that even seemingly minor events can develop into something much more severe), the effects upon organisations can be 'terminal'.

This means that the organisation itself could fail, and certainly, there could be harm to its workforce, its stakeholders and its wider interests. At the most extreme end of that spectrum, and in the case of high-impact kinetic risks, this can mean loss of life. Given, therefore, that there is a degree of extremeness, then it is important to try to understand why organisations still fail to prepare effectively when the impacts should be quite clear. In short, given the clear potential for highly damaging impacts, why do organisations and their people fail to jump out of the way of a speeding train?

Resilience management – Capability and culture

It is relatively easy, I know, to write down the answers to life's problems in isolation and without context. The limitations of theory can generally be most vulnerable to challenge when there are attempts to apply them in the workplace. Also, although there is an immense amount of opinion and theory put forward daily from all quarters concerning human behaviour and its effect on others (such as, by implication, political, economic, social and technological impacts), it is also worth considering ideas, theories and opinions on the less easily quantifiable and controllable aspects and attributes of behaviour. Therefore, to complement the human-caused discussion, we should also examine thoughts on ecological and environmental issues, natural disaster patterns and weather flows. Where does the multifaceted and multi-level – not to mention massive in scale – informed and uninformed body of thought about the future of the world take us? Not only that, but how do our own attitudes to these issues affect our ability to recognise the opportunities and dangers that they present? Do we feel powerless, overwhelmed and therefore static in the face of these challenges? I think that many of us do.

The consequent limitations that are self-inflicted by our behaviours, our inability and unwillingness to countenance and apply the rapidity and flexibility of thought that are essential are problematic. To meet the demands of a rapidly and flexibly developing risk landscape, these may be significant factors in the inability to prepare for and respond to the impacts that threaten to cause significant damage to us. Does the basic human condition predicate against the effective adoption and implementation of resilience measures and processes? We should think about how we are able to categorise problems, how we are unable to categorise others, and assess to what extent that we are simply and generically unable to meet the demands that the more fluid and mobile risk landscape places upon us; at least when we must take into consideration the mindsets and approaches that we carry with us.

Behaviour is entrenched and can cause significant problems for individuals and organisations. Worryingly, if there is little or no didactic source for us to develop thoughts, ideas and responses that will allow us to plan to mitigate against global interconnected risks, the disadvantage is exacerbated by the conclusions of studies, such as that of Briggs and Edwards (2006).[32] They indicated that the 'resilience'

---

[32] Briggs, R. and Edwards, C., (2006), *The Business of Resilience*, London: Demos.

profession has a long way to go before it can adequately provide intellectually agile and threat aware management that is able not only to plan but also to align its plans with business – and convince business that these plans are relevant and will contribute effectively to organisational capability both in the long and short term. This report still seems to reflect some of the behaviours within individuals and organisations that may or may not be generational or even gender related. For those who work within organisations similar to those surveyed within that report, it may be instructive to think about how the 'sector' may have changed. I think that behind all the more recent terminologies and approaches espoused by some individuals and organisations, the answer is likely to be 'not much'.

The selection and allocation of resource for resilience

The consideration of resource, especially when thinking about organisational behaviour, is related to how effective our people may be, and how effective the organisation itself is in recognising potential risks and what it wants to do about them.

People within the organisation need to have been trained so that they are able to undertake a particular role or their routine role more effectively when a crisis takes place. Training can be formal, informal, structured, in person, online or in any other variation. The training should be appropriate for the organisation and for the individual, to ensure that at all levels the correct level of preparedness is put in place. It is important to ensure that senior management are trained in crises as much as those who are dealing with the operational elements of the business; the pressure will grow for the senior levels of the organisation as the crisis develops. Importantly, the training need is not exclusive to one group or another. Training should be focused, provide precise outcomes and be matched to the needs of the organisation. If it is not, what is the training for and why are we paying for it?

We have mentioned testing and validation, and again this is something that must be used alongside training, to ensure that we have the best possible confidence in our organisation to be able to meet its needs. Similarly, we have mentioned resourcing and the need to have in place enough people, properly equipped, to be able to carry out their role. They also need to be *authorised* to carry out activities based upon resilience planning and perhaps their role within the organisation. At some point, people will feel that they are required to act outside their normal area of responsibility or authorisation. It will be important that the process for giving authorisation, or the decision-making process, are encompassed within organisational plans. It is not desirable for the organisation's team members to hold back from deciding because they feel they are not authorised, when in fact they are. Most crucially and importantly, when issues arise and we are faced with problems, we, as organisations and individuals, will be required to do something and to act. That commitment needs to be fulfilled.

Not only do we need to ensure that our people are in place and resourced, but also that they have the physical and psychological attributes to be able to meet the demands that will be placed upon them. Physical and mental robustness will be highly desirable when the organisation is required to face challenging times and events. Teams will need to operate for long periods of time with challenging and high-stress situations, and there may be less rest and recuperation available to them than they would prefer, especially in a high-tempo crisis. This may be unavoidable, and if it is the case, then the right people need to be in the correct roles. Although we know when we are training and exercising that there will be an endpoint; the end of a real crisis, incident or event may be less easy to predict. In such situations our capabilities will be stretched to their limits.

Not only physically but mentally. We need to ensure that our people are in a good position concerning their mental health. Something that is missed quite often is the post incident activity, which allows us to not only assess how we performed as an organisation, but also to ensure that our people feel that they can access support and guidance, especially if there have been traumatic events. Every individual will have their own issues to manage, and this should be considered by the organisation. Mental health and consideration of domestic and home life issues will need to be encompassed in thinking, planning and employment. This 'decompression' and the reinforcement of positive thinking when people will have been involved in crucial, pressurised decision making with consequences, is essential. It is a positive that we have become much more aware of well-being and mental health in the workplace. This awareness must extend to support for individuals and teams under sustained and high consequence pressure.

Attributes of prepared organisations

Organisations are not just about groups of individuals, but in our context are about being homogenous, effective units that are adaptable, flexible and able to meet and manage resilience challenges. Prepared organisations will have specific well-developed attributes that are, or can be, put in place to give an effective response capability.

Plans are essential. Plans need to have been properly conceived, designed, written, effectively tested and updated where necessary. If we do not do this, then we will find that when we are tested for real, we are not able to face the challenge effectively. Plans need to be accessible, current and focused on the organisational aims and objectives, while identifying actions that need to be carried out by appropriate levels of personnel within and throughout the organisation. Plans will also consider external stakeholders and influences, and in many organisations, there will be a need for their supply chain and stakeholders to demonstrate compliance by having their own plans in place. Plans must be inclusive and based upon careful thought and consultation. As you have seen and will see, plans and ensuring their effectiveness are a key theme in our discussions of resilient thinking.

Resources support for plans. The organisation that fails to allocate effective resources to an organisational capability as planned will not perform well when it faces a resilience challenge. Resources will include people, materials, equipment and time. These will need to be considered not only in the context of pre-planning, but also what needs to be put in place in the short, medium and long term. Also, they will need to incorporate what may need to be changed in the face of changes to a crisis profile. The organisation will need to be able to demonstrate and understand that it not only has the resources that it would like, but also consider what contingency it will need to have to enable additional resources to be diverted into a crisis response when the demand is raised. The question of spare and contingency resource/fallback/reserve is a challenge for many organisations, as they can be seen and treated as 'available'. In an ideal world, contingency reserves should be used only when needed; not as an overdraft or 'rainy day' backup for routine financial and material resource needs.

Validation. Ensuring that our plans will work through skills and capability is extremely important for the application of plans to reality, and is something that should be achieved through training and testing. This must be at the core of a crisis organisational capability. Effective validation will mean that the organisation will be able to face a crisis with a degree of confidence, and knowing that the appropriate people are in the appropriate roles to deal with problems. The validation function should also ensure that if there are deficiencies in capability or any other aspect of the plan, they are addressed. This may incorporate the need to change either the plan, the resources that are allocated to it, or even the personnel who are named by role to fulfil a particular crisis management activity. There will need to be a significant degree of pragmatism applied here so that there is no doubt that the organisational aim has a priority rather than the preferences of individuals within it.

Knowledge is essential. This means that the responding organisation needs not only to know itself what its aims and objectives are, but also what the resilience response options need to be. There also needs to be knowledge of the capabilities of the individuals and teams who will be involved within the organisational response, so that the organisation can rely upon its plans and ensure that it can face a crisis with a degree of confidence. This requirement for knowledge complements the validation need, where the measurement of capability is based not only on the activities that happen, but how they align with plans and the organisational resilience aims. The organisation also needs to be clear about the types of knowledge needed. At some levels it will be about knowing what to do if instructions are needed and how to respond. At other levels it will be about managing the critical aspects of the organisation and keeping functionality alive. It may be about having the depth of knowledge and understanding of risk, crisis and emergency management in depth. Whatever the level or function it *will* be about the responsibility of the organisation to hire and employ people who have the necessary knowledge to operate effectively when things inevitably go wrong.

Learning capabilities for the organisation. The organisation must be able to be in a position where it has learned from various sources about what it and organisations in general can do to mitigate the effects and impacts of crises. Learning can often be overlooked in busy and resource-challenged organisations. This can be especially problematic when considering that resilience knowledge development and learning will need to compete with other business learning and development requirements for resource and funding. When crises are not happening, and the requirement for search specific knowledge development and learning is not so apparent, then the challenge will potentially be quite significant. It would clearly be imprudent to avoid investment in resilience learning and development across the organisation in preference for an ad hoc response. However, realism needs to be applied, and the relative importance of resilience will naturally have the potential to be overlooked until that knowledge is needed.

Currency and forward thinking. Prepared organisations will know their context and environment in their normal organisational business, and have an ability to consider what may impact upon them. There will be a risk register within most organisations that will be designed to deal with business risk; and there should also be a resilience risk assessment embedded within that to identify where there will be areas of concern that may arise. Resilience should not be a 'bolt on' to an existing risk assessment structure, but should be explicitly linked to it, as it will have an influence upon organisational capability. Although some organisations will have an organic or inherent capability for conducting assessments of what may be happening or what could happen to the organisation, many organisations will not. However well-developed this thinking may or may not be – the baseline capability should not prevent organisations from being able to consider and take stock of issues that may have an impact upon them and planning accordingly. That may well be a governance requirement or a compliance need. Well prepared and resilient organisations will have placed considerable emphasis on this to ensure that not only lip service is paid, but that the capability is robust and dependable. At some point in the development of such capabilities, it can be useful to employ external consultancies that bring scrutiny, validation and a 'critical friend' approach to the organisation's thinking.

Maintained focus. When a problem occurs, focusing on what is critical is important for the organisation. It can be quite challenging for this to take place, especially when the pace of a problem begins to envelop the organisation, and there are multiple activities with varying demands upon management and resource. Focus in this context is the concentration on the aim of recovering from the crisis or issue effectively. Although it may not necessarily be the case that meetings should take place constantly, it is crucial to be constantly monitoring what is happening within the organisation, and the impacts that are arising routinely. This allows the organisation to detect anomalies and abnormalities as they happen. This monitoring should inform what needs to be done in the focused response to a particular problem arising in the context of a wider crisis development. For example, how might the organisation feel the minor 'tremors' from some problem that is bubbling in the resilience web. To achieve this successfully will involve the maintenance not only of the focused response, but also of the focus on the aims and objectives of the organisation. The two are intertwined and should not diverge; this is another important justification for resilience management to be an embedded capability with which the organisation is comfortable and assured.

Resilience requires flexible thinkers and a blameless culture. There will be times when decisions need to be made that may not necessarily reflect what is written in plans. There will also be times when organisational team members will need to act upon their own initiative, and take decisions that would normally have been taken either further up the management ladder or by another department. However, flexible thinkers will be essential, as they will need to make their decisions and informed discussions based upon an understanding of not what the outcome will be, but what it could be once it has been subject to thought and management. *Flexible thinkers,* may also be *disruptors and innovators*. These types will often be stifled and even marginalised in some organisations. I would contend that such organisations will not be as well prepared as those who include, if not embrace, them.

The organisation will also need to ensure that it has the availability to call upon external expertise and resource when necessary. No organisation will have all the organic material and capability to be able to meet the demands of a particularly complicated crisis. Multiple organisations, agencies and regulating bodies may all provide the necessary guidance and support when things become too challenging for them to manage. This is something that should be considered as part of the stakeholder management process in any case. As we have just mentioned in the context of currency and forward thinking, there should also be a consideration for the hiring in of consultants or other supporting elements who will be able to provide a capability over and beyond what the organisation already has. If it is considered that the organisation will be fully engaged with trying to maintain its momentum through a crisis, the use of a consultant can be helpful, as it will allow the organisation to continue with a nonorganic, impartial influence and management structure in place to assist and guide it through the problem. These resources can bring significant return on investment when deployed and used well. Similarly, and especially if we have a wide range of stakeholders, suppliers and venture partners, there may be an equally wide range of knowledge and support available. More importantly, as those entities will be linked to the organisation because they bring value (otherwise what is their purpose?); their input may well be more than just desirable, it may be critical.

Communication flow, especially when a situation is moving quickly, can sometimes be difficult to maintain. When there are multiple decisions to be made and multiple priorities to be followed, it can also be difficult for management to ensure that the reasons *why* activities are being carried out are clearly laid out. It will be a significant help for those who are required to carry out tasks if they understand why they are doing so, rather than just being told what to do. The aim should not necessarily be to justify a particular action, but to give an insight for the individuals concerned into the reasons for the decisions that are taken and the actions that are required. Understanding this will have an influence on their performance. Communication should also be timely and accurate. Within the organisation this is essential for maintaining capability; when communicating outside the organisation it is essential for assurance, reassurance, confidence and viability. Communication, as we have mentioned, is a core element of effective crisis management, and failure to communicate has repeatedly led to organisational failings when it mattered most. The failure to communicate effectively even more so. There is a litany of failures to effectively communicate in the history of crisis response, choose any number of examples – look them up and learn about them.

Agility and innovation. If it is assumed that organisations have a plan in place, and that they are looking to implement that plan when a crisis hits, they also need to be able to develop a capability to be agile and to innovate. The plan forms a basis; the difference between a simple plan and the highly effective response, is the agility and innovative thinking of those within the organisation so that they can rapidly respond to the changes within the crisis risk profile, and to decide on and recommend appropriate actions. Speed of thought, and the ability to discuss and evaluate the options will be critical to success. They will be based upon informed judgement, knowledge and analysis, and will be essential for the effective delivery of capability in the face of what may otherwise be an overwhelming set of circumstances. The burden of resilience is on the whole organisation rather than a core response team alone; and drawing on wider capability will give an edge. Therefore it makes sense to ensure that the organisation invests time, effort and resources in developing agility in its people; and that should not just be confined to managers.

Ambition. All organisations will want to maintain their ambition towards achieving aims, objectives and vision. The maintenance of this ambition is quite important as it ensures that the organisation has something upon which it can focus rather than simply survival. There will be times when surviving a particular aspect of a resilience challenge is overriding, however, the equal issue is that at some points the organisation will need to be thinking about how it can emerge on the other side of a crisis in a better position than when it started. It will need to be able to compete and operate better than its competitors in what may be a resurgent operating environment. Those organisations that understand the requirement to maintain their ambition and focus on the future will be able to set performance goals even during a crisis, so that they are able to emerge on the other side of the problem in good shape and form. If the overall aim of resilience management is to ensure that the organisation can maintain its position; it must maintain its purpose. The slower to respond and less able to resume the momentum the organisation is, the chances are higher that it will be in the lower quartiles of the resilience 'league table'. Naturally, if your organisation does sit in that lower quartile, you need to be able to move out of it. You can assume that other organisations are not necessarily going to sit back and remain in that quartile with you. With that in mind, it is worth considering whether you should compete or fail.

Human factors in organisational resilience

In thinking about human factors, our focus should not be as much on the drawing of lines and diagrams concerning the necessary and required structures and systems. It is more important to focus on deep, people-centred activity that is essential for the organisation to develop in appropriate ways and in the face of global change.

What we must consider within the system is not only the structures and capabilities, but also the *human interaction* that is essential for the organisation to work in appropriate ways and to manage resilience. Organisations should look to develop capability such that their people can live and work while neither compromising nor hampering the effectiveness of resilience. The overlay of humanity upon the complex ideas concerning structural layout is something that is critical to the development of this organisational and organic understanding process. We should also recognise that we have human-based systems to develop that can be subject to both technology-based practices and approaches, and the highly developed electronic and information networks that support them. However, organisations must have an equally well-developed people-centred focus. The aim of this focus should be to ensure that we are comfortable and capable working in the face of much more intelligent and knowledgeable network systems that to some extent are able to operate without our input; and this challenge is not going to recede. All of this is against a background of global scale challenges that continue to consolidate and increase.

In the 'digital age', we need to recognise that technology is taking organisations forward, and that AI changes the way that we work and, in effect, our future. However, it is critical to ensure that not only do we have the technology to enable us to move forward, but also that we are able to manage and be managed by that technology to its best advantage. Human beings are not machines, and organisational technologies will need to be designed and used such that they are optimised to meet our needs. Intertwined with that is that people need to be able to operate effectively and comfortably for extended periods in an 'always-on' world. Machines do not become tired and frustrated, they don't have financial and family worries, they are not easily distracted. That can be to their advantage rather than that of the human individual, and will be, to some extent, an advantage for the organisation. However, we employ humans, they are an asset that must be developed and utilised effectively in concert with this technology and its benefits.

In organisational resilience, overload and overtasking can have significant impact, and there is merit in focusing on developing support and welfare, and identifying strengths within our workforce such that we can make the best of these technological capabilities now and in the future. Human beings have specific requirements and capabilities that we must be able to recognise and optimise so that we are able to get the best from our people and therefore from our organisations. If we consider that we are looking at a system rather than a group of components, this means that we are using human beings who may or may not be willing or capable of meeting our needs. As we have mentioned, organisations also need to monitor performance and signs of feedback to ensure that they can continue to meet requirements effectively without breaking down and causing other elements of the system to fail because of consequent errors and problems. Human beings do require such maintenance, and of course when they do fail it can be spectacular. They do have the capability to mask their own errors and problems much more effectively perhaps than technology systems alone can. This can mean that errors and deficiencies risk being ignored and hidden as much as they can be made in the first place.

In considering the organisational resilience system, we should recognise that every human has a story, and every human requires organisational attention to ensure that they are performing to the best of their ability, and in response to the pressures that we place upon them. The limitations and parameters that human beings can impose on organisations (in direct contrast to and in parallel with the improvements and exceptional capabilities that they can bring), can be significant inhibitors of the organisation. Flexibility may require the organisation to move away from what is written on paper to something that is able to interact and develop in a more holistic and synergistic operating context and environment. People matter; and even with the ongoing and developing ideas related to AI and the 'sci-fi' concept of robot and automation taking over many human tasks, although sentience remains, and the human mind and brainpower provide a driving force behind innovation and development of capability; we must ensure that we include that human factor into our overall development of organisational capability for resilience.

Change, of course, is a challenge all of its own. It is probably most often characterised by how much resistance it faces rather than its effect. You may have seen or heard of the Kubler-Ross Change Curve, which originally came from a study into grief after bereavement.[33] More than likely you will have had change, probably cultural, in mind when thinking about its influence on your organisation. The Kubler-Ross model and our experience show that change takes time to internalise and accept; and organisations are not immune to this; their people even less so. The challenge in the resilience context is to some extent considering change as much as any of the specific technical and specialist skills that we might need. Even in the face of extreme challenges, such as pandemics, economic depression, political skulduggery and conflict, the inability to accept change remains a barrier to progress. If our experience in general is that change does not make much difference to us, we tend not to embrace it rapidly. Why should we?

How about thinking about what may be coming that will force big change, and in turn micro changes in any number, and that will affect your thinking? Not problems that have already happened; such as COVID-19, as they have happened, and we have changed already, even if we do not quite realise it. Ultimately, your resilience capability

---

[33] Kubler-Ross, E., (1969), *On Death and Dying*, Macmillan, New York.

depends on the way that you manage what you can, and yourself, to navigate change as much as anything else.

Failure, cause and effect

Any number of case studies will highlight the problems caused by human factors and the simple errors and omissions that can grow into immense consequential loss of both life and material. When this happens, because the consequences are so great and the causes can be so seemingly minor, we really do need to have taken the time and made the effort to understand where these gaps can arise, and the almost unique place of human failure within organisational resilience as a cause of significant problems. Even where failures can be smoothed over and hidden, or even forgotten, about in some other areas of minor consequence and effect, it matters greatly when the further impacts are such that an organisation can fail. This is serious, it is fundamental to survival that we understand it. We should therefore aim to define and refine our understanding not only of how things work but also how our limitations and successes as individuals can influence outcomes fundamentally. After all, successes are celebrated; failures should be regretted, scrutinised and instructive. For every organisational failure across any and all of the areas of activity that we cover in this book and in many more that we don't, we need to understand cause and effect. We are moving on in this regard from focusing overly on the cause of the problems and more heavily onto the examination and understanding of how behaviours affected impacts. How did our inability to implement the positive and overcome the negatives of the organisational and individual traits that we have discussed in this chapter so far, make the whole thing worse? How could we avoid the same or similar thing happening again. How much better at resilience could we be? And what about our organisation and its traits?

Hierarchies and power

Notwithstanding the way that organisations and their people feel they might wish to behave, the various influences upon them cause them to follow routes to solutions. This may be based upon various influencing factors that impinge upon human thinking and the capability to make rational decisions. If these constraining factors exist, it is useful to think about how their qualities have an influence – positive or negative – on the organisation. The qualities of organisational structure merit our attention again; and if we think about those, we can perhaps then think about how we might address, change or refine them.

Questioning the level of hierarchical qualification to decide. It is not a given that a particular person in a particular role at a particular level of seniority has a particular capability to be responsible for a particular type of stress problem. The problem that is facing the organisation may well fall outside the experience and capability of that management individual. However, it is common to see that within organisations, those who are entrusted with leadership and management roles feel that they are compelled to lead and take decisions. Sometimes they do this to show initiative and because they feel that they should do something. Sometimes they do this without consulting with experts. Many resilience professionals find this a challenging issue; especially when the results of such actions are not necessarily effective or positive. The problem is that we have the potential for *fait accomplis* to take place or be put in place. If those are not the right ones there may well need to be a significant amount of time, resource and effort spent on recovering and repairing the damage.

Resistance to valid contributions. Human behaviour is something that becomes more defined when things go wrong and decision making is needed. Excluding expertise and advice is something that seems to crop up quite often. There are many cases littering organisational histories where those who have valid contributions to make are ignored or overruled by those who feel that they know better. These issues when they do arise can be significant and impactful. The difficulty facing the consultant or manager who is attempting to influence those at a higher level and who feel that they have higher responsibilities, is that they may not be the person who is 'carrying the can' – especially in the eyes of the senior level manager, and therefore their contribution is less valid. I include this from a personal perspective. I don't claim to be an expert, and don't claim to be always right. However, I do know that for every recommendation and attempted contribution that I have offered employers in my specialism over the years, there has been an equal amount that have been ignored or overruled. Do I find that frustrating and annoying? I think so; as would anyone else. This has included everything from physical security to corporate risk management, to crisis response and business continuity. Those are my specialisms and to have my input ignored will naturally sting a little; and I am sure it is not just me who has faced these hubris-laden behaviours.

Questioning arrogance and entitlement. Human beings can be arrogant and when this is a trait that is not checked and managed, or challenged, then there will be situations whereby organisations will not work effectively. Deeply personal traits such as this are especially challenging to deal with. However, it is something that the resilient thinker should be aware of so that they are able to either allow for it or plan to meet the issues that this may cause. These undesirable and essentially human traits are normally quite evident as they can chafe, especially when they are demonstrated by the usual suspects: male, suit-wearing go-getters. However, arrogance and entitlement can come in different forms. You and your colleagues may be quietly arrogant and expect what you believe you are entitled to. Those traits can be shown, if not immediately obvious, by most of us to some degree. Regardless if this is happening in your boardroom or your HR department, it may block progress; and the wheels may come off your work very quickly if soft power is applied by those exhibiting these traits.

What is in it for me? Human nature being what it is, there will always be a degree of self-centrism and ego involved in any decision-making process. If there is a blame culture proven to exist within the organisation, then there will be some significant soul searching to be done as the person who is responsible for a particular course of action wrangles with the problems that may face them if they make an error or mistake. This can be problematic, and again, as with arrogance it is important to understand how to manage it. At every level within the organisation there will come a point where a value judgement is made by an individual about what the benefit is to them following a particular route. The decision taken will then influence the outcome. As with other traits, it may be that these attributes only become visible over time and as we become familiar with our work colleagues. Who can be relied upon to commit to a decision and course of action, and who can be relied upon to be unreliable? It will be worth your while finding out.

Compliance and deference

Traditionally, organisations were perhaps based upon the will of the leadership being imposed upon those within the organisations, and requiring them to follow a particular route or course of action. There are many who believe that those days are behind us and that organisations are now groups of equals all working together towards the same goals. The prevalence of this belief, probably deluded to some extent, seems to be the result of social media's wishful thinking rather than an observation of reality. Despite progress in that direction, the challenge will be in the type of organisation where compliance and deference are expected at lower levels, and therefore there is no rational challenge able to be made to a decision-making process that is either flawed or dangerous. Again, I have observed this in quite a few organisations that have a veneer or illusion put across that the inclusive matrix of management is in place, when it is absolutely not. There is some naivety I think in believing that running organisations by multi-level agency, consent and consultation are what organisations want or need. What many want, even though they dare not openly admit it, is for their workforce to do what they are told to do, in the timescales expected. This requires compliance with decisions made and deference to higher authority. It is also increasingly hidden behind fluff and obfuscation as 'authority' is perhaps not seen to be a positive aspect of any strategy or management process.

It can be very difficult to overcome the issues related to compliance and deference within the organisation, especially, as mentioned, if we have a blame culture. Human beings have long memories and can recall where problems may have arisen during times of stress. For that reason, it can often be difficult to commit to a decision or course of action that may backfire upon an individual or organisation. Workplace management and relations are always a challenge for everyone. Nobody likes to be told what to do; nobody likes to have their authority or decisions challenged or disputed. The minefield of organisational management is thickly sown with potential problems and is wide, long and often without definable perimeters.

Self-analysis

With these traits being prevalent in organisations and individuals, further exploration may be of value. Expanding a little more on behavioural science and the study of it can be highly valuable for the development of organisational capability and improvements. The idea of behavioural science as something that goes beyond simply psychology and looks more closely at interaction and its impact on others is something that should be particularly close to our study of cause and effect in organisations and the effectiveness of resilient thinking. There are many influences on our ability to understand how we behave; and of course, for every action that we carry out there is a reaction from those who carry out their own responsibilities that may impact upon our activity. Some of these reactions can be quite challenging when brought to the surface.

The challenges that do arise because of behaviours can be hard to accept. If we analyse the organisation considering some of the traits that we have already discussed, we may be able to anticipate effectively. For example, for every protective measure that attempts to secure an organisation and to alleviate loss there is an internal adversary who is seeking to circumvent or breach such protective measures. The problem is that they may not feel or be seen as an adversary; they may just not 'get it' or want to. In the case of legislation or regulatory activity there might be an internal opponent or political/ideological adversary who is vehemently opposed to certain legislation or regulation for their own benefit or of those around them. This is normal human behaviour. The requirement to understand behaviours and the impact of interaction is crucial to effective organisational resilience, as it is not simply a case of the imposition of processes and ideas (and how they may not be universally welcome), but also the understanding that there will be an impact. When this happens, our intended actions can be stopped, diverted or diluted, and we must be prepared to either change or modify our own initial ideas or behaviour in response to the behaviours of other human beings. We can therefore become *reactive to reaction to our own initial action.*

Naturally, the actions that we take will depend on the severity of the impact, any amount of compromise that may need to be imposed or accepted, or any sanctions that may be required. These are all part of understanding cause, effect and human motivations, and the frustrations of placing plans and behavioural requirements in a human context and structure.

Therefore, we must begin to understand at an early stage that whatever we do put in place or even contemplate as actionable requirements will be workable. The outcome is always going to be dependent upon the reactions of those around us, as stakeholders, who we either affect or will affect our capabilities in the short or long term. We can take as a prime example the global problems that occurred when governments attempted to impose their own carefully thought-out plans without considering the full human and societal 'overlay'. COVID-19 imposed a set of restrictions upon populations that effectively required them to withdraw from their human interactions and wider societal behaviours. For many, this entailed the loss of their anchor points of work and social behaviour, and being guided by advice that in many cases, it is fair to say, they did not understand. Certainly in free democracies these restrictions were outside of our previous lived experience, and we moved from being able to be trusted with our own decision making to being directed quite stringently about what was permissible and what was not.

The problem then arose where populations reached a point where compliance became a restriction that they were no longer prepared to tolerate. After several months of restrictions, people returned to some semblance of normal life as soon as they felt they were able to. In many countries and societies this resulted in unmanageable breaking and breaching of the restrictions that governments had put in place, and indicated quite clearly that the best laid plans would not stand in the face of human behaviours. To an extent, this could have been anticipated, although the scale of the large-scale emergence from compliance by those who flocked to public spaces and hospitality venues in pleasant weather challenged the government, law enforcement and a wider component of the population who did not wish to break the regulations for various reasons. Most importantly, even when people were dying in significant numbers globally, the desire to be 'free' overrode caution and societal efforts towards infection control.

The problem, perhaps, behind our civilised societies, is that we sometimes behave in a primordial way. The term 'primordial', for many, recalls images of prehistoric swamps with early humans wandering about with makeshift weapons, hunting and surviving. The term really refers to the beginning of time and therefore how we have always been. If we think about how humans have behaved since then, there are particular sub-functions, behaviours and parameters that constitute what Power (2017)[34] referred to and credited back to Foulkes (1964)[35] in relation to primordial 'images'. Power (2017, 92) asked rhetorically:

> *"What might primordial images be, and where were and are they imagined? They are shared in the Unconscious and are what all people experience; images of father, mother, birth, eating, defecating, breathing, sex, growth,*

---

[34] Power, K., (2017), On the Primordial Origins of Group Analysis and their Relation to the Creative Nature of Humanity, *Group Analysis*, *50* (1), pp. 91–103.

[35] Foulkes, S.H., (1964), *Therapeutic Group Analysis*, London: George Allen and Unwin.

decay, murder, destruction, death, sun, moon, light and dark, night, circle, group, parting, mourning and so on."

Both Foulkes and Power were talking concepts, theories and trait analysis around the 'hard-wired' behaviours of humans. There are perhaps some parallels to Maslow's (1943)[36] often quoted 'hierarchy of needs' and human motivation. Going back to our responses as societies and humans in relation to the perceived impacts of the COVID-19 pandemic, it may well be that the primordial images are closer to the surface than may be comfortable for us to accept. The bubbling to the surface of behaviours of crowds indicated that primordial actions could exist, and in concert with 'herd behaviour', the impact on wider society, we have seen to be very negative. Trotter (1914)[37] coined the phrase 'herd behaviour' that we perhaps recognise; but has become more in evidence in the 2020s, perhaps another manifestation of social media's power. However, and whatever the base influence on response, there is a clear indication that humans will react and 'push back' in the face of direction and the requirement to be compliant.

Is it the primordial, such as Power's referred to 'sun' image that drew crowds in huge numbers to parks and seaside towns to congregate and flout social distancing rules that were designed to save lives; and did that urge overcome the real threat of death? Do we separate and segregate our thinking to ignore or deprioritise actions that fuse our hard

---

[36] Maslow, A.H., (1943), A theory of human motivation, *Psychological Review.* 50 (4): 370–96.

[37] Trotter, W., (1914), *The Instincts of the Herd in Peace and War.*

wiring? Perhaps the take of Bifulco and Pecchinenda[38] contributed:

> *"This kind of segregation and separation is also related to the increasing infrequency in which we encounter death, by virtue of the improved hygienic sanitary conditions and of a certain social pacification. Consider, for example, the decline of child mortality or the reduction – at least in the West – of epidemics, famines, wars, etc."*

In the context of organisational resilience, the social pacification is perhaps not only that we perceive war and pestilence to be someone else's problem, but also that we are desensitised. The constant and controlled imagery that confronts us in films, TV, gaming and social discourse tends to render the impacts of life changing (and life ending) events as something 'other'. It happens remotely to others and with no impact on us. Therefore it cannot be perceived as a concern that overrides our freedoms.

Staw et al[39] talked of a failure to alter practices in response to change, and being locked into incorrect and negative processes as a result of being unable to deal with the dynamics of change. Clearly, this is an issue that should concern us as resilient thinkers, as we consider not

---

[38] Bifulco, L., & Pecchinenda, G., (2018), The representation of death in modern society, Funes. *Journal of Narratives and Social Sciences*, 2, 1–7.

[39] Staw, B.M., Sandelands, L.E. and Dutton, J. E., (1981), Threat-rigidity effects in organizational behavior: A multilevel analysis, *Administrative Science Quarterly*, Vol. 26 No. 4, pp. 501–24.

necessarily the risk itself; but the ability of the organisation to deal with it all once the problem has been identified. As a person who deals with academic theory as well as its application, I believe that it is important to understand that observations and identification of issues that manifest themselves in theory come from looking at how organisations operate. So this idea of threat rigidity means that we are not able or willing to act effectively because we have self-confirmed that the only options are those that we want to take. This, in turn, means that potentially, regardless of the nature of the risk, we will not be able to understand our own failings and act accordingly. That is an even bigger risk than the risk itself, if we are unable or unwilling to see clearly and analyse ourselves well.

It is not only individuals, but groups of them who compound the problem. Wenger[40] – defined 'communities of practice' as groups of people who share a concern or a passion for something they do, and learn how to do it better as they interact regularly. This is an interesting concept; and Wenger offers it as a very positive method of developing learning organisations. However, on the negative side, communities of practice can soon drop into Janis's (1972)[41] groupthink again, when a group makes faulty decisions because group pressures lead to a deterioration of *"mental efficiency, reality testing, and*

---

[40] Graven, M., Lerman, S. and Wenger, E., (1998), Communities of practice: Learning, meaning and identity, *Journal of Mathematics Teacher Education* 6, 185–194 (2003) https://doi.org/10.1023/A:1023947624004.

[41] Janis, I L, (1972), *Victims of Groupthink*, New York: Houghton Mifflin.

moral judgment". So, we can see that there are probably traits within any organisation that combine the positives of communities of practice with a negative of groupthinking. Alongside that, we can consolidate and corroborate our own views and decide that we are going to react in a particular way towards a particular problem. It appears that there is a clear danger in discussing and deciding upon responses in groups; and we need to be aware of this as an important component of our planning and risk impact management processes.

It's interesting that we can reach the point where a positive idea can be equated with a negative concept. It's not only the academic theories that provide insight into why particular mitigation issues may arise; we need to revisit our own behaviours and ideals. If we don't really understand anything beyond those ideas that we have built and self-reinforced, either individually or as groups, then this can lead to either misplaced confidence or a lack of confidence in stepping beyond what we don't really know. Clearly, it would be sensible to be able to understand and appreciate before acting proactively in response to developing and emerging risks and threats. But if we don't want to understand, or if we find it too difficult, or if we are in a situation where our own particular area of the organisation needs to be defended against the influence or potential for being taken over by another; then we have the potential for weakening the organisation. Whether we exhibit individual or group traits that are positive or negative, or may be a blend of both, it is important to understand them.

Spooks and snipers

Coming away from the academic discourse a little, the more prosaic understanding of who may be challenging you either overtly or behind the scenes is worth some attention. If everything in your world is going right, you may be working under some misapprehension. In any structured society, and by society I also mean our social and working groups, there are people who are out to get you. There are spooks and there are snipers; and by that I do not mean state spies or soldiers with rifles – but those who are out of your view and working behind the scenes, sometimes as part of wider activity but other times directly against you, to cause impact, or to discredit or 'damage' you in many ways. We know that we have some hard-wired behaviours; but there are others who are deliberate in thought, intent and action.

Right now, today, someone you know will be having a negative thought about you. It may be a colleague or employee at work, or a 'friend', or someone you know who is a competitor for status or income. Tactics they may use could include gossip, influencing others to work against you, undermining your decisions, counter-briefing and deliberately re-interpreting what you say or do to cause problems for you. Subterfuge and smartness to frustrate your efforts and discredit and diminish you may be something that happens quite constantly at several levels. These hidden activities, collaborative and hushed, will debilitate you, affect your ability to interact and manage, and can be damaging before you even realise – if you ever do. These are 'spook' tactics to disable adversary capability and are often only detected once the damage is done. If you are aware of this you may detect their fingerprints in conversations or communications where their influence can be seen and felt. I have worked with and detected this behaviour on several occasions; it is damaging and negative.

Then there are the snipers. The analogy is a little simpler here. Every time you raise yourself out of cover, become noticeable because you are looking to act or make change, there will be someone who has a problem with it. The next thing is that someone takes a 'shot'. They may miss or they may stop you in your tracks; and if you do manage to avoid being hit, at the very least you will become less inclined to raise your head, break cover and be the distinctive person that organisations need and can ill-afford to have as hesitant leaders and managers.

It's all down to human nature of course. Normally envy or something similar; and Duffy, Shaw and Schaubroeck provide a useful treatise on the nuances of workplace envy and its constituent elements that helps understand this human trait and its impacts.[42] If you are a 'tall poppy' – and most managers and those who want to interact socially with colleagues are; or if you are successful, even looking to make positive change, the spooks and snipers are lining up and settling in to make their move and cut you down.

---

[42] Duffy, M.K., Shaw, J.D. and Schaubroeck, J.M., (2008), Envy in organizational life, *Envy: Theory and research*, pp.167–189.

Paranoia? The Cambridge Dictionary identifies that as: *"an extreme and unreasonable feeling that other people do not like you or are going to harm or criticize you."* The reality is that even the saintliest of us have other people who do not like us, and although they may not physically harm us there is much that they can do to make life difficult. Overcoming the challenge caused by spooks and snipers – if we want to be valuable as friends, colleagues, employees, employers and leaders or managers – is not as simple as backing off or taking cover to reduce impact. A counterattack makes the victim a perpetrator, and given that we all need to be able to lead our social and working lives as those around us need us to do; what are the options?

In terms of the commitment to the resilient organisation, the optimal method for dealing with negativity and these understandable human traits is to work around them. Although we all want to be liked and happy in our jobs, it is perhaps more sensible to understand that that cannot be us all the time. When the challenges come, the spooks and snipers will either step up or step down. What will matter more will be the response and the capability; and perhaps then they will realise that negative behaviours are exactly that; and are of no use to the organisation at all. If that is true in a crisis, it will still be true in the return to routine, if they are still there. The challenge for you as an individual is in choosing your time to counter their actions.

Summarising organisational behaviour

Organisations are complex, complicated and multi-faceted, and there will always be some tension between what the organisation wants and what the individual can, or is willing, to give. The behaviour of our people sets the tone and capability for our organisational resilience. We have discussed the reasons why we take particular actions and approaches, and why inaction can be a damaging outcome of our behaviours and attitudes. For the organisation to succeed, it needs to optimise the outputs from its people when they are under pressure, and the key to doing that it is to work with them when they are not.

Individual and cultural approaches can make a difference; spotting, nurturing and developing positive talents within the organisation will allow us to develop and put in place future capabilities. The real challenge is in leading this capability development. Every other social media post seems to be focused on leadership and how to do it, and I would guess that 75 percent of those who offer their thoughts have had little experience of the challenges of leadership. Although leadership may or may not involve discussions, consulting the team and asking everyone's opinion, it will boil down to what the designated leader does when the pressure is on. That will be when the leader looks around and finds that he or she is relatively alone, and when everyone who does not want to step up looks to you for direction and your signature on the decision.

In resilience disciplines and professions, leadership capability in all aspects of your role is essential. There are many potentials for you to fail and falter, and it should be your mission to ensure that you, and those entrusted to work with you, minimise those risks. To achieve this you will need to blend knowledge, interpersonal and relationship management skills, empathy and organisational focus. If you are helped by inspirational TED talks then by all means use them, if you need to read books about it then please do. However, the underpinning need is to lead your band of behaviour-led sisters and brothers to success in resilience. Recognise their faults, concerns, strengths and prejudices alongside your own.

Having thought about behaviours, we will look in the next chapter at barriers to effective thinking, and ideas about approaches to take as we develop a mindset for the resilient thinker.

Here are your resilient thinker think points from this chapter:

1. Thinking about your organisation, to what extent do individual and collective behaviours influence its resilience capability?

2. Given that we should be able to build an understanding of the negative impacts that *could* occur when things go wrong, how effective is your organisation at planning for them?

3. To what extent does your organisation consider the physical resourcing of roles and the suitability of specific individuals for pressurised tasks?

4. How effectively does your organisation develop its thinking and actions? Is 'Groupthink' prevalent? Are you able to identify other human behavioural aspects that should be addressed?

5. Training and preparing for challenges are essential. To what extent does your organisation think about and put in place training for its critical staff?

CHAPTER 7: BREAKING FREE FROM CONVENTIONAL THOUGHT

> *"Never accept ultimatums, conventional wisdom or absolutes."*
>
> **Christopher Reeve**

We have thought about the way the world is going and the challenges that we face; and we have also considered how difficult it can be to face and manage them. We've talked about organisational resilience, focused on crisis and about the way that we as humans think and behave. It is easy for us to rely on support to help our thinking and action; and we do need tools to help us. But there is something else. If we were good at resilient thinking, then perhaps we wouldn't be caught out so much; and we need to ensure that we add a little 'sizzle' to our capabilities.

In this chapter we will cover the need to move on from the idea that models and frameworks are fully effective, and think about the need to develop originality in thought. Conventional thinking is needed, wild and uncontrolled thinking perhaps less so. However, now is the time for those who are learning what our new world is teaching us, to challenge what is conventional. It is perhaps more important than it has ever been to squeeze out conventional thought and the concept of what works well. Sometimes, and seemingly more often, the old ways are being proven to be ineffective and irrelevant in the face of dynamic change.

The twenty-first century checklister

Up to this point, we have only briefly discussed the checklist culture, and the idea that it can be useful for some people to rely upon frameworks to provide them with the guidance that they need to conduct their essential activities. This is fine if you want to be limited and engender a dependence upon recycled information that may not necessarily be applicable in all cases. The fact that flexibility, one of the most overused and under-applied words in management, is probably a fundamental requirement for the effective response and recovery process, can tend to be forgotten in checklist culture. Here's a thought: you would think that the inherent flexibility and almost immeasurable wealth of information available to us on the Internet would allow us to free our thoughts slightly and to become a more adaptable and flexible group of professionals. Well, that may be the case for some of us, but for others the Internet and the growth of information capability in the twenty-first century is actually allowing the checklist culture to thrive, increase and permeate.

To understand the scale of this issue, let's consider the plethora of templates, free programmes, planning guidelines, 'buy a course or consultancy from us' sites, or any of the many other available easy-to-complete, corner-cutting, plagiarism-developing resources that are available to us all electronically. Let's also admit, we have all either looked at them or used them in some context or other at some time since the Web became the core of our lives. I do not believe that there is anything wrong with that, and like many things in life, moderation in use can be beneficial and provide real utility. However, like many things in life, overuse and dependency can very rapidly become a negative thing. The cheap and easy processes that allow us to access other people's materials and thought processes, and sometimes these materials and thought processes themselves, have been modelled on others' work, and effectively make us lazy. Think about this: if, during your appraisal at work, or even casually, your boss said to you that in their opinion you were lazy and a corner-cutter – how would you feel? How would you feel if they said that you were an inveterate cheat who copied other people's materials and passed them off as your own by changing words, phrases and content, as a short cut to meeting your needs?

Even more importantly, how do you feel about yourself when you've been entrusted with developing strong and workable plans specific to your organisation, and you've borrowed somebody else's material? And, even more importantly than that, deep in your heart of hearts, do you really feel that what you've borrowed is going to be effective? It is worth asking you these questions, because, if you feel uncomfortable about any of these (and I suggest that you should), then you aren't naturally a checklister. Although that is good news for you and probably for your organisation, you do need to be aware that the Internet and the resources that are available to you can change you from a fine, upstanding, self-sufficient, thinking and adaptive professional into a borrower. And although there may be benefits, this cannot be beneficial in specific circumstances for specific organisations. Have you ever tried on a 'one-size-fits-all' item of clothing? It may chafe in places or be excessively baggy in others – and it will rarely do the job satisfactorily because it is about convenience and low cost, rather than 'fitness for purpose'.

The culture of borrowing and adapting material is actually becoming a pandemic within many industries, as the capability of the Internet and social networking sites, in particular, continues to grow. Let's be absolutely clear here, we are not advocating in any way that the Internet and the infinite resources available are a bad thing in themselves; that would be to ignore their revolutionary and transformational power and effect. But, and it is a big 'but', once we add in human beings with their natural competitiveness, vanity, desire to be seen to be performing better than their peers and colleagues, etc. the plagiarism from the Internet begins! A question to ask yourself is this: within your peer group, your network and organisational colleagues (perhaps those you meet at conferences and seminars), how many of them know in depth about the many and multifaceted elements of resilience? The simple answer to that is this: very few. And where did they get their knowledge, and how can they apply it if it is not their own?

We all know some things; in some areas we have more depth of knowledge than in others; in some areas we are specialists; and in others we have no clue whatsoever. That is the truth without exception within the world of resilience, in fact in every aspect of life. The thing to do now is to wander across to the Internet, go and have a look at the specialist and professional groups on social networking sites, and see how many self-professed experts and 'thought leaders' there are. Even more importantly, take a close look at what the self-professed experts are posting on the sites. At first glance, it often looks like they are providing you with information that they have gleaned from their wide and deep knowledge and experience. In most cases they aren't. In fact, most of them are trawling sites, feeds and communities, and recycling them without any additional comment, qualification, innovative thought or valuable insight. Their activity is not about the growth of knowledge; it is not about providing any development of ideas based around the items that are posted; it is often more about 'Look at me, aren't I knowledgeable – give me a job'. And that, for me, is a case of deception, because in many cases if you do press for further comment or information from many of these individuals, you often get no response whatsoever. Why? Because they do not really know what they're talking about; in fact, they're not talking about anything new at all – they're just telling you what somebody else has said!

So, what you have there are the fully up-to-date, very networked and very aware individuals who are falling back on the age-old behavioural processes often associated with the very worst of resilience managers. 'This is what it says, read it.' Wouldn't you prefer it to be something like, 'This is what it says; read it, and also this is my viewpoint. I'm interested in learning about other viewpoints and ways in which we can, as a profession and industry, improve our capabilities'? What we are getting in most instances is worse and more damaging than empty noise. The frustration can be that many subjects are ripe for debate, some of them are ripe for development, and some of them may even be ripe for inclusion within forward-looking organisations to improve resilience. But a simple post that says: '20% of IT companies worried about cyber threats' posted by Joe Smith (this week's top influencer) and followed by a link to a news website tells us nothing much about anything. If we get into the habit of telling people nothing about anything, but dressing it up as something about something, and we are perceived to be reliant upon irrelevant information, or that which can be reoriented to suit us, then we are doing ourselves, the resilience profession and, ultimately, our employers, a major disservice. What is missing is the analysis, the evaluation and the value.

Which brings us on to another type of checklister: the type of person who has learned something on a course, or has read it in a book, and now considers their theory to be the main and overriding one with which we should all comply. Even more depressing is the type of person who has written a particular document, good as it may be, and then expects us all to accept it without question. And then there are the recognisable 'industry leaders' who are involved in the inner circle of some kind of group, society or association, who consider themselves to be the absolute oracles of everything, and who expect us to gaze in awe at their mighty brains and at the fantastic work that they do. A by-the-numbers checklister, one who speaks rather than listens; sends rather than receives; and shouts, figuratively, when they could offer analysis, perspectives and *ideas* is not an asset. They can be intimidating; they have influence and often powerful networks, and they are able to shape policies – sometimes at national level – which may be misguided and may offer no help or assistance to individuals or organisations whose aim is to become more resilient. And sometimes we can see all these traits and attributes combining in national-scale initiatives, policies and standards that are the outcome of ego-based groupthink, knowledge arrogance echo chambers.

Now, we all know that none of us are perfect; it would not be right for me to sit here in judgement, effusively writing disrespectful statements about different people who may well be at the top of their game in their particular field. But it is important to ensure that whatever anybody says, no matter how much they tell you that they know, no matter how much they could convince you that their way is the correct way, no matter how intimidating they and their colleagues may be, and no matter how much you want to be their friend, you should not be afraid to question, criticise, argue and debate. You have every right to challenge checklisters and 'experts', and every right to offer your version of how things should be. I believe it is not just a right, but a duty. However, if you do not take the opportunity to test knowledge, and to add your own, the pursuit of resilience and best practice in what is a developing 'industry' may as well stop right now. Who knows, you may actually reach the satisfying point where you expose the checklister's weaknesses, and by doing so, offer a new model for the resilience organisation of the future. That takes us away from a static, mundane, constant reiteration of old tropes that are maintained by those who benefit from them. It takes us forward into the inclusive, challenging world of disruptive thinking and innovation. And this is not only challenging because it is about new ideas and fresh blood, but also because overt and passive resistance to such change will come from all directions.

The failings of experience

Close your eyes, think hard and in your mind's eye envision the resilience professional: experienced, knowledgeable, confident, capable, drives a nice car? The perfect resilience professional will have a good balance of all these attributes, and if you do really well, then you get the car. However, one of the most coveted attributes when I ask colleagues and peers about what they need from resilience professionals is often 'experience'. There is nothing wrong with that whatsoever; experience is a good thing, as it allows us to become extremely knowledgeable about most things that may happen to us in the future. This is because what we have learned in the past is going to allow us to become far more adaptable and versatile when faced with whatever may come next, and it is going to make us far better than our peers in every respect.

However, this is only partially true. Although experience is of value, there is quite a lot about the culture of the experienced professional that is potentially worrying. I, personally, think that nobody learns much that is universally applicable from experience. And what I mean by this is that experience is something that happens to us, and our responses to it are based upon our perceptions of what happened, how we felt, our own reactions and how successful we felt we were. So, if there are two of us in a room and we both have had exactly the same experiences from the day of our birth (and even that is impossible), and the same thing happens to both of us at the same point in time while we are in that room, do you think that our experience and the lessons we learn from it will be exactly the same? Of course not, perception is everything and the human mind, wonderful as it is, allows us to put our own 'spin' on everything that happens to us. Therefore, experience can never be properly shared because it belongs to one person only. Shared experiences in groups are never fully shared because every experience is different in many ways.

Now, in a similar way to the checklist, let's think about our experienced professionals in our sector. The old and bold, or even the young and smart, absolutely believe that their experience equips them to be able to face the future confidently and capably. Well, they are halfway there, but their experience is theirs and theirs alone; they will take their experience and they will bend and shape it to suit whatever the next event will be. They will use anecdotal knowledge and the memories of their own experiences to shape responses, and if you are really unlucky, they could shape yours as well. This is the world according to them, and may not necessarily be the world that we need to live in. How many times have you read a document, a newspaper article, a blog or online article that says somewhere in it, 'in my experience', or 'when I was …'? It may all be very entertaining, some of it may be applicable, some of it may be extremely useful, but it is not the basis for future planning. These experience stories do have value in training and education, especially when considering case studies and lessons learned. However, they will not form the underpinning pattern for response as a standard.

Experiences can be recalled and replicated; but not necessarily reapplied. Just because you have experienced something at a point in time, in a certain place, under certain conditions, it does not mean that the experience is applicable at any time ever again. Everything around you changes by the second – conditions change, people change, the weather changes – and influences like this (some micro, some macro and some imperceptible) will affect the outcomes next time round. So, all of those people who rely on their experience as being the core of their capability, need, I suggest, to start to think about adding a little more colour to their palette. In a dynamic, growing industry, where threats and risks change, where the benign environment changes, and where things can happen extremely quickly and without warning, or even slowly and with plenty of warning, those who rely upon the flawed idea of experience as the main generator of capability for the organisation – or even for themselves – will find themselves staring at a potential nightmare, as they are overtaken by events that their experience has not equipped them to cope with. Meanwhile, it may be the hour for the innovator. In an age where technology and new challenges are outstripping our ability to cope; it seems even more vital to understand that experience is of value only when it is applicable. When it is not applicable, it is baggage.

More than anything else, the thing that makes the checklisters and the experience-mongers not only inappropriate, but downright dangerous to an organisation, is that they think and believe that they know the answers. They may well know some of the answers; they may know most of the answers. In fact, they may be that 0.0001 percent who really do know all the answers. For all of us, in reality, there is a significant gap between most people's self-regard and their capability; so how come our industry seems to have more than its fair share of them? And how come our industry seems to have more than its fair share of checklisters? Well, I go back to the same old story, men with loud voices, who are fond of their own opinions, who have a degree of expertise in a particular area and are keen to show through their competitive nature that what they know is more valuable than what their colleagues know.

Now add in some good old institutional arrogance, an awareness of rank structure that may have been gleaned from the military or the police (but not always), some aspiration and some ambition, and you've got a very turgid mix. I'm wondering whether people like this exist in every other area of business, or whether it's just ours? The problem is that in the resilience 'sector', the type of failure caused by checklisters and by the type of people we are talking about here can be significant, damaging and irreversible.

In fact, let's be more specific – in the worst cases, where the gravity of situations and risks demands everything that we are not talking about here, in order to be able to provide balanced thinking and forward-looking assessment and management capabilities, the result of failure can be fatal. And this is the difference that is important to remember at this point: in some, but not all, areas of our industry and sector, people can die because of our inability to do what we are here to do. It is important to remember also that nothing should stand in the way of our ability to maintain security, continuity, resilience and the protection of our own people. Consequently and logically, we should begin to think about excluding egos and ambitions, our own fantastic world view, the plan that we wrote and is so good because we wrote it, etc. Because I do not know about you, but if it is me who is responsible for a fatal problem because of who I am and personal behaviours that I could have fixed, I'm not going to be feeling too good about it.

To make things really work, to get your organisation to do things that you really want to do, to be resilient and to be competitive, balance and nuance are the way ahead. Ego, posturing and the relentless pursuit of outperforming our colleagues and competitors, so that we look good at the expense of everything else, belongs on a sports field – not in the serious business of resilience.

Experience	Learning	? Neither

Experience	Learning	Neither
• Acquired expertise • Many case studies • 'Battle hardened' • Networks • System and process knowledge • Reputation	• Analytical approach • Subject knowledge • Networks • System and process knowledge • Cross-discipline Awareness	• New approach • Willing to learn • Freedom to innovate • Lack of experiential bias • Not exposed to weak learning

• Preloaded ideas • Superiority complex • Reapplying history • Networks • Set in ways/lack of currency • Reputation	• Lack of experience • Superiority complex • Theory rather than 'real world' • Lack of networks	• No experience • Little or no leaning • New to everything • No networks • Outsider until proven

Figure 25: Experience

There are various interpretations and attitudes towards the relative merits, advantages and disadvantages of those who have experience, those who have a learning qualification and perhaps those who come into the industry with neither. Does the person with experience have the full range of requirements to be effective and successful? Is the brainy academic the answer? Or is it time for new blood with no baggage to make its mark?

Perhaps it depends on your own status and where you came from. Each 'type' has its merits, and each has its drawbacks. The table offers some ideas for you to think about and perhaps to consider your views about what you aspire to be, or how you think your ideal resilience professional's profile should look.

Is it a good idea to use most of the 'good' elements of experience and learning and combine with the approach of the person who is neither? Do the 'good' elements compensate for the problems that the 'bad' may cause? It's your choice. However, if you are intimidated and shouted down by those who would benefit from you being afraid to contribute, you will not be able to contribute.

Continuity of operations

As the title of this chapter is 'Breaking free from conventional thought', it is probably an appropriate time to start thinking about what we can actually do in different ways to meet the challenges that may be facing us as resilience professionals. We're not going to go through a checklist, that's for sure, but we should begin to think about what is in place, how things are done and how they can be done differently (if they need to be done differently) to be able to ensure that organisational resilience is something that can be achieved in a cost-effective way – and that means including current risks and, logically, those that may develop in the future.

At this juncture, it is probably quite useful to think about what conventional thought is. Of course we have already talked about the checklisters, the 'Sir Humphreys', and the experience trap. In general terms, we know that we need to conduct people planning and resilience thinking to match organisational processes. But so far, we haven't really come up with any good ideas about how we're going to do it. The first question to ask is, 'Will conventional thought do the job?' Is it good enough just to be able to do what everybody else has been doing, without innovation and without looking forward in any great detail? Some people will say that it is, and perhaps they are right to some degree. If you are comfortable with the parameters within which you operate, and you are reasonably confident that you can meet any potential problems that may face you within those parameters, then perhaps you will be all right and you can relax. But, if we work on the principle that we are continually trying to improve, and if we are trying to look to excel as a competitive organisation, then we should consider thinking a little harder than our competitors and trying to outsmart the development of threats and risks that may appear in the future. What is certain is that your adversaries will be innovating whether you do or not.

If we offered a checklist during this part of the book it would actually negate the whole thing, and it would be an absolute waste of time reading any further. So, how should we orient our thoughts towards a point where we can begin to innovate and start to look at ways of improving what we do and how we do it in the future? Personally, I'm a big believer in the blank page. It is always useful to be able to very carefully consider absolutely everything that could come into the mix when you are thinking about anything that has any kind of organic life or potential for behavioural change about it. I believe that in the same way that checklisters and experience can have limits to their value, being able to open your mind matters a lot. This is where you need to start doing what you did when you were a child and before it was trained out of you: you need to start to imagine things. If you take a child and put them in an empty room with a cardboard box, they will make something of it. Leave them for half an hour and a cardboard box could be a car, a spaceship, or a house, or filled with imaginary friends – but it will be something that they have thought about, imagined and created in their mind. They may have used a little bit of experience, and they may have applied a little bit of experience to their imaginative approach, but, in the main in their little head, they will have gone off into a flight of fancy and will be developing stories, discussions and interactions without any prompting from anyone.

So why not take a similar approach when looking at what is facing you and your organisation? You do not have to make up wild imaginary risks. But why not think with a little more fluidity about the frameworks that you are in, and think about how things can develop, and how they can become better and worse based upon developments, interdependencies and interactions. How do we respond? How would we like to respond? How do our peers and superiors want us to respond? And how can we develop the capability to respond? If we do it by the numbers, you can guarantee that we will not do it satisfactorily. If we do it by application of thought, we will perhaps have a better chance of doing things better. There is no need to go off on flights of fancy because that would be dangerous, but there is every need to think about the things that you may not be thinking about just now. And while you're opening your mind, really start to think about perception. That means, think about what you see and what you interpret, and then try to put it in the context of an organisation and a competitive environment that may not necessarily see things your way. Try to understand and accommodate in your free thinking the perceptions of others.

Every incident in every way means something different to everyone who is involved. Think about your organisation: what is a problem for your company is not necessarily a problem for the company next door to you that produces different things for different customers within different timescales. Of course, if an asteroid lands on your building, then it will probably have some impact upon them as well, but, in the main, everyone is affected in different ways. Therefore, there is no best-fit plan, there is no best-fit solution for any event at any time under any conditions, which will be replicable the next time it happens. This can be quite difficult to cater for, and I am not suggesting for a moment that whatever plans you have will not be fit to mitigate the effect of a particular event and its impact upon your organisation. In fact, quite the contrary: it is important that the plans are in place. But the main and underpinning point here is that plans are single-use only – and after every event they will invariably need to be amended. Now, how often does that happen?

Whatever approach is taken, most importantly, the plans that are in place need to be written on the basis that they make sense. They need to be based upon the realities that face your business and your organisation, and they need to provide you with the capability to respond. They do not need to tie you down to a particular flowchart that does not allow you the latitude to respond; or does not allow you to branch off into different directions, should needs be; and that has not been planned properly, with the necessary levels of redundancy and supporting linkages to ensure that, when things do go wrong, and you do have to deviate from the plan, you have an escape route. The linkage of all the elements contained in any plan is important, just as in any other chain-type structure. No matter how it is constructed, there needs to be a strong bond between the various elements that combines to provide an all-inclusive yet flexible capability. We talk about 'chains' a lot, and they are often used as representative symbols for continuity in particular. When you think about it in a little more detail, chains are flexible, they hold together various components, they can be locked or unlocked, they can be short or long, and normally they are quite difficult to break. If your chain, or your capability planning, is strong in the right points, links the right elements and is constructed of the right materials, then you have continuity.

As we are still working on the concept of not being too prescriptive here, it is important again to consider how you would do things differently based upon what we have been talking about so far. Importantly, do you consider yourself to be a flexible, thinking, resilient person in a flexible, thinking, resilient organisation? If not, is it your fault, or is it that of the organisation that expects you to be working to rigid processes?

The stovepipe and the silo (again)

If we think back to earlier chapters, we mentioned briefly the issues related to stovepipe or silo management. There are many different functions and personalities within every organisation, many of them conflict, and in most organisations, to some degree, there will always be cases of people getting on with their own business and not really being too interested ih what everyone else is doing. This is another fundamental aspect of human nature, and when you throw in the issue of competitiveness within organisations, then you can sometimes find that it is quite difficult to break, to any great effect, stovepipe or silo approaches. You can write it in your documents, you can plan for it, you can brief your people, but, at the end of the day, human nature will always prevail.

I do not want to repeat much in this section about the issues relating to stovepipe and silo management, but it may be useful to take things a stage further and to consider how we often think in isolation about what we are doing, and to consider the implications a little more. I think that most people would agree that, in business, one of the main drivers for our activity is to contribute to the bottom line and to maintain profitability. We need to maintain a competitive edge and to look for opportunities wherever and whenever we can. Of course, in our area of the business, we need to ensure that resilience is built in (at least, that is an aspiration), and we are probably all firmly of the belief that this will contribute towards success. But what about all those other members of the team who are frantically seeking to contribute to the bottom line, so that they can get their bonus, or climb the promotion ladder and reach the peak within the business? Do they care about little old you and your specific area? In general, probably not, until their own performance is hit.

If we think about organisational growth, expansion and relationship building, it is good to think about the tools that we employ. When you are seeking to set up a new partnership or joint venture, or even to launch a new product or service, there is a great deal of activity that is required. You need to do a significant amount of schmoozing, relationship building, planning and discussion, all that kind of thing. You will probably carry out due diligence upon an organisation – it would make sense if you did – and you will carry out the necessary legal and regulatory preparations. All good stuff, all part of effective enterprise risk management and good corporate governance. But what about your own people? How do you stop them from damaging the resilience of your organisation in their keenness to seal the deal? How many conversations do they have, business meetings with potential partners, social and other discussions, as part of the whole preparatory process, for which they are not prepared or informed, or during which they let their guard down and allow information to seep across to someone who may potentially be a competitor? The focus on getting the business will, in their view, override other considerations, and sometimes issues such as security, continuity and other hindering processes may not particularly be within their field of vision. This is dangerous silo thinking. This is not about lines of control within the organisation, or management discussions about line diagrams and who reports to whom. This is about thinking only about one element of a continuous and merged process that together will protect the business and allow it to grow. An unguarded and immature approach to building relationships and to setting up partnerships with those who are external to our organisation and who may cause damage in the longer term is, frankly, stupid. And we should also ensure that we consider the negative effects of this within the organisation, where impacts may also be felt.

Your Field of Vision - maintaining your focus

Growth
Beat competition
Market and advertise
Bring in and use talent
Seize opportunities
Global activity
Innovate
Exploit technology

Outside your Field of Vision?

Competitor intelligence gathering
Fraud and scam
Insider risks
Cyber exposure and risks
Joint venture and partnership resilience

Outside your Field of Vision?

Logistic and supply chain risks and gaps
Governance and legislative change
Political impacts
Social change
Threats and adversaries

Your focus: Achieve the Business Aim

Figure 26: Field of vision

Within your organisation there will be a legitimate and required focus on the things that the business needs to do to achieve its aims. The workforce will be as focused on their own work as you will be on yours, and the activities that they are required to carry out. In looking outward, but in keeping and maintaining focus and effort only on their own areas, they perhaps will not notice or be aware of the risks and threats that may be lurking around and outside their field of vision.

In the resilience context, where we are seeking to maintain our organisational 'life', this aspect of behaviour needs to be monitored and managed. Our people may simply not be aware that everything that they do will have attendant issues or risks that could have damaging effects upon the organisation. So, if they cannot see what is out there, first of all you will need to be their eyes, and second, you need to try to get them to widen their field of vision to include the threats.

I think it is a law of physics that widening the field of view reduces focus, or something like that. I think it is also a law of humanity that people concentrate on what interests and rewards them. So, you have a real challenge to try to make this work.

You may be mentally nodding your head here because I can bet that you have either been involved in or have witnessed situations like this – where your organisation has chased the result and forgotten about the disablers that may damage the organisation in the longer term. So, when we're thinking about knocking down the silos, we need to think not only about the traditional ideas of management within the organisation, but also, and critically importantly, about getting our own people to open their field of vision and to understand the various blended issues affecting us in the wider context. But, make no mistake, this will be a challenge, because you're going to have to convince those who are chasing the dollar that they must consider things more widely. The target-driven, results-focused organisation with which you are probably involved, has little time for you and your resilience principles, which basically add friction and slow down processes. This is where you must be a thinker once again. More importantly, this is where you must begin to influence your colleagues that they themselves need to start thinking a little more and working away from their own mental checklist about how to swing the deal. Maybe this is aspirational, and maybe we should just settle for the fact that we should come in later and bolt on the various solutions to the problems that are engendered during negotiation and partnership processes.

However, it would be better if we could really influence the organisation to break down silos.

But this is all really tricky, because in simple terms, we are back to the same old principle that human beings are going to spoil your fun and frustrate your efforts. Everyone within your organisation at your level wants to do better than you. Some people within your organisation at your level, and those who are below you, who want to fill your shoes, want to see you fail. There is no point in becoming paranoid about this because it's just one of those facts of life. So you need to consider how you make it work, so that you do not fail, so that the organisation does not fail, and so that we meet the target of achieving resilience. And, fundamentally, forget about what others may have as their objectives for you; consider your own thinking and actions.

Thinking your way out of it

When I worked in a university, some time ago, someone who was involved in the more 'artistic' educational programmes that we provided used the term 'non-creatives' for those who were not involved in that arty type of activity. I thought that was a bit disparaging, and this got me thinking and starting to consider whether we are creative enough in our thinking within resilience and related activities and functions. Clearly, we are bound by regulation and legislation, and the need to provide specific asset-protection functions to our employers, clients and stakeholders. But do we need to adhere rigidly to frameworks in our thought processes, or could we be more creative in our approach to providing protection for organisations?

So, the question is: where else can we provide creative approaches to our business and functions? Where does creative and innovative thought allow us to really add value to organisational capability? We have, I think, endured endless discussions on the various functions of resilience management and its place within the organisation, and I think that the fostering of creativity and of new approaches to the problems that face resilience may be something that can add real value. Although we seem to accept that we can expect various levels of buy-in or otherwise from our organisations, there must be new ways of doing things that will really allow us to align with organisational priorities, to develop excellence and, thus, a real and meaningful capability to protect assets and ensure organisational survival.

Of course, there will be obstacles. There always are. However, a creative and innovative approach – the new way of looking at things – may provide us with ways to overcome those obstacles and to achieve our objectives in a more efficient and effective way than perhaps we have done in the past – or even are doing now. There, then, is the challenge: creativity is not the sole domain of advertising people and designers, and perhaps we should develop and claim a little bit of creativity for ourselves. It is a fundamental personal and organisational trait for progress in challenging circumstances.

The concept of creative dissent

Although we continue to talk about the positioning and acceptance of resilience management (you know: getting the c-suite to buy-in, developing aligned programmes, contribution to bottom line, etc.), perhaps we should be considering other management issues that could help our organisations. If we can assume that we leave our egos at home and save our 'look at me, I'm great' approach for our kids, and try to be brave enough to accept that sometimes there is risk in ordinary management decision processes (failure and blame), then there may be some helpful approaches to take that may really help to move you and your organisation forward.

One of these could be the adoption and encouragement of creative dissent. It is easy to be a yes-man/-woman; letting decisions go by without rocking the boat can avoid getting you noticed for the wrong reasons and stop you being picked on when the accusations begin to fly. But it can be extremely useful to sometimes challenge the decisions that you are faced with and to contribute your own opinions and ideas. So why don't more people do it? Why do people tend to put up with bad ideas (and bad management decisions) and their consequences – making their views known only to their colleagues in hushed tones, or their spouses when they get home at the end of another frustrating day? Is it fear, is it blame culture, or is it over-caution?

Perhaps, for many – especially the good old standard ex-military and law-enforcement types – there is a hard-wired response to decisions from above that ensures that we do what we are asked to the best of our ability – because that is the way that success is measured in our experience. Deference shows that we are mirroring our leaders; and that is the way to get ahead. For others, it is fear of the blame game, or maybe even of losing status by rocking the boat – which could mean that they fear becoming left out of the decision-making process completely. And that fear is certainly not without justification; I have seen it and experienced it.

But what about the tried and tested methods of debate and discussion? Why not question decisions and offer creative alternatives? Why do many managers find it difficult to indicate to their hierarchy that there could be another way? Can dissent ever be creative, or is it always seen in a negative light in your organisation and stamped out? Does your top team see you as an innovator and contributor, or as the person or department who is constantly pushing back? Is the perception that you are like that based on thinking that you have a negative attitude rather than a wish for improvement? I suppose it depends upon your organisation and how much risk is involved – how much is at stake for you? Only you can make that judgement, but one of the worst feelings possible is looking back and wishing that you had done things differently when you had the opportunity. And if not now, when will you take it?

Summary

The resilience sectors are, like any other, congested with their fair share of static thinkers and pontificators. Networks are strong, and there are many who feel that they are entitled to recycle their experience and second-hand knowledge. I am of the firm opinion that this is a major contributor to a general lack of ability to move forwards. Entrenched views, preferred approaches and dogma simply impede the ability to think and act differently. I am convinced that the current prevalence of particular types of people is not only untenable, but has the potential to cause real and damaging effects when properly tested.

This, of course, gives an opportunity to think about and apply a little ingenuity and freshness of approach. Unless you want things to stay as they are; I certainly do not. It is perhaps depressing, perhaps unsurprising, that in the second edition of *Resilient Thinking*, I reviewed this and the following chapter and left them fundamentally unchanged from the first publication ten years earlier. Despite all the accelerated changes and surprises that shouldn't have happened, but did, in that decade, the same old networks are in place with the same behaviours and the same ideas. Many of the networks that follow them repeat the same behaviours and recycle the same arguments and activities with only limited innovation. It shouldn't surprise us that checklisters roam the Earth, and that the issues that we discussed here are the great immovables. But they are. There are too many people working in resilience who are out of their depth and knowledge set. To avoid becoming a checklister, become a thinker and challenge the normalcies that expose us and our organisations to risk, and will do so ad infinitum, unless you make the change.

I believe that the great hope for resilient thinking will come in the new approaches that those who were born from 2005 onwards or thereabouts will bring. With new attitudes, different mindsets, openness and flexibility, perhaps the necessary change will come. In the meantime, as the climate closes in, our accepted world order fragments and economies, wars and viruses cripple our societies, we cannot stand by and wait for the new thinking to arrive. We need to move on from conventional thinking; it is of little value to us.

Here are your resilient thinker think points from this chapter:

1. In your personal and organisational planning for incidents and issues, to what extent do checklists and frameworks form the basis of proposed actions?

2. How important, do you personally think, is it to have the flexibility to go 'off-piste' when circumstances change?

3. To what extent do you think that checklists and frameworks have advantages over 'off-piste' thinking and actions?

4. In your organisation (and assuming that silos exist in some areas), what is your assessment of the need for them? Who espouses them and why?

5. To what extent is dissent or disruptive thinking tolerated or accepted in your organisation, if at all? Do you think it should be?

CHAPTER 8: PROBLEMS AND RESPONSES

> *"We cannot solve our problems with the same thinking we used when we created them."*
>
> **Albert Einstein**

Resilient thinking is about considering and finding ways to overcome impacts and to meet the challenges that risks throw at us. In this chapter, we consider the issues related to some core risk problems – we're also going to review some ideas about the stasis of thought that we need to overcome to be effective. The need to face problems and to be able to come up with solutions is without doubt a challenge; but responding to problems does need that thinking approach. Being able to look beyond what is presented to us as guidance, good practice and frameworks to follow, is an essential attribute of resilient thinking.

A little analysis can go a long way and may differentiate between the successful and the failed response.

Facing problems

At this stage and reflecting the general approach that we have taken in *Resilient Thinking*, we are not going to provide any checklists, or refer you to any standards or any other framework answers to difficult questions. This is not because frameworks do not have value – they do. However, the idea is that we need to consider the thinking processes that need to be undertaken or at least considered by an effective resilience professional who is going to make the effort to work over and above what somebody else has written for them. The next thing for them to do is to use what is provided between their ears to ensure that any resilience processes, planned or otherwise, are successful. There are not going to be any great psychological theories proposed, but if, by the end of this chapter, you are thinking a little bit more than you were at the start of it, then we are getting somewhere.

You can devise all the risk management processes in the world, as many BIA lists as you can handle and have plans everywhere, but if you haven't faced up to the problems that are facing you before you start any resilience process, then you are going to miss your mark completely. While pulling together this book, I have been asking a few questions about attitudes to risk, continuity, disaster recovery or whatever definition you would like to overlay onto the organisational ability to survive and operate. It is staggering, truly staggering, that so many people, who are so well respected, insist upon imposing their own view upon others and on recommending systems and processes (often, but not always) that they themselves have devised, as the solution to all our problems. And it is not just rogue individuals, but whole organisations that can demonstrate those behaviours. I think that's a little conceited, and although we absolutely should refer to the expertise that exists within the industry, we should also be a little iconoclastic. Nothing and no-one is beyond question; no organisation should be above some disruptive thinking; there is no rationale for resistance or refusal to improve capability through innovation.

Risk assessment, risk management and impact analysis are some of those particular areas that generate much discussion from the 'experts' about what can be included when scoping the problem and what perhaps cannot. Some will argue that you cannot assess the probability of threats becoming a risk with any degree of accuracy; some are convinced that the requirement to scope out every risk or potential problem is absolutely essential to the survival of an organisation. Others say that we are wasting time considering every possible option for risk and impact and response to them, and that we should have plans that are fairly generic, and which can be adapted to suit the particular incidents that may affect us. There are, of course, reasons for these views above and beyond the normal 'do it because I say it is right'; there are also time and resource constraints that mean that some organisations cannot expend the time and effort on facing as many problems as they should. It is all understandable, reasonable and normal; there are many drivers, as we have discussed, for perceptions, views and attitudes. What we need to do is think about getting around the blockages and obstructions that are put in our way.

I am quite perplexed and am still trying to understand what this issue is that some people have with actually facing up to problems. What is wrong with considering everything that can go wrong and at least thinking about it? Why is it so difficult to understand that things can happen to you, that it is not always going to be someone else, and that, consequently, you need to be prepared? It's not really a difficult concept to understand – the fact that you need to expend some brainpower and think about things a little more. The COVID-19 pandemic again raises its head as an example of an initial inability to respond effectively, helping it to spread and develop. In hindsight, there may not have been many options to take; however, the fact remains that the response could have been more effective and better than it was. The thinking was not as effective as it could be.

Personally, I'm a big believer in the brainstorm. Why not get every stakeholder with a particular interest in, or functional responsibility for, a particular problem together into a room, or even a bar, and think about the issues facing your organisation frankly and openly? Why not leave egos at the door and value everyone's input? Why not consider the delivery driver's view of issues within your logistics chain? Why not discuss with the head of cleaning services the routines and issues that are related to janitorial work within your organisational building, where they go and what they do, and any related resilience issues? The 'why not' will tend to be around the inability to understand that even those outside decision groups have ideas; they may not have a say in things, but they may have some answers. And look at your plans, look at them right now, and consider whether they are really fit to meet the problems that are facing you. If they aren't, it is time to get your thinking cap on.

Thinking

You're not really doing as much thinking about things as perhaps you may believe. If we do accept that most of us are conditioned by what we do, our life view and our need to make our lives simpler and easier than they might be, we fit results into what suits us, our ambition and our comfort. We shape our actions to make us feel better about what we do. But we need to think more widely than the self-centre. Building on the idea of creativity that we mentioned earlier, it helps to be creative in considering the types of events that may happen and cause damage to an organisation. The problems that can be caused by underestimating or misestimating will far outweigh any time, effort and thought that you have expended on this kind of activity.

Clearly, overestimating can be as bad as not thinking enough; it can cost time and money – but that's risk for you. But in general, over*thinking* is not something that is a negative. Sometimes it is worthwhile noodling around with ideas and concepts to find the answers. Thinking is not a bad thing, and like education, is an investment well-made.

The types of events that can affect business are wide and varied, and can arise without any particular level of warning. The types of triggers for an event that could face an organisation are normally and quite effectively grouped by most into the areas covered by PESTEL/PESTEL-type risk assessments. As with everything else, we do need to dig a little deeper than the headline. There are many subdivisions and sub-types of events that can occur under these main 'headings', and it is prudent to plan for as many as possible that may affect the organisation. Before planning to respond, it is sensible to conduct the risk assessment in the first phase of activity. We'll come back to risk later in the chapter, but being a thinker and being creative, suffice it to say at this stage that all possible events that may have a potential impact on the organisation should be considered. It is also useful here to ponder terms, such as 'trigger', which may summon a vision of a rapid, kinetic or 'explosive' event. These threats will be no less serious than those which arise rapidly, and they need to be considered, catered for and managed.

It's worth remembering at this point also that it may not all be bad. Sometimes the outcomes of events will provide us with the ability to move forward from where we were, having identified where the problems were and learned the lessons. It would be preferable if we were able to learn the lessons from other organisations, rather than from our own, but sometimes it happens that way. I think that the proactive and competitive organisation should seek to take every advantage from what a negative outcome may initially be, and aim to improve processes and, thus, performance, by the introduction of commensurate learning processes. So, not only should we be looking forward to what may be coming next, but we should be looking around us to see who else has succumbed to the various pitfalls of operating against the background of risk. The 'landscape' in every sector is littered with the burning wreckage of poor risk planning and the outcomes of actions taken or omitted from a response.

Event and incident blending

A lot of people use mental pictures to envisage formats and timelines for their response processes; some even write them down. And, although the overall responses of organisations should be to anticipate, respond and recover sufficiently from an event, there is probably a prevalent view in many businesses that responses should be phased or time sequenced. This reflects the widely held, but erroneous, view that the components of resilience are completely different and separate. Admittedly there are different functions, specialisms, lines of activity, resource processes and degrees of understanding required – but are they really all that different?

Sometimes it can be useful to stop and take stock. Look at your own business or organisation and ask yourself a question: 'Do things flow here?' Initially, and probably in many of its core activities, the flow will be there. It may differ in different areas, departments and business units. But in terms of your general organisational activities, and the synergies and linkages between various components and departments, do things move as smoothly and as well as they could? What could be done better, more efficiently and with more support from the whole team – top to bottom? How can you take what is probably a multidiscipline activity and make it work like the purring, well-oiled machine that you want your stakeholders to believe it is? And is your current flow an illusion based on the stories that the organisation tells itself?

As with most management models and processes, a good place to start is by understanding what your organisation actually means to itself. Is it all about profit, or does it have nobler, philanthropic motives? Is the pursuit of excellence the driver for everything that happens? Are your people allowed to fail, or do you live and operate in a blame culture where, when things go wrong, the priority is finding out whose fault it was, rather than addressing the problem? If you can understand who you are, and if your team can understand who they are, and what they are trying to achieve, then you probably have a fighting chance of putting in place and following processes that allow you all to achieve, at least, most of the things that you are trying to do. If you do not know what you are doing, and if you do not know what you're aiming for, then you do not really need to worry about what is blocking you from getting there. This is simply because there is unlikely to ever be a realistic chance of you getting there.

If we apply the same general questions that are discussed above to your organisational resilience functions, then you have potential for failure right across the board. If you do not understand what you are doing your activities for, who can play their part, how and why, and if you do not have some latitude for error, at least in the planning stages, then you are probably doomed, if not to failure, then at least to continual crisis management as your norm. So, how do we make resilience flow? Do we actually need to make resilience flow, or is it a case that the blockages are built in because of what it is and how it needs to be implemented across the organisation? Straightforwardly, do we think that we are at a point now where we have a good general understanding of the applications and requirements for effective resilience management at least on paper – or do we have many miles to go? And if we do have many miles to go – what is the best route to a satisfactory destination? Perhaps we can come back to thinking about planning.

A good plan should result in a truly resilient organisation. Planning represents preparedness; thinking about what could come next and having the resources and the will to be able to recover from incidents and events that may impact upon the organisation. Devising a comprehensive, fit-for-purpose and effective plan is a complex process; however, many organisations really do not expend an appropriate amount of time and effort (not to mention money) on planning. As we have mentioned quite a few times now, what you do is a pain in the backside for your organisation – most find your work inconvenient at best, unwanted at worst – and, if you're unlucky, a waste of money. Given that challenge, one that is inherent to resilience work, the high stakes require high levels of effort.

If we were to take the easy option we could write a plan, publish it without involving any effort or input from other organisational departments and distribute it. Into the drawer it goes, the plan is written, never to be seen again. Easy? Yes. Effective? No, and no again. The good news is that effective planning for resilient organisations – and all their functions – is achievable. The bad news is that it is most definitely not easy. As a resilience professional, planning is a fundamental part of your job that you need to get right.

Planning is not 'sexy' in the same way that installing a fantastic new surveillance/access control/detection system/software program may be, or organising and running the protection for one of your organisation's main movers on an overseas trip. It is certainly not as profile building as you wearing your best clothes as you win a little Perspex trophy at your in-house awards. But if you do not invest the necessary time and effort – and get your organisation to do the same using your knowledge, experience, capability and charm – then you can forget the sexy jobs and the awards because you probably won't have a job at all; and you certainly will not be a winner.

For the resilient thinker, the devising of the plan that protects the organisation – top to bottom, inside out and reaching out to its external linkages – should be the ultimate challenge and its success the ultimate reward. This means that there is an investment required in time and effort on your part. You can ask for inputs; you can get other people to write it for you and you can devolve some of the responsibility for producing subcomponents to other people. However, in the final analysis, you can outsource a great deal, but you cannot outsource diligence. As a resilient thinker, as a resilience professional, it is you who will lead your organisational capability. It may never be fully recognised, and you may wait a long time for your work to be appreciated and to demonstrate benefits. However, it will come if you do your job well.

So, we're back to planning fundamentals again. Now some people may think I'm contradicting myself here because a plan is a checklist; and I'll concede that to some extent that is true, but the plan that is put together and used solely as a checklist will be flawed. It will be expected to happen in a certain way, to certain timescales, using certain resources.

A good plan, an effective plan, is to use that cliché, a 'living document', and that means that checklists are out. Checklists are for those who have trouble thinking aide memoires are needed by those who cannot remember things. If we turn to thinking about your plans and how they are written (if, that is, they are your responsibility), answer these questions:

> **Did you write it yourself? And is that a good or bad thing?**
>
> **Did you start from a blank page? And is that a good or bad thing?**
>
> **Did you copy and paste any content? And is that a good or bad thing?**
>
> **Did you have it checked and verified? Will it work?**
>
> **Did you let both internal and external stakeholders know where it is?**

Figure 27: Some questions about planning

There will be various responses to the question. But, as an example, if you did cut and paste, then it isn't your plan. You cannot possibly understand it as well as someone who has designed and delivered their bespoke plan. Think about when you make a presentation or must deliver a briefing that someone else has written – it is never the same as one that you have written yourself. You will falter, have blank moments and perhaps bluff your way through, but it is not and never will be from your mind. If you're responsible for developing the plan and you do not know it (and that goes for the 'owner' of every sub-plan of yours), then it won't work. So, perhaps you can see that it is crucial that you ensure that your 'buy-in' to this is real. To make plans work, you must get people to really contribute based upon a commitment, which means that investing in the idea of doing it properly is crucial. Remember always (silos again) that all the other departments that you will deal with are interested in getting on with their jobs, and not necessarily in helping you with yours, so you need to think very carefully about how you can make it all work.

The cut-and-paste epidemic is quite a thing. Not so long ago, and some of you won't remember this, when we were writing plans and documents, we actually used to cut paragraphs and sentences from previous versions of documents and paste them into our new updated copies before having them retyped in a new format. Believe me, this used to be the quickest, and probably the most efficient, way of getting large documents updated and amended. Of course, nowadays cut-and-paste means highlighting a section, a couple of clicks and moving information around. That makes it even easier than the old way. That, in turn, makes it a seductive and widespread method of changing someone else's material to suit you. Cut-and-paste is a cheat, and if you cheat your organisation in a resilience context, then at some point the cheating will be exposed by an error or omission. The question that you really and honestly must ask yourself is: 'Am I prepared to compromise or am I going to do things properly?' With all the pressures that we all face in our daily lives, the temptation to take the easier route is there. However, compromise is by its nature a dilution of purpose; and when purpose is needed, it can negatively affect outcomes.

No matter how you get to the point of putting your plan together, whether you've imagined, plagiarised, listened to a checklister, become a checklister, included lots of experience, consulted all areas, understood the business, cut and pasted, etc. you will have a type of plan as an output. If it is a big, thick document with lots of drawings, some colour and maybe even some pictures, you may well feel justified in standing back with a degree of pride and feeling that you have achieved your aim. Of course, that depends on what your aim is; if you want to keep the bosses happy with some lovely desktop publishing to meet a tenuous audit requirement, then you could be in clover. Equally, and probably conversely, you need to have put in place something that is going to work. Plans come in various types and forms, but I think there are some pretty standard types that most current plans match. The types of plans and how they are implemented can combine or can be combined to positive or negative effects with various shades of impact.

Here are some:

Bad plan with no implementation. You probably have a sizeable problem here. The quality of the plan will not really matter because nobody is reading or using it. As it is a bad plan it is likely that there will not have been much thought or knowledge put into it.

Bad plan with partial implementation. In this case you will have some elements of the organisation doing bad things, some doing bad things partially and some doing nothing effective.

Bad plan with full implementation. Perhaps the biggest problem. This will probably give the same effect as would a bad plan with no implementation. However, if you have spent time, effort, and money on training and implementing the plan, it has cost you twice.

Good plan with no implementation. All the time, effort, and money you have invested here is meaningless. Nobody is using it.

Good plan with partial implementation. We're still not there yet. Everything is written and the right people have been consulted. It's all good. For some of the organisation anyway...

Good plan with full implementation. Relax. Good work all round and money well spent. I don't think so – how long do you think a good plan will remain relevant? Can you maintain the effort to implement it fully in the long-term?

Figure 28: Bad plan, good plan

The fact is that the best plans in the world are only as good in time and space as at the point when you devise them. Your plan will match one place, one time and one set of people focused on one particular mission. The key to writing effective plans is that it requires work, work and more work. Reaching the nirvana of the effective plan will need you to exercise all your skills and to think, really think, about it.

Thinking like your problem

I believe that in order to be able to plan effectively, you need to think like your problem. Clearly, a risk is not a thinking entity. That is true to some extent, unless a premeditated malicious act is being carried out against your organisation. However, a problem that may develop into a real crisis or serious incident is often the result of various influences, actions and consequences. But there is a tendency for problems to behave in ways that we cannot predict. Firstly, problems will fill the gaps that you leave. You can guarantee that if you have a hole in your plan, if you haven't thought of something (or cannot be bothered), then the problem will find it, squeeze into it, and bring complexity and difficulty to your resilience efforts. Understanding that vulnerability is a crucial and critical aspect of effective resilient thinking.

Secondly, problems rarely do what you ask them to. Just because you have a plan in place, and just because you have allocated resources to that particular plan, it does not necessarily mean that the problem that you are facing is going to respond to or be mitigated by the plan's implementation. You need to be ready for that. So you need to consider – do you have contingencies for your contingencies, and do you have backup plans for your backup plans? Have you identified gaps? What you do need to do is to think about where gaps might be, about their potential extent and depth. Also, what caused the gaps in the first place? All of these are considerations of the fluidity, complexities and traits of risks that are caused by dynamics, influences and consequences.

Thirdly, a problem will only get worse if you leave it unattended. If you choose to ignore a small problem, you can guarantee that it will become a big problem. As a resilience professional, you do not really want to be facing big problems. I believe that it is far better to be able to mitigate and reduce problems when they are small and relatively ineffectual, before they become huge and unmanageable. It's common sense really, but it is surprising that human nature will often blind us to the fact that a problem is there – we worry about facing it, we sometimes refuse to really consider all the issues that are involved and then it is too late. Therefore, when you're coming up with your planning process and when you're thinking about all these great ideas you can use to manage the problem, you need to also consider some of the 'what-ifs?'. What will be the consequences of getting your planning wrong (and some of your planning will always be wrong)? And you need to think carefully, honestly and self-critically to ensure that you avoid the issues caused by not facing reality.

Questions that help and hinder

What happens if I do it?   **What happens if I don't do it?**

What happens if I wait?   **What happens if I get it wrong?**

Will it be my fault?   **Who can help?**

Figure 29: What happens?

Being brave and addressing the issues of consequence is a fundamental component of thinking and successful resilience. If you are arrogant, unknowledgeable, ignorant, stupid or crazy enough to consider that you will be able to put in place a foolproof plan, guess who the fool will be? Your aim should be to be able to answer these questions with care and clarity.

8: Problems and responses

Risks

At this point, I would like to come back to one of the fundamental areas of contention in resilience: the often-discussed, argued-over and mangled subject of risk assessment.

In modern society, general threats become risks with impact at international and national strategic levels, but also they can have adverse effects on individual organisations, groups of businesses and other enterprise organisations. This is because the consequential impacts of these risks have the potential to spread beyond initial points of protection failure and even to change in effect as they move onwards and develop from their causal point of origin. Therefore, it is important to recognise and act upon such threats before they become too difficult to manage, control and mitigate. There are thousands and millions of threats and risks, multiple combinations of various elements that can have an effect or impact upon any organisation. Some people get themselves all tangled up in debates about whether a threat is equal to a risk, whether a risk is a threat, whether either of them are valid planning tools. Some people and organisations never even consider any aspect of it. Most need to understand the whole thing with increased and improved clarity and application of thought.

It's my view that risk assessment and risk management have a crucial role to play in limiting the effects of threats upon organisations. A considered and forward-looking risk management process with realistic and flexible mitigation planning will provide an organisation with the ability to evaluate emerging risks, and to put in place effective countermeasures and associated processes and procedures. It sort of makes sense that an ability to consider the multiplicity of issues that could influence the organisation, and to plan based upon that consideration, is better than doing nothing at all. This is also preferable to ignoring a particular element or type of risk just because we do not believe in risk management as a valid management tool. And it is important to know that there are some evangelists who have no confidence in risk management at all, as they see it as guesswork and an inexact science. Of course risk management is not a science, neither is it an art. It is a knowledge-enabled skill.

There is no doubt that there are some grey areas, and that the whole issue of resilience risk, threat and management is complex and evolving. It necessitates concerted efforts to provide any chance of countering the threats and limiting their effectiveness. However, this is not to say that focused and well-thought-out planning and preparation cannot be effective in managing risks to satisfactory (note I have not said 'perfect') conclusions. Primarily, fundamental to any successful planning and implementation of response and mitigation measures is the need to ensure that activities are based upon correct assessment. This could be achieved by making some attempt to mitigate risks either by manipulating the threat (which is unlikely), or by configuring the organisation to respond or protect itself and its processes so that it can maintain resilience – and that seems to make sense.

If we want to ensure that we can limit the damage and continue to operate, then we should consider the option of using the full range of risk management functions. However, there is some credence to be given to the anti-risk evangelist view that unpredictability is one of several factors that can hamper effective risk management. And risk management also requires agility of thought and a degree of commitment from the target organisation itself, which may not be forthcoming. In effect, risk management itself runs the risk of being ineffective; much like any other dynamic process. Those who say that you cannot estimate with a great degree of accuracy the elements of risk or threat that have the potential to affect your organisation really believe that, and with some reason. However, the complexity does not simply lie in the difficulty in thinking about forecasting. The capability to manage a fluid and dynamic situation effectively can often be hampered by the fact that we put in place mental frameworks and images to characterise our ideas. To illustrate, let's talk about the classic, simplistic interpretation of risk assessment.

THE BASIC RISK TRIANGLE

Figure 30: Risk triangle

Here we have a simple risk triangle. There are three main and interlinked components:

1. **Probability (or whatever you want to call it)** – the degree to which something may happen.
2. **Impact (or whatever you want to call it)** – the degree to which there is an effect.

3. Management (or whatever you want to call it) –
options for dealing with risk.

This type of diagram and variants of it are very useful to
allow us to consider risks and what we can do about them.
It's really straightforward – guess the probability, ask
around and see what the impacts might be, then simply plan
a response. I think that for some individuals and
organisations that really does give the illusion of having
completed a complex risk assessment.

Now that has been set into your head as a template diagram
that provides an illustration of the linkage between various
elements of risk management. If this is the way you've been
taught to view risk management, then the next thing you
start to do is to put values on it. So, if you have been taught
that you should assign numbers or values to each of the
three sides of the triangle and then multiply them together,
then you've begun to think that everything should be
mathematical. In fact, a lot of organisations rely upon this
mathematical interpretation of this simple risk triangle and
its outcomes by multiplying numbers and then producing
easy-to-interpret values. It is literally formulaic and
simplistic.

In reality, the risk triangle should look different and be
more complex. Even thinking about the simplest of risks
may involve many sub-facets and influences that may help
you to come to a valid conclusion only if you consider them
in detail. But, of course, a risk dodecahedron would be a
terrible thing. If we assume that we are going to use a risk
triangle, then we can redraw it with all the additional
thoughts and intangibles that make it a more useful,
thought-provoking diagram. In other words, although it's
more difficult and takes a little more thought, you can take

something simple and, by using your head, transform it into an effective assessment and management 'tool'. And if you're going to use tools, they may as well be effective and fit for purpose.

THE THINKING RISK TRIANGLE

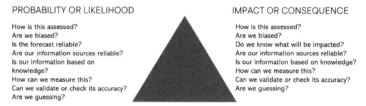

PROBABILITY OR LIKELIHOOD

How is this assessed?
Are we biased?
Is the forecast reliable?
Are our information sources reliable?
Is our information based on knowledge?
How can we measure this?
Can we validate or check its accuracy?
Are we guessing?

IMPACT OR CONSEQUENCE

How is this assessed?
Are we biased?
Do we know what will be impacted?
Are our information sources reliable?
Is our information based on knowledge?
How can we measure this?
Can we validate or check its accuracy?
Are we guessing?

MITIGATION, MANAGEMENT OR CONTROLS

Do we know how to mitigate based on our assessment of Probability and Impact?
Are we physically and financially resourced to mitigate the risks that we believe we have identified?
Have we analysed and considered *in depth* what will need to be done and what further impacts there may be?
Are we prepared really? Not lip service or written plans that we have not questioned. But really prepared?

Figure 31: Risk triangle added

This annotated version of the same outline diagram provides us with a lot more to think about, and, if we take a self-critical approach when putting together a risk and threat model, then we will be in a far better place to provide a plan for the organisation that will really meet its needs. By incorporating enabling questions, which in themselves should generate further enabling questions, we make things more complicated, but arguably more effective.

Thinking again about numbers, I for one am not really convinced that we can simply put a numerical value on probability and impact alongside management, and then throw them into a simple equation and produce effective outputs. So, instead, we write down something like *Figure 32*.

Figure 32: Risk equation and formulaic thinking – How variable are the numbers and their meanings?

Figure 32 does look straightforward, easy to understand and useful. But what can happen if it is done incorrectly is, first of all, that we can assign incorrect values to all the elements. Those values may have been hurriedly thought out or not thought out much at all. This, in turn, will automatically skew any effective assessment outcomes. The trap here is that we are going for a simple numerical ranking process, whereby it is easy for us to consider the risks with the highest value in simple terms and deal with them. But, if we haven't done the assessment correctly, then it does not mean anything. Any one of those figures, when incorrectly assessed, can cause the assessment to be incorrect overall. Too low and you are going to have gaps and you are going to fail. Too high and you will expend disproportionate effort and resources – neither is good. I was never very good at maths at school – but if you are, then why don't you think about this and figure out how many different permutations of numbers you can achieve for a particular risk, if you set values of between one and ten for the three elements of risk assessment? And, if you think even more carefully about this, then you can probably see that multiple permutations can create multiple uncertainties. It follows, then, that the basis of a good risk assessment process and plan requires us to address accurately all the variables on that framework, and then apply them to the organisation honestly and in a thinking, self-critical way.

We have looked at many facets of a complicated problem, and I think we can agree that the components of the whole planning and resilience question need to be subject to deep and detailed evaluation. And, of course, this takes time. However, we need to be clear about some simple requirements. Invest the time, effort and thought, and your plan will have a good chance of working – if you cannot afford the time, effort, energy and worry of doing this process in detail, then you need to be able to prepare for the consequences. You have some simple options.

You always have options

Do nothing. Is this always a 'no go' option?

Let someone else worry about it. Often used, but what are the potential problems?

Put in place some appropriate measures.

Put in place every measure that you can think of.

Figure 33: Options

All of these options will be attractive to you at various levels and times, and for various reasons. What you decide to do is your choice, based upon all the influences and concerns you face. Whichever one you choose, there will be consequences. These consequences will vary in severity, speed and impact. But be under no illusion – they will be there.

The pond and the pebble

We talked about forward thinking earlier in the book, and hopefully we are warming to the idea that we need to consider consequences. When I mentioned to my wife what would be in the contents list for this book and talked about the pool and the pebble she said to me, "That's a bit of a cliché." I agreed (I always agree with her, actually – it works), but, as we already know, clichés get used for many things that we use a lot and normally use because they are useful! So, we're going to pause on the bank of a notional pond and reflect upon what happens when a pebble is thrown into it. Where does the pebble end up? Does it affect the top, middle and bottom layers, and where do the ripples go? Also, what happens when the ripples hit the edge of the pond? We're going to take this analogy to its absolute limit now. You can approach it in two ways, I suppose: either as an illustration of impact and consequential effect (which you should be thinking of in your planning), or, if you like and it's your day off, as a little story about a peaceful, still pond and its shattered tranquillity.

Your organisation is metaphorically the pond. It has a surface – the thing that is discernible to the outside world – and this will, ideally, be tranquil and calm. However, under the surface is where the action is: big fish, little fish and all sorts of different pond life with different motivations and life cycles are moving around in there. Some are reliant on others to survive and operate; others will be working fairly unilaterally in their actions. On the edges of the pond will be all the other organisms that depend on the pond to exist. Plants, animals and the pond itself will need to survive by being fed a regular supply of water and other nutrients, sustenance, resources and energy, including sunlight. No matter how big the pond is, no matter what depends on it to survive, the pond must rely on others to stay alive. In the ideal world, we will have achieved the natural balance, where everybody and everything gets what they need from someone or something else in this system, and the circle of life is maintained. This is your organisation and its multiple dependencies going about their normal routine, daily life and operations.

However, one day, it all changes, and the pebble hits the surface of the pond. It does not really matter where it comes from. It could be thrown, it could have been dropped from space, but it hits the surface and disturbs the pattern of life in the pond. This pebble will affect the balance and structures that exist within the pond, and will have evolved over time because of the following effects.

The size of the pebble is an issue. If it's a tiny little pebble it won't be a real problem. There will probably be limited impact and limited disturbance, and the wider pond will not really be disrupted to any great degree. If the pebble is a big one, things could be different; there will be a big splash with lots of ripples and major disturbance. In a similar way, although one tiny little pebble may not have a major effect, lots of tiny little pebbles impacting the surface at the same time might have a different outcome. There will certainly

8: *Problems and responses*

be additional disruptions in many locations that may challenge stability and calm to some extent.

The depth of penetration into the pond. If our pebble penetrates right down into the depths of the pond and hits the bottom it may well throw up some silt, which could make the water cloudy and difficult to navigate for the pond life. How many layers of pond life will it pass by, or even hit, on its way down? If everyone and everything is lucky, it's just going to go straight to the bottom with minor effect. But life isn't normally about being lucky, and the fact that there will be some impact in some way can never be ruled out or ignored.

What happens when the pebble's effects reach the edge of the pond? If all the ripples that the pebble generates go to the edge of the pond, they can damage the peripheral elements that support and supply the pond itself. How big will the ripples be and to what extent will the damage take place? To what extent will the *status quo* have changed?

The short-term changes can become long-term problems. Let's say that the pebble is a big one, and that it hits the pond's biggest player or predator flush on the head on its way in and down to the bottom. So that player is now out, and we have a gap in the normal process and life of the pond. The balance is disrupted, and a change has taken place that will have long-term effects on the pond itself. Others will fill the gap, and there will be differences, changes and alterations to patterns and processes that previously existed.

So, we can see that there are impacts and consequences from this unforeseen event that has hit our organisation in the form of this pond and caused various problems or issues. What we then need to consider is to make sure that the next time it happens, or has the potential to happen, we put in place some protection or contingency plan. There are probably many ways of ensuring that the pebble does not hit the pond, that it does not penetrate all the way to the bottom, and that the ripples do not hit the edge and cause any further collateral and consequential damage. The trick, of course, is to try to think about how putting in place those measures would impact upon the ecosystem of the pond itself. You need a strategy that does not involve simply filling the pond with concrete. Naturally that would be a solution; however, mitigation by cessation of core activity and purpose is arguably not an optimal solution.

A thinking strategy

'Strategy' is a word that is often used by organisations and their managers to attempt to define the 'big picture' and their long-term aspirations and plans. But, in many cases, although the strategy may have been designed, understood and implemented in some isolation by the higher levels in the organisation, there may not be clarity of understanding (and implementation) at middle and lower levels. Now, this may not be a problem in routine and day-to-day operations, where most employees will be familiar with what they need to do, to what standards and in what timescales, but things can change. When there is considerable pressure in terms of time, resourcing or information demands, coupled with the need to manage and operate in difficult and unfamiliar circumstances, the need to understand the organisation's strategy becomes really important.

Simply and fundamentally, a comprehensive strategy that can be understood and applied throughout the organisation is crucial to the successful management and 'steering' of the business through its routine life, let alone through resilience events. And if you're a manager, this is where you come in. Every organisation, in enacting a strategy, will look to its managers to make things work, to drive processes forward, to understand where you want to be and how you are going to get there, and, in the context of issues related to resilience, you should perhaps consider the planning and implementation issues that we have discussed so far. The reason for this is that when things do go wrong, and the organisation looks to you for solutions, you will need to be able to work to that strategy.

To make things work, effective strategy and subsequent processes should focus on the long-term viability and sustainability of an organisation in both benign and malign environments. Businesses need to be equally effective and robust when things are going badly and when they are going well. And it is important to remember at this point why we are doing all this: we are aiming to maintain operations and our products and services, whatever they may be, and to continue to generate income. It is of minor interest to stakeholders and interested parties *how* the organisation plans to achieve its strategic objectives – what is of interest is that the objectives are achieved to a satisfactory level. Perspectives on corporate strategy and resilience planning may vary in detail, but all should focus on achieving organisational capability in adversity and continuity of critical business functions before, during and after a contingency event. This should ensure an ability to move forward, ideally improving upon pre-event status and leading to strengthened organisational performance.

In effect, the organisational strategy and its success or failure will be critically dependent upon the interactions between itself and various external and internal factors. If there is a real problem, an organisation that only focuses on one or another aspect may find itself in trouble. If the business fails to address its own weaknesses in a timely and appropriate manner, no strategy aimed at reducing external impacts will save it. So, a thinking strategy needs to be put in place. That means one that is sensible, logical, workable and real. You can have all the management-speak in place in your strategies that you will ever need or try to imagine. But you must, absolutely must, ensure that it can transfer into reality. There is of course a challenge with reality; and that is that every one of us has a different reality in our worldview; and that can lead to problems for management.

Research and what it revealed

A few years ago I conducted some research into the readiness of security managers (as good a representative group as any other set of specialists), to envisage the threats facing businesses from emerging risks. I asked a representative number of security managers about their ability to face interconnected future risks and my findings were quite enlightening. Here's what happened.

In assessing the readiness of individuals and organisations to face emerging global and interconnected risks, the study that I carried out not only considered what these security managers and practitioners were capable of visualising and achieving, but also attempted to divine the levels of willingness and foresight to embrace concepts outside their 'comfort zone'. The levels of expertise, experience, and academic and intellectual flexibility, as well as the attitude of respondents to security management as a dynamic function, rather than a reactive checklist-based strategy, was one of the areas that I felt would be a fundamental contributor to their ability to meet the challenges posed –

or, conversely, to their inability to manage issues effectively.

I began by researching the available literature and published works about 'what might be coming' – new and emerging risks that may be beyond their initial experience set – and balancing the published views and conclusions against the results of questions that I asked security managers. It turned out that clear disparities emerged between what is reasonably expected to happen in the future – both near and long term – and the recognition by a significant proportion of the security management grouping that the future would present significant risks to their organisations beyond those which exist at the moment.

Moreover, the view of security as a professionally managed function varied significantly between what my research suggested that the manager needs to function effectively and security management's own view of its capabilities. The evidence was quite strong that there was a real reluctance to engage with risks and to face the difficulties that they may cause. I felt that, from my study, a stance where change resistance appeared to be almost embedded and endemic within businesses did not augur well for the viability of the traditional security function in its current form. And that it created another potential level of vulnerability.

My studies indicated that if the risks were real, dynamic and growing, they didn't seem to be recognised as sufficiently threatening for the security managers to consider significant refinement or review of current practices, and thus to change approach, attitude and knowledge levels. Despite being provided with a list of emerging risks that could affect them, security managers, in indicating that their focus had not shifted from traditional security threats, gave a worrying insight into framework thinking. Perhaps more worryingly, there was no significant indication that they would be shifting that focus in new directions in the near future. I thought about this a little more and I concluded that, although unpalatable, this is perhaps understandable; despite the literature making dark predictions, much of it could be (and perhaps justifiably is, to some) considered to be sensationalist and speculative. 'Oil shock', anyone?

Many busy and otherwise focused managers felt that forecasts of major global impacts were difficult to measure and envisage until the events happened. And this led me towards further thoughts and conclusions. I felt that it would be a naive and near-sighted security manager and business organisation that failed by omission or ignorance to notice forecast indicators and to begin to consider meeting new challenges. An example was that despite mention being made of pandemic measures in business planning, there was little real evidence that anything concrete or effective was in effect being done. I think that, as I write this book, most people believe pandemics to be a buzzword, rather than a risk/impact issue.

Although it is simple and straightforward to make such statements in an academic study, change is difficult to achieve in reality because, as we have been discussing, there are not only attitudinal issues, but also knowledge gaps. Despite the literature and general trends in resilience management that aspire towards a better-prepared and more capable profession, the significant element of security personnel, who considered experience to be equally or more viable as a business enabler than academic ability or general business skills, was a depressing indicator of the intellectual and attitudinal strides that will be required to move forward. When individuals do not know what they need, and their own organisation cannot see them as business enablers, but rather as restrictive rule enforcers, there is a significant and worrying danger of both elements missing the point of resilience's existence within a modern and progressive business.

In the same way that emerging risks have converged to form a significant threat to business well-being and security, the threat from within is also because of a convergence of incapability, attitude and ignorance. If it was determined by my study that there is a capability gap, a lack of awareness and a disappointing lack of willingness by managers and their employers to break out of a mould, it would be important to make recommendations that not only recognise that these deficiencies do exist, but also provide a realistic basis for change.

What was more, it was not only that the checklisters had problems in being equipped to face the risks, but it was also clearly evident that the majority of organisations paid a degree of lip service to emerging risks, and were clearly focused on the traditional range of security issues. This understandable approach is a result not only of business bottom-line focus, but also of the poor profile of security managers who need to learn and develop the skills and abilities necessary to link the risks to the business and to persuade the organisation of the value of 'soft skills'. These appeared to be less evident in security management than they should be, and this is where the more enlightened resilient thinker should come in. Because such skills are complementary to the experience and to the core security knowledge and abilities necessary to conduct effective security operations, it is equally essential that businesses and individuals are guided towards recognising and acting upon this need. Communication and engagement skills should be an integral part of any corporate or organisational development programme. It became clear to me that many organisations are sailing ahead without any awareness of the 'icebergs' that may be before them, and, more dangerously, are not consulting or listening to those who could protect them against disaster. Maybe that's because those who could be consulted or listened to have little of value to say.

At the core of this research, and clearly evidenced throughout responses, there lay the issue of conservatism. The experienced second-careerist resilience manager remained indicative of the majority of respondents, and the clear and alarming evidence was that the proportion of those who value experience over education remains high. Responses also indicated that there is almost a blissful and defiant unawareness of formal risk and impact management processes, and of the global effects of security risks. This attitudinal deficiency will, no doubt, be difficult to address and rectify; however, the organisations and individuals involved do need to do this in order to survive and to capitalise on any opportunities that may arise in the long term. Clearly, the 'traditionalist' is poorly equipped to assess and address newly arising issues, and the process of attitudinal reprogramming requires them to recognise not only that they are deficient, but also that they do need to change.

In summary, and to realistically address the disparities between capabilities and risks posed, I concluded that a process of enlightenment is the way ahead. Criminology and traditional risk management are central to the concerns of security managers; willingness to change and to consider emerging risks was a difficult concept for security managers to face. The results of the research indicated not only that emerging risks (assuming that they are real) are continuing to arise, as theorised in published literature, but also that security management is, on the whole, conservative and risk averse. Security is dominated by the narrowly focused, which has little clear recognition not only of the risks, but also of its own educational and development needs. There has, regrettably, been little change in my observation of these traits in the security and other resilience sectors.

Global business is competitive, and global risks can have debilitating and potentially business-fatal consequential effects. Those organisations and individuals that cannot, or will not, recognise the evidence before them, are destined to be less competitive than those that proactively face the challenges. Only when the current minority becomes the future majority, and open and free thought overcomes conservatism, will the linked resilience issues be truly and adequately addressable. The role of the resilient thinker is to make that difference and to address the issues. If you are equipped with an understanding of the task ahead, the attributes of resilience and how to engage with the challenges that are before you; then you are in a promising position for success. As we draw towards the conclusion of the book, I believe that it is important to reflect upon our ability and will to change and to become more than a defensive, static, reactive capability.

Here are your resilient thinker think points from this chapter:

1. In your organisation, to what extent do you think that team members focus on what their own objectives are? How much do you feel that focus may be to the detriment of the strategic organisational objectives?

2. How effective do you feel that the organisational approach to risk may be?

3. To what extent do you assess that those responsible for risk in the organisation understand risks and can therefore manage risks effectively?

4. In your organisation, to what extent are there 'filters' in place that change risk reporting to avoid blame and repercussions?

5. Is your resilience function demonstrably diverse in all respects? Do you think it is time that things changed? Why?

CHAPTER 9: CONCLUSIONS

"You are what you do, not what you say you'll do. "

Carl Jung

Organisational resilience needs expertise and rationality; it needs people who are committed and who understand what both the organisation and they themselves are doing. We need guidance and frameworks, and there is utility in using models, but they need to be used sensibly and carefully, and they need to be applied by thinkers who know what they are aiming for and what they are talking about. I believe that because of the issues we have talked about in this book, there are huge gaps in knowledge, capability and awareness that can cause significant problems. With the evidenced gaps in some areas and the reluctance or inability to engage with threats and to properly protect organisations, there is an opportunity for motivated and capable resilience thinkers to move things forward. If you can see this, and if you think that you fit the requirement, then there must be a place for you.

A significant issue for effective resilience is that of getting over ourselves. The problem, even with resilient thinking, is we just don't know enough about what may come. That said, for every 'Black Swan' there will be a measurable and identifiable probable risk that does not require us to work too hard on predictions. Likewise and perhaps conversely, for every in-place assessment of a management process, there is potential for a more detailed evaluation and analysis of the resilience components and their applications, which may benefit from much more developed organisational understandings. But, overall, we tend to either misunderstand or to actively avoid sharing that understanding unless it is at a price or stokes our own ego.

Looking into the future is problematic. New risks are bubbling up now, they are shifting, changing, linking and disengaging. We know something about some of them, and we know something about ourselves – where our paths cross is a challenging thing to know and predict; and it is vital for us and our organisations to understand that we should and must have a view not only on what that point of intersection may be, but what we know about ourselves to be able to reach the other side of the intersection. In the future, in fact right now, the 'traditional' resilience professional is the tech-savvy and constantly current younger generation. Therefore, there is potential for change to happen and the past of resilience, based on hierarchies and barriers, rather than flexibility and agility in thought and action, may yet fade away. Or we may be seduced along a route that bypasses where the more damaging long-term issues may be. But change *does* compel us to change; resistance to that is naturally detrimental.

Although we can observe change, we also need to anticipate what it may mean. Politically and economically, China is moving more quickly and decisively than ever; the Cold War is back. India and other nations are aligning themselves where they think the wealth and growth will be. Socially, the interconnected global community has found its voice. Economically, the patterns of the twentieth century are being disassembled and changed. Organisationally and individually, the effective resilience response to this is to consider the negative effects of bias, examine our structures and linkages and to have the 'airline experience': lose our baggage. It is a matter of choice, of course, but we should do this because behaviours and attitudes are changing all around us; and we need to keep pace. The inability to recognise and act upon the huge pivot of the twenty-first century will be more than simply harmful; it will be catastrophic.

And when we think about our ability to change, we need to understand whether we really can. One of the things that exercises my mind is the idea that others have a view of what the resilience type of person is. It is often based on the view that resilience people are a certain 'type'. Whether you are thick-skinned or not, should it concern you? I think that it should, because if you generate hostility, apathy or resistance rather than positivity and co-operation, then you will not be the agent for organisational improvement and resilience that you need to be.

We need to think also about the task at hand; and it is not a small one. All organisations, if they are to survive and thrive in adversity, require a resilience 'function' of some sort. It seems inevitable that that function may be performed by an undermanned, undervalued department (and, as such, may be somewhat 'weak'). More rarely, it may be fully resourced and staffed with the capability to meet all issues and to plan and prepare thoroughly and effectively. Some organisational cultures, and the people who work for those organisations, understand and support the resilience function; others all but ignore it, and, in the worst cases, the organisation may be hostile. But, despite all that, we all know that resilience – what we do – is important and that the company cannot go on without it being effective. Resilience is special.

Actually, no it isn't. Resilience is one of many business-enabling functions that is as important as all the others – but it is not special and, when done badly and by poor managers, it can be a liability in time, resource and negativity. As we have discussed, there is a constantly reheated argument as to the effectiveness of the alignment of resilience functions and getting the business to buy in, and to understand, that everyone is on the same side: 'If only (for example) security were more integrated into the rest of the business …/Nobody likes us or understands what we do …/That probably wouldn't have happened if the company had understood security …'

In general, people do understand the need for resilience. They know that theft is wrong, violence is fearful, terrorism is dangerous, and that leaving access doors and computers unlocked is insecure. The problem is that as much as we debate the aspiration for our part of the organisation to be really important, to most people, it just is not. They have lives to lead and jobs to do, and in many cases all that you bring to the party is a niggling inconvenience that they feel that they could quite happily live without. So, when it comes to that perennial 'let's get buy-in and support from the board and get people to understand the huge importance of resilience', we could be debating this for a long time because I am not sure that it is ever going to be a universal trend. Resilience issues happen to other people and therefore you are often representing an abstract concept rather than something tangible for the organisation and its people to think about.

Why do we feel the need to stand at the foot of the table looking upwards at what we perceive to be our more valued colleagues and departments, with a mixture of envy, anger and frustration that they just do not get it? Why don't they understand our role's importance, even though there is a headline resilience issue somewhere in the news every single day? This whole area is debated in depth in varied guises on an almost constant basis, which suggests that something is wrong. But it is mainly debated by us. Outside our community, it is much more difficult to find major debates going on about why businesses should value and integrate resilience more. The main debates in your organisation will be about how much money should or should not be spent, even more than on 'culture', 'buy-in', 'awareness' – because in the main there is no perception of a need to discuss it. You are there, you are needed, you are paid for and you need to do your job. So get on with it and leave people alone; that's what they want.

Procedures can still be effective without anyone caring about them because they must be. Remember our aircraft from Chapter 2? Well, on all aircrafts, procedures are carried out to prepare for take-off, safety briefs are offered to disinterested passengers and, generally, there is that efficient series of activities carried out. Whether the 'culture' of the passengers is aligned or not, and whether they are aware or not – nobody gets off the ground until the checks are complete. Ask the cabin crew whether they feel valued – you know the answer. When things start to go wrong, however, who will the passengers be looking to then?

Life is a journey, and it is probably true for the great majority of us that we will never stop learning. There is an infinite amount of knowledge out there: things that we know from experience, either our own or that of others; things that are there, but we haven't heard about; things that we are taught in training or education; and things that are over the horizon for all of us and we haven't really conceived as yet. I am interested in the mindset of humans as we climb the social and professional ladder: do we start to believe that we do not need to learn so much? Is it sufficient to build a knowledge base and then to finesse that knowledge as we develop?

As we have said previously, we all know someone who thinks that they know something about everything; and in most cases it is probably true that the reality does not necessarily match the self-view of the individual concerned. I personally feel that I learn something new every day – whether it is in my own area of specialism or in general terms – and I actively seek out the development of knowledge and understanding so that I can do my job better – and, in my own case, help others to develop their own knowledge and understanding. Is everybody doing that, and do they need to? Is it about attitude, perception, opportunities or something else? Is it arrogance, self-delusion or justified self-confidence that is in play? Or is there no problem at all?

I met someone, while writing this book, who was discussing with me his views on security-related subjects. He clearly regarded himself as something of an expert in most matters (don't we all?). In my discussions with him, it became clear that, despite his knowledge and experience, both of which were significant – there was a bit of a flaw. No matter how much we discussed and debated various elements from organisational resilience to planning physical security – he was always right! I was essentially force-fed his opinions and views for about three hours, and I do not think that he actually heard a word that I offered back to him.

It was more than a little disconcerting that a person who has significant responsibility in security management can only see things his way. Even more worrying was a lack of willingness to consider the other person's viewpoint. It started to dawn on me that he was, in fact, so rooted in and respectful of his own qualities, experience and knowledge that he could not find space in his mindset for any ideas or concepts at variance with them.

It was also interesting to see how he assumed (rightly or wrongly, but certainly on no demonstrable evidence) that his experience and knowledge were more valuable and relevant to a range of security scenarios than mine and those of the other people in the group. Falling back upon the supporting rationale of some of his thoughts, he used the 'I could tell you this, but I would have to kill you' approach – which failed to convince most of those in the room. In summary, this fellow came across as a know-it-all who did more to undermine his own argument than any one of us could have done, had we been given the opportunity! I think that there are lots of people like him out there. No, I know there are; so do you – you have met them. If you haven't, it might be you.

For every overbearing know-it-all in our business, there is probably an equally large number of those who take the easy route. The planning and implementation of resilience measures to protect assets and maintain continuity can be a long, involved and detailed process. It can also be something that is far more simple and rapid. In general terms, it is probably a safe assumption to make that the simple, rapid method will be less thorough – therefore less effective – and probably cheaper than more detailed and protracted efforts. Clearly, that does not automatically make it better value. What will make it better value is the return on investment by high-quality, organisationally oriented team members – you. Hopefully at this stage we can agree that resilient thinkers need to be characterised by effort and analysis.

On the managerial and organisational-process front, a strong organisation will address the need to adopt business-aligned and integrated resilience management structures, endorsed and supported by the board/c-suite/top team or whatever the *mot du jour* may be. There will be structured and aligned policies and procedures, security awareness programmes, plans, publicity campaigns and activities. If the organisation does not see what you are trying to achieve, it will invariably not be their fault.

Protecting the assets of an organisation of any size involves a blended and assimilated approach, I feel. It is quite negative to build protective measures that are difficult to employ and perhaps are perceived as cumbersome or a waste of time. It is quite positive to build the mythical 'awareness and culture' that we often read about but find quite challenging to achieve.

So, resilient thinkers, is there a better way? First of all, we really do need to recognise our deficiencies and failings. Are we flexible in thought, do we understand risks and impacts, do we believe in anticipation of risk probability at all; or are we impact or 'all-hazards' focused? Is it our way or no way? Do we understand that if our organisations want things 'their' way, then our approach may need to change? In other words, are we effective in our role by knowing our business and what it needs, then *able and willing* to meet its needs? If not, we may have a problem.

Of course, as human beings we are totally focused on ourselves. We may not want to admit it, but everything that we do is about making our own existence the best that it can be. Altruistic acts such as helping others, giving to

charity, protecting our loved ones, etc. will benefit others –
but they also make our own lives better. We are naturally
egocentric; and in resilience we should accommodate that
and understand that what we are doing is not led by us, nor
really influenced by us at all. If there was not an
organisation to protect, and adversaries or unwanted events
to affect it – we could all concentrate on ourselves and get
on with living life. But life is not like that.

Making organisations resilient, and enhancing our
contributions to that, means that we need to self-analyse
first of all and try to figure out what we need to focus on,
and which parts of our perceptions and biases, viewpoints
and prejudices we should modify. We should try to learn
more, grow our experience, see how others do things, share
our own knowledge and enthusiasm. Effective
organisational resilience can be achieved by collaboration
and understanding of what is required and what is not. This
is the first step of any risk analysis in any case; and should
be extended to the personal approach of resilience
professionals. Barriers are great, but thoughts and ideas
need to come in, while preconceptions, prejudices and our
own little world views and egos may need to be kept at bay.

I would like to think that at some point we get over our self-
centred silo views concerning what we are. Business
continuity management, risk, impact, security, crisis,
disaster response and emergency management, are all
variations on a theme, different tonalities in a necessarily
coherent aim of providing resilient organisations. It's a little
like an orchestra; lots of players with some more prominent
and noisy than others. But only by following direction does
everyone understand that by seeing the primacy and
importance of each other's roles in the performance, and
knowing what success sounds like, the whole thing will

work. It helps if the conductor waves his baton and points his finger at the right time, and we all know who the great composers are. In resilience, it would be great to see the elements coming together properly at last. What about a big conference where we get all sides together and really examine this? I will if you will; but I doubt I'll see it in my lifetime – too many niches to preserve. Too many egos competing for space and money.

Real resilience is about mindsets and approach. And the idea that a stint in the military, law enforcement or the emergency services makes us an 'expert' is plain wrong. Holistic resilience and its interface with corporate and noncorporate organisations is wide reaching, wide ranging and requires multiple skills and awareness levels that we should aspire to reach. Resources and planning, good intentions and blame are immaterial when the test proves that there are multiple failings in recognising and dealing with criticality, cause, effect and impact. Not only that (and we are probably better at this), we need to consider and analyse what went wrong and does go wrong with other organisations and where and how they got things wrong. On occasions, the management of risk is about taking risk and breaking free from our coded and programmed history, ideas, prejudices and mindsets.

Exposure to different thinking, broader ideas and the building of new knowledge is available to everyone, everywhere. The wealth of knowledge and capability that can be accessed via a simple web search can of course be overwhelming; especially if you haven't had much access to the basics and fundamentals. Which model is optimal? Should I be a cyber specialist (and is there a market for me)? What about physical security? Does networking actually work your net or is it standing around eating little prawns on skewers? How can I become accomplished at resilience when there seem to be 1,001 expert opinions and viewpoints about what is good, not so good or in fashion at any one time with any one group of 'experts'?

Security, risk and resilience are not difficult subject areas and functions. Despite the buzzwords and complicated frameworks that appear repeatedly, and that seem to focus on the development of disciplines as 'black arts', anyone can become adept and influential. Simplifying the process of learning, removing organisational, institutional and sometimes personal barriers against entry, can all help to give access to what some observers may see as a closed world from the outside.

For those entering the 'sector'; well there isn't really a sector; security, risk and resilience are functions not sectors. There are plenty of opportunities, and if you can find the areas where the enlightened are then you can shine with them. Although there are some organisations that think that being a former police officer or military is enough to light up a new career in these areas (invariably it won't be); the opportunities are wider than that. In the new world we inhabit – thinkers, doers and knowledgeable equals are needed, regardless of whether you choose to wear double denim, pinstripes or any other outfit. You do need the ambition and the ability to learn. Be different and disrupt while you can – you'll be old one day and then you can conform. Resilience can be your future and your capabilities are needed. Make the leap.

Familiarity breeds contempt and lack of familiarity should breed inquisitiveness. Step back ten years or so and think about all the things we didn't like about our society and lives. Most of those are probably still there with an additional layer of seismic uncertainties now continuing to deepen. Brexit, Covid, nationalism, big war, political alignments, energy, cost of living, mass migration, climate. Lots to think about and much to be afraid of. To get ahead of this and move beyond absorption, the challenge is to be more inquisitive and become familiar with what is coming before it has an impact. We can live in the moment and be the mole in 'whack-a-mole', or be the one with the mallet and be prepared. Preparation doesn't mean that we can change what is coming; but we can and should manage impacts on ourselves and what matters to us. We can do that. Save for a rainy day, change your job, change yourself, work a little further forward into the future; it requires application and your best efforts. The past is gone, although it informs our future. The present is what we cope with. The future is where our thinking needs to be. The way we were is not where we are going. Be resilient and look ahead, the rear-view mirror is for what is behind us.

Over to you …

FURTHER READING

IT Governance Publishing (ITGP) is the world's leading publisher for governance and compliance. Our industry-leading pocket guides, books, training resources and toolkits are written by real-world practitioners and thought leaders. They are used globally by audiences of all levels, from students to C-suite executives.

Our high-quality publications cover all IT governance, risk and compliance frameworks and are available in a range of formats. This ensures our customers can access the information they need in the way they need it.

Our other publications about business continuity and resilience include:

- *ISO 22301:2019 and business continuity management – Understand how to plan, implement and enhance a business continuity management system (BCMS)* by Alan Calder, *www.itgovernancepublishing.co.uk/product/iso-22301-2019-and-business-continuity-management-understand-how-to-plan-implement-and-enhance-a-business-continuity-management-system-bcms*

- *ISO 22301:2019 – An introduction to a business continuity management system (BCMS)* by Alan Calder, *www.itgovernancepublishing.co.uk/product/iso-22301-2019-an-introduction-to-a-business-continuity-management-system-bcms*

Further reading

- *Well-being in the workplace – A guide to resilience for individuals and teams* by Sarah Cook, *www.itgovernancepublishing.co.uk/product/well-being-in-the-workplace*

For more information on ITGP and branded publishing services, and to view our full list of publications, visit *www.itgovernancepublishing.co.uk*.

To receive regular updates from ITGP, including information on new publications in your area(s) of interest, sign up for our newsletter at *www.itgovernancepublishing.co.uk/topic/newsletter*.

Branded publishing

Through our branded publishing service, you can customise ITGP publications with your company's branding.

Find out more at *www.itgovernancepublishing.co.uk/topic/branded-publishing-services*.

Related services

ITGP is part of GRC International Group, which offers a comprehensive range of complementary products and services to help organisations meet their objectives.

For a full range of resources on business continuity visit *www.itgovernance.co.uk/shop/category/bcm-and-iso-22301*.

Training services

The IT Governance training programme is built on our extensive practical experience designing and implementing management systems based on ISO standards, best practice and regulations.

Our courses help attendees develop practical skills and comply with contractual and regulatory requirements. They also support career development via recognised qualifications.

Learn more about our training courses and view the full course catalogue at *www.itgovernance.co.uk/training*.

Professional services and consultancy

We are a leading global consultancy of IT governance, risk management and compliance solutions. We advise businesses around the world on their most critical issues and present cost-saving and risk-reducing solutions based on international best practice and frameworks.

We offer a wide range of delivery methods to suit all budgets, timescales and preferred project approaches.

Find out how our consultancy services can help your organisation at *www.itgovernance.co.uk/consulting*.

Industry news

Want to stay up to date with the latest developments and resources in the IT governance and compliance market? Subscribe to our Weekly Round-up newsletter and we will send you mobile-friendly emails with fresh news and features about your preferred areas of interest, as well as unmissable offers and free resources to help you successfully start your projects. *www.itgovernance.co.uk/weekly-round-up*.

Milton Keynes UK
Ingram Content Group UK Ltd.
UKHW020046161123
432630UK00011B/105

9 781787 784192